I CAN'T BELIEVE
IT'S A BIGGER AND
BETTER UPDATED
UNOFFICIAL
SIMPSONS GUIDE

I CAN'T BELIEVE IT'S A BIGGER AND BETTER UPDATED UNOFFICIAL SIMPSONS GUIDE

Warren Martyn and Adrian Wood

Virgin

This edition published in 2000 by
Virgin Publishing Ltd
Thames Wharf Studios
Rainville Road
London W6 9HA

First published in 1997

ISBN 0 7535 0495 2

A catalogue record for this book is available
from the British Library.

Typeset by Galleon Typesetting, Ipswich
Printed and bound in Great Britain by
Mackays of Chatham PLC

CONTENTS

ACKNOWLEDGEMENTS

The authors would like to thank the following for their advice and assistance in the compilation of this book: John Ainsworth, John Binns, Jo Brooks, Paul Cornell, Neil Corry, Peter Darvill-Evans, George Fergus, Mike Fillis, Peter Griffiths, Shaun Lyon, John McLay, David Miller, Carnie O'Grady, Jim Sangster, Cavan Scott, Steven J. Sensibar (for helpful nitpicking), Charlie Thompson, and extra special thanks to Mark Phippen and Kathy Sullivan, without whom . . .

We also recommend the www.snpp.com site as the very best. Apart from hours spent using it for double-checking, and correcting our notes, we found it exceedingly well put together, lots of fun and with a trillion (well, almost) links to other useful sites. Keep it up, guys . . .

And Warren Martyn would like to dedicate this revised edition to Lily May Merrett, who arrived on the day this was finished.

Introduction

Before we start we'd like to explain the purpose of this book
– and say a few words about what it is and what it isn't.

This is a book designed for an aficionado of *The Simpsons*
rather than the novice. Unlike some other episode guidebooks
we're not really setting out to take our chosen series to bits, or
to provide detailed behind-the-scenes information. What follows is more of an *aide-mémoire*, a map to direct you through
the 226 episodes. It was created because we wanted something like it on our own bookshelves – something to guide an
ardent *Simpsons* viewer to their favourite episode or a particular scene, and to provide footnotes to some of the more
obscure texts to which the series refers.

Put simply, we think *The Simpsons* is one of the best TV
shows ever made, and quite probably the defining document
of life as it's lived in the West in the later part of the twentieth
century. It's startling to find a TV series that's not good every
now and again, or good for a while before turning sour, but
consistently excellent in all areas – acting, animation and
scripting – over eight years.

We've taken each episode and boiled its contents down into
the following categories.

Episode Number and Title: Hardly any of *The Simpsons*
episodes carry an on-screen title. The titles used in this book
are those used for publicity purposes by Gracie Films and
Twentieth-Century Fox. The episode numbers appear at the
end of each episode. The episodes are listed in the order in
which they were transmitted by the Fox Network in North
America.

Premise: The basic plot of the episode. We've been careful
not to reveal too much or reveal any twists in the plot for
readers who haven't seen that particular show.

Features: A basic cast list of featured regular characters (except the family themselves) in the episode, listed in order of appearance. We've done our best to spot cameos from regulars in the background of scenes.

Couch: A description of the sequence at the start of the majority of episodes in which the Simpsons rush in to their living room – and something unusual occurs.

And introducing: The first appearance of a regular character.

Trivia: A collection of the most pertinent bits of fictional trivia (for example, a reference to another episode or a particularly amusing name for a product) to be found in an episode.

Homage: In which we've attempted to detail all the references to films, TV and books that we can find in that episode. We've tried to grab as many of these as we can, but in a series as complex and homage-packed as *The Simpsons* some things will inevitably have slipped past us. We've been careful, for the sake of younger readers, to include references that may appear obvious to older ones.

Notes for Brits/Notes for the Uneducated: When an episode relies on the audience's knowledge of a certain American public figure or institution for its comic impact we've included an explanatory word in the 'Notes for Brits' section. When the same is true for a person or institution who isn't part of the mainstream of popular culture we explain it in the 'Notes for the Uneducated' section.

Look out for: Much of the humour in *The Simpsons* is visual, but where we can we've made reference to the funniest incidents or encounters in an episode.

Notes: This is where we pass judgement on the episode covered. We very quickly ran out of superlatives. But this section contains our observations on favourite scenes, memorable moments, especially good lines, etc.

In addition there are sub-categories relating to certain characters or situations which you'll discover as you move through the book. For example, there's a section for Homer's Mmmmms as he contemplates various foodstuffs, and another for all the dumb B-movies you may remember Troy McClure from.

Principal Credits

Cast of Characters

In the main body of the book we've listed the regular characters who appear in each episode apart from the family. Just to act as a reminder here are a few words on each of them, together with the voice credit where known.

Snowball II and **Santa's Little Helper** (Frank Weller): The Simpsons' cat and dog respectively. The first Snowball, beloved by Lisa, was run over and replaced. Santa's Little Helper was obtained by Homer and Bart in the first episode.

Grampa (Abe Simpson) (Dan Castellaneta): Homer's bad-tempered, senile and pineapple-headed father.

Grandma Simpson (Glenn Close/Tress MacNeille): Homer's long-lost mother who he thought had been dead for years. After faking his own death, Homer was delighted to finally meet her and make up for lost time. She's an intoxicating, upbeat, vivacious ex-hippie who took the young Homer to Woodstock, and she's currently on the run from the vengeful Montgomery Burns.

Patty and **Selma Bouvier** (Julie Kavner): Marge's unmarried, chainsmoking, curly-haired Homer-hating sisters. Selma's been married several times but it always seems to end in disaster, and to console her she's got a pet iguana called Jub Jub. Patty's resigned – almost – to the single life. It's easy to tell Patty and Selma apart – Patty's necklace has round beads, Selma's necklace has oval beads.

Grandma Jackie Bouvier (Julie Kavner): Marge's miserable mother, who's not too happy with the way her daughters have turned out. She looks like an older version of Patty or Selma.

Mr Charles Montgomery 'Monty' Burns (Harry Shearer): The villainous, ancient boss of the Springfield Nuclear Power plant. He resembles a praying mantis, is fond of drumming his fingers together, disposing of his employees using elaborate traps, and saying 'Excellent'. He tends to forget who Homer is, despite their many encounters.

Waylon Smithers (Harry Shearer): Mr Burns' obsequious bespectacled assistant. He's been licking Mr Burns' shoes for so long that he's fallen hopelessly in love with him. Collects Malibu Stacey dolls and is a big Abba fan. He helps Mr Burns to remember who Homer is by telling him 'That's Homer Simpson, sir'.

Lenny (Harry Shearer) and **Carl** (Hank Azaria): Homer's closest colleagues at the power plant. Lenny's the white one (who looks and sounds a bit like Chew-Chew from Hanna Barbera's sixties cartoon Top Cat), Carl's the black one.

Principal Seymour Skinner (Harry Shearer): The Vietnam vet principal of Springfield Elementary. Original name: Armin Tamzarian. Nickname: Spanky. Possibly as much out of touch with the world outside school as it's possible to be. He's dominated by his mother Agnes (Tress MacNeille), with whom he still lives.

Ms Edna Krabappel (Marcia Wallace): Bart's teacher, embittered after her husband left her for a younger woman. She likes to smoke and to cackle deprecatingly.

Miss Hoover (Pamela Hayden): Lisa's mousy, bespectacled teacher, who has not very well concealed right-wing beliefs and a lonely personal life.

Mr Largo (Harry Shearer): Lisa's music teacher, with flowing white hair and baton. He favours the precise approach, so Lisa's freestyle approach is not to his liking.

Otto Mans (Harry Shearer): A laid-back, long-haired heavy metal fan whose Walkman is permanently playing. Could be the worst driver in the world. Driver of the Springfield Elementary school bus.

Groundskeeper Willie (Dan Castellaneta): Red-headed, red-bearded Scottish groundskeeper at Springfield Elementary.

He has no time for the softly-softly approach of modern teaching methods, and will rip off his shirt at the slightest sign of crisis in order to reveal his rippling biceps.

Lunchlady Doris (Doris Grau): Acerbic ash-flicking lunchlady at Springfield Elementary. She's got no respect for the kids or whatever gruesome dish she's cooking.

Superintendent Chalmers (Hank Azaria): The schools' inspector who's the bane of Principal Skinner's life. He always seems to turn up at the worst possible moment.

Milhouse van Houten (Pamela Hayden): Bart's best friend. A nerd, but not too much of a nerd. He obviously takes after his parents, Kirk (Hank Azaria) and Luanne (Maggie Roswell).

Martin Prince (Russi Taylor): The squeaky-voiced chubby teacher's pet of Springfield Elementary.

Wendell (Nancy Cartwright): Curly-haired classmate of Bart who gets sick at the slightest provocation.

Sherri and **Terri** (Russi Taylor): Identical twin girls who exist only to smirk and titter.

Nelson Muntz (Nancy Cartwright): The hulking, tyrannosaur-mouth bully of Bart's class. He's renowned for his mocking 'ha-ha'.

Lewis and **Richard** (both Nancy Cartwright): Nondescript friends of Bart. Lewis is black with curly hair, Richard is white with a quiff.

Jimbo Jones (Pamela Hayden), **Kearney** and **Dolph** (both Nancy Cartwright): The three worst kids at school. Jimbo wears a woolly hat, Kearney is an overgrown skinhead, and Dolph has hunched shoulders and wears shorts.

Janey Hagstrom (Pamela Hayden) and **Allison Taylor** (Winona Ryder): Nondescript friends of Lisa.

Ralph Wiggum (Nancy Cartwright): Son of Chief Wiggum. So backward he could be disturbed. He likes to eat glue and miss the point.

Bleedin' Gums Murphy (Ron Taylor): Jazz legend and Lisa's sax-playing mentor.

Uter (Russi Taylor): German exchange student at Springfield Elementary. He wears lederhosen and is sometimes confused with Martin by the novice viewer.

Barney Gumble (Dan Castellaneta): Homer's best friend. A hopeless, single, penniless, shambling alcoholic.

The two barflies: Two guys who hang out in Moe's Tavern with Homer and Barney. They don't do much but drink.

Jasper (Harry Shearer): A white-bearded friend of Grampa's who lives with him in the Springfield Retirement Castle. He's perhaps even less in touch with reality than Grampa.

Herman (Harry Shearer): The owner of Springfield's Military Antiques store. He has an atomic bomb he wouldn't mind setting off one day – and only one arm.

Cletus (Hank Azaria): A young hillbilly, married to the delectable Brandi. Between them they have more children than they can count (at least sixteen, plus an assortment of dogs). They live on a ramshackle farm just outside Springfield.

The Flanderses: The Simpsons' God-fearing next-door neighbours. Ned Flanders (Harry Shearer) is so painfully affable he'll let Homer borrow anything. He has a wife, Maude Flanders (Maggie Roswell) and two sons, Rod and Todd (both Nancy Cartwright).

Ruth Powers (Pamela Reed): Marge's neighbour and good friend, who has a daughter Laura (Sara Gilbert).

The Winfields (Harry Shearer and Maggie Roswell): The Simpsons' other set of neighbours. A sweet old couple.

Hans Moleman (Dan Castellaneta): An apparently very old man who can't see, can't drive and hobbles pathetically around Springfield issuing cryptic comments.

Chief Clancy Wiggum (Hank Azaria): Springfield's staggeringly incompetent Chief of Police. He has blue hair, likes eating doughnuts, and wears his police badge on the wrong side. He is married to Sarah and has two children, one of whom is Ralph.

Mayor 'Diamond' Joe Quimby (Dan Castellaneta): Springfield's corrupt mayor.

Lou and **Eddie** (both Harry Shearer): Chief Wiggum's equally incompetent sidekicks.

Krusty the Klown, aka **Herschel Krustofsky** (Dan Castellaneta): The ever-popular host of the Krusty the Klown show on local television, and proprietor of a myriad spin-off products and dodgy merchandising deals. He likes smoking cigars, throwing money away, and reading pornography. He's often accompanied by his chimp, Mr Teeny.

Sideshow Bob Terwilliger (Kelsey Grammer): Krusty's silent stooge for many years. He revealed himself to be a well-read, plummy-voiced Englishman with a mad desire to seize power, raise cultural standards, and to kill Bart.

Sideshow Mel (Dan Castellaneta): Sideshow Bob's replacement – another, much less violent, plummy-voiced Englishman. He is married to Barbara.

Itchy and **Scratchy:** The gruesome cat and mouse cartoon duo beloved of Krusty's viewers. Itchy's the mouse, Scratchy's the cat.

Arnie Pie (Dan Castellaneta): Springfield's eye-in-the-sky traffic reporter.

Kent Brockman (Harry Shearer): Springfield's top reporter and host of *Eye On Springfield* and his opinion slot *My Two*

Cents. Always keen to stir trouble, cause an unnecessary panic, and seem important. His real name is Kenny Brockelstein.

Scott Christian (Dan Castellaneta): Kent's less blame-apportioning but more sardonic colleague.

Bill and **Marty** at KBBL (Harry Shearer, Hank Azaria): The DJs at Springfield's radio station, always ready with a dumb observation.

Rev. Timothy Lovejoy (Harry Shearer): The pastor of the First Church of Springfield. He gets very confused by religion and would rather play with his model trains. His wife Helen (Maggie Roswell) is a notorious gossip. They have a daughter, Jessica (Meryl Streep).

Miss Allbright (Maggie Roswell): Bart and Lisa's long-suffering Sunday-school teacher, who never seems to have the answers either are looking for.

Troy McClure (Phil Hartman): A B-movie actor whose career has slipped still further down the lists of the casting directors. He'll do anything.

Rainier Wolfcastle (Hank Azaria): German-born tough guy who plays McBain in the popular series of action movies.

Bumblebee Man (Dan Castellaneta): The star of an inexplicable Spanish comedy series that always seems to be rerunning in Springfield. His real name is Pedro.

Moe Szyslak (Hank Azaria): The hapless, pennypinching and not too bright bartender and owner of Moe's Tavern. He has a lot of strange secrets and is the victim of prank 'Can I Speak To . . . ?' telephone calls made by Bart.

Apu Nahasapeemapetilon (Hank Azaria): Indian proprietor of Springfield's convenience store, the Kwik-E-Mart. He's not too fussy about what he's selling. Bart often visits him for a squishee drink. Catchphrase: 'Thank you, please come again.'

Snake (Harry Shearer): The plummy-voiced one-man crime wave of Springfield. Tattooed, unshaven, and terribly polite.

Dr Hibbert (Harry Shearer): The jocular family doctor to the Simpsons. He likes to break bad news with a smile on his face and has a wife called Sylvia and two kids.

Lionel Hutz (Phil Hartman): The world's worst lawyer. Often used by the Simpsons.

Dr Nick Riviera (Hank Azaria): The world's worst doctor. Often used by the Simpsons.

Dr Marvin Monroe (Harry Shearer): The world's worst psychologist/counsellor. Often used by the Simpsons.

Dr John Frink (Hank Azaria): A bespectacled scientist with a number of crazy devices to his name and not much of an idea about science.

Don Tony D'Amico (Joe Mantegna): The godfather of Springfield's criminal underworld.

Gil (Harry Shearer): Hapless businessman whose every endeavour ends in disaster. He is married but his wife is having an affair with someone called Fred.

Captain McCallister (Harry Shearer): The white-bearded, pipe-smoking proprietor of the Frying Dutchman seafood restaurant.

Spotty Boy (Hank Azaria): An acned teenager trapped by an endless variety of dead-end jobs.

Android's Dungeon Guy: The nacho-guzzling, Internet-fixated, *Dr Who* marathonning 'sexless food tube' who's the proprietor of Springfield's SF and comics store. He wears unflattering shorts and has a ponytail.

Judge Snyder (Harry Shearer): Springfield's local lawgiver, usually driven mad by the townsfolk, particularly if their lawyer is Lionel Hutz.

Kodos and **Kang** (Hank Azaria, Harry Shearer): Three-eyed, many-tentacled squid-like aliens fom the planet Rigel. They circle Earth constantly, awaiting the opportunity to invade, or perhaps just to do some entertaining aboard their saucer.

The Tracey Ullman Show

The British comedian made her name on the BBC with leading roles in sketch shows such as *A Kick Up The Eighties* (1981–4) and *Three of a Kind* (1981–3), but then transferred her talents to records with the albums, 'You Broke My Heart In 17 Places' (1983) and 'You Caught Me Out' (1984). In 1987, having moved to the US, she starred in *The Tracey Ullman Show*, a sketch show which won the Fox Broadcasting Network its first Emmy. The show ran until 1990, and between 1987 and 1989 featured a series of short animations by Matt Groening, best known then for his cartoon strip, *Life is Hell*, featuring a group of maniacally depressed rabbits and dwarves of dubious sexual orientation in fezzes. The cartoon shorts for *The Tracey Ullman Show* were known as *The Simpsons* and for the first two runs were broken into segments and played at various points during the show. For the third block, they were one-off five-minute stories, the family also appearing in the show's main title sequence saying 'hi' to Tracey. Voicing the characters were two Tracey Ullman show regulars Julie Kavner and Dan Castellaneta as Mom and Dad (changed to Mrs Simpson and Mr Simpson from Season Two), along with Yeardley Smith and Nancy Cartwright as Lisa and Bart. For the first short, Liz Georges was credited as Maggie, who gurgled 'g'night'.

The animation for the first twenty odd shows was very crude with the characters gradually transmuting into the now familiar characters of today. Homer had a little more hair, Maggie and Lisa had very punky spiked hair and Marge's famous blue coiffure was quite short. And after 'Bart's Haircut' (Short 18), the boy's hair attained its now traditional look. Marge, by the way, is never referred to by name, always just as 'Mom'. As the shorts went on other characters would crop up such as Grampa (looking very similar to how he does in *The Simpsons* TV show), Krusty the Clown (not Klown) and Itchy and Scratchy.

The Episodes

What follows is a run-down on the shorts in the order they were transmitted, with a few odd notes along the way.

Season One (1987) – 7 Shorts

Short 01	Good Night

Introduces the whole family.

Short 02	Watching Television
Short 03	Bart Jumps
Short 04	Babysitting Maggie

Marge's hair noticeably taller

Short 05	The Pacifier
Short 06	Burp Contest
Short 07	Eating Dinner

Season Two (1987-8) – 22 Shorts

Short 09	Making Faces

Julie Kavner credited as Mrs Simpson

Short 14	The Funeral

Dan Castellaneta credited as Mr Simpson. This runs more like a traditional *The Simpsons* episode, with the family away from the house for the first time. Uncle Hubert introduced (he's dead, by the way). Lisa plays with a *Life is Hell* rabbit – a motif that crops up many times over the subsequent shows.

Short 10	Maggie's Brain

The bizarre humour and dream sequences of this one are good portents of what is to come when the show proper starts.

Short 08	Football
Short 12	House of Cards
Short 15	Bart and Dad Eat Dinner

Homer's dire dietary habits are seeded here, although Bart does not share them.

Short 13	Space Patrol

14

Short 18   Bart's Haircut
'What the hell did you do to my hair' – Bart cusses for the first time!

Short 20   World War III
Short 16   The Perfect Crime
Short 17   Scary Stories
Short 19   Grampa and the Kids
Grampa is introduced – his wicked humour is very prevalent. The Happy Little Elves are mentioned for the first time.

Short 11   Gone Fishin'
Short 21   Skateboarding
Short 22   The Pagans
Short 23   The Closet
Here we see *The Simpsons* formula really shaping up well. The genesis of many future *Simpsons* episodes.

Short 24   The Aquarium
Short 25   Family Portrait
Short 26   Bart's Hiccups
Short 27   The Money Jar
Lisa has matured into the familiar Lisa.

Short 29   The Art Museum
Pure Simpsons mayhem, no doubt helped by the first appearances of catch phrases such as 'Ay Carumba', 'Don't have a cow, man' and 'Why, you little . . .'

Short 28   Zoo Story
A wonderful moment when the monkey family look just like the Simpsons. The sort of visual gag expanded and magnified on the regular episodes.

Season Three (1988–9) – 19 Shorts

Short 30   Shut Up Simpsons
Homer called Homer for the first time (by Grampa and Bart). The traditional hand-round-the-throat-popping-eyes strangling images appears properly for the first time (it's hinted at back in Short 25 – Family Portrait).

Short 35   The Shell Game

Short 38   The Bart Simpson Show

First appearance of The Itchy and Scratchy Show – Homer considers it too violent.

Short 33   Punching Bag

Lisa is a bit more feminist. And the legendary first appearance of 'D'oh!'

Short 40   Simpsons Christmas

The whole short features Bart's rendition of ' 'Twas the Night Before Christmas' – the sort of literary reference that would litter the Treehouse of Horror episodes.

Short 39   The Krusty the Clown Show

Introduces Krusty, whose live show is accompanied by Itchy and Scratchy, The Happy Little Elves and Chunky the Pig. And for the first time, 'I'm Bart Simpson. Who the hell are you?'

Short 34   Bart the Hero

Short 41   Bart's Little Fantasy

Short 37   Scary Movie

Lisa wants to see 'Return of the Happy Little Elves' but Bart takes her and Maggie to 'Revenge of the Space Mutants'. More portents to the future . . .

Short 32   Home Hypnotism

Short 31   Shoplifting

Short 36   Echo Canyon

Short 44   Bathtime

Short 45   Bart's Nightmare

A sequel to Short 35, The Shell Game, including dialogue from that short. And on breaking a jar, Bart yells, 'I didn't do it!'

Short 46   Bart of the Jungle

Short 47   Family Therapy

Short 42   Maggie In Peril – Chapter One

Short 43   Maggie In Peril – The Thrilling Conclusion

Short 48   TV Simpsons

And the rest, as they say, is history . . .

First Season

1989–1990
13 Episodes

1
7G08:

'The Simpsons Christmas Special'
(aka 'Simpsons Roasting on an Open Fire')

Written by Mimi Pond   **Directed by** David Silverman
Also starring: JoAnn Harris, Pamela Hayden

Premise: There's to be no Christmas bonus in Homer's pay packet this year. And Marge's savings are sacrificed to rescue Bart from a scrape at a tattoo parlour. It looks like the Simpsons' festivities will be frugal – unless Homer can find success as a department store Santa Claus.

Features: Grampa, Patty and Selma.

Couch: There's none of the usual title sequence at all.

And introducing: Principal Skinner, Mr Largo, Milhouse, Janey, Sherri and Terri, Wendell, Lewis, Richard, Ned Flanders, Rod Flanders, Mr Burns, Moe, Barney. We hear Smithers on a loudspeaker at the power plant, but he's not seen until 'Homer's Odyssey'.

Trivia: The Springfield Mall contains The Happy Sailor Tattoo Parlor and The Popcorn Shack. Homer shops for cheapo gifts at Circus of Values. Springfield's local newspaper is the *Springfield Snooper* (in this episode only – it's the *Shopper* when featured in other episodes), and its racecourse is Springfield Downs. Lisa is an enthusiastic viewer of the Happy Little Elves' Christmas special ('This Christmas we're going to be sad little elves!'), and among the detritus at the racecourse is our first sighting of Duff beer. Santa's Little Helper is discovered by Homer and Bart in a dog track race. The other dogs in the race are called Whirlwind, Quadruped, Dog o' War and Fido. This episode was made after 'Homer's Odyssey', but shown before it, and so Homer is already safety inspector at the plant, breaking the first season's continuity.

Notes: Circumstances dictated that this was the first trans-mitted episode, and it's pretty standard early fare, with the series not quite hitting its stride. The opening scenes at the pageant are especially cutesy and all-American. The realism of the first season is much apparent, with only the laser used to remove Bart's tattoo hinting at what the series will become. 'The Simpsons Christmas Special' is the on-screen title; 'Simpsons Roasting on an Open Fire' is the title used to publicise the episode.

2
7G02:
'Bart the Genius'

Written by Jon Vitti   **Directed by** David Silverman
Also starring: JoAnn Harris, Pamela Hayden, Russi Taylor
Special guest voice: Marcia Wallace (as Ms Krabappel)

Premise: Bart swaps papers with Martin Prince at an IQ test. He's referred to the Enriched Learning Center for Gifted Children (proprietor Dr J. Loren Pryor). His new school's laid-back liberal ethos suits him fine – until he's asked to show evidence of his neglected genius.

Features: Principal Skinner, Milhouse. The screening of episodes out of production order spoils a neat visual gag introducing Skinner, in which a graffito of him sprayed by Bart on a school wall fades into his actual face.

Couch: The Simpsons rush in and sit down with such force that Bart is ejected into the air. He topples back to earth as the main title credits roll across the family's TV.

And introducing: Martin Prince, Ms Krabappel.

Trivia: Bart's breakfeast cereal is Frosty Krusty Flakes, and he has a Krusty lunchbox and a framed photo of Krusty at his bedside. The books on the shelf at the Enriched Learning Center include: *Pushkin*, *Life of Leonardo*, *Crime and Punishment*, *Nana* by Emile Zola, *Shakespeare I–XV*, *Dante's Inferno*, *Babylonian Myths*, *Design of Computers*, *Moby Dick*, *Paradise Lost*, *The Iliad* by Homer, *The Odyssey* by Homer, *Candide*, *Astrophysics* and *Balzac*. There's also a Radioactive Man comic. Kids at the Enriched Learning Center have *Brideshead Revisited* and Anatoly Karpov lunchboxes.

Notes for the Uneducated: Jane Goodall is a British ethologist and an authority on wild chimpanzees: she lived alongside them for her researches.

Look out for: Look closely at what Maggie's doing at the beginning of this episode – it could be that she is the undiscovered Simpson genius.

Notes: Superbly written and directed, often a literal child's-eye view of education, the first *Simpsons* episode proper is a classic. These twenty minutes cemented Bart's position as a cultural icon and a hero to all underachievers, and managed a good few kicks at the hothouse schools along the way. Especially worthy of note is the sequence where Bart visualises his maths problem, the viewing of which should be a required part of teacher training.

3
7G03:
'Homer's Odyssey'

Written by Jay Kogen and Wallace Wolodarsky
Directed by Wesley Archer
Also starring: Christopher Collins, Pamela Hayden,
Sam McMurray, Russi Taylor
Special guest voice: Marcia Wallace (as Ms Krabappel)

Premise: Homer is fired from his job as technical supervisor at the Springfield nuclear plant. Unable to provide for his family, he contemplates ending it all – until he discovers a new life path as a campaigner for safety.

Features: Ms Krabappel, Milhouse, Sherri and Terri, Wendell, Moe, Barney, Mr Burns. The screening of episodes out of production order pre-empts a brilliant introductory scene for Mr Burns in this episode – the camera pulls out from the crowd of protestors outside the plant and finds him standing looking down at them from his office, the angle of the shot emphasising his massive cranium and villainous expression.

Couch: The Simpsons hit the sofa with such force that it collapses.

And introducing: Otto, Smithers (who appears very tanned), Moe's two barflies, Mr and Mrs Winfield, Wiggum, and Jasper. It's hard to tell, but the guy who nearly runs Homer down looks like Hans Moleman.

Trivia: Homer watches Loaf Time: The Cable Network for the Unemployed. There's 'El Barto' graffiti on both the school and the city hall. Apart from the waste dump and tyre yard, Springfield has a state prison. The guard at the gate is watching Krusty on TV, and Homer eats frosty doughnuts. We get our first glimpse of the three-eyed fish and see a Duff Beer commercial. Bart's report card states that he has U grades in Science, Reading and Writing, Fs in Social Studies and Math, and a D for Physical Ed. Marge used to be a roller waitress at Berger's Burgers.

Homage: Playing in Moe's Tavern during Homer's darkest hour is Patsy Cline's 1961 hit 'I Fall To Pieces'.

Notes for the Uneducated: 'John Henry Was A Steel Driving Man' is a folk song dating from the nineteenth century.

Hello, can I speak to: I. P. Freely.

That's Homer Simpson, sir: 'he used to work here in the plant.'

Notes: More of the series' framework is established, with the first of many employment problems for Homer. The story rather fizzles out at the end, but there are many good moments, especially in the power plant.

4

7G04:

'There's No Disgrace Like Home'

Written by Al Jean and Mike Reiss
Directed by Gegg Vanzo, Kent Butterworth
Also starring: Maggie Roswell, Pamela Hayden

Premise: Shamed by the behaviour of his family at Mr Burns' annual workers' picnic, Homer enrols the Simpsons at Dr Marvin Monroe's Family Therapy Center (motto: 'family bliss or double your money back').

Features: Mr Burns, Smithers, Moe, Barney.

Couch: Homer is squeezed out on to the floor.

And introducing: Eddie and Lou, Dr Marvin Monroe, Itchy and Scratchy. (There's a guy drinking in Moe's Tavern that looks a bit like Lenny.)

Trivia: Some of the gelatin desserts at the picnic have been shaped like parts of the nuclear plant. The Happy Little Elves make another appearance. The Family Therapy Center's phone number is 1-800-555-HUGS.

Homage: Stately Burns Manor looks a lot like Kane's castle in *Citizen Kane* (Orson Welles, 1941). The cry 'One of us! One of us!' comes from the final scene of *Freaks* (Tod Browning, 1932).

Itchy and Scratchy in: An unnamed, very generic Tom & Jerry style cartoon. It looks like Scratchy is doing the unthinkable and preparing to savage Itchy with an axe at the end of the clip, suggesting that their roles had not been delineated at this stage of the series' production. We don't see the theme tune or even hear their names.

Mmmmm: . . . marshmallow.

Notes: It's very strange to see Homer pawning the TV set in an attempt to save the family; if this episode had come later Marge would surely have taken this stance. A neat swipe at family counselling with some great set pieces; we're especially fond of the perfect version of the Simpsons and the electric-shock aversion therapy. This was the first episode shown by the BBC in the UK when they finally got round to transmitting the show.

5
7G05:
'Bart the General'

Written by John Swartzwelder
Directed by David Silverman
Also starring: Susan Blu, JoAnn Harris, Pamela Hayden

Premise: Bart is being bullied. He teams up with Grampa to battle bully Nelson Muntz, aided by Herman, owner of Springfield's Military Antiques Store and also owner of rather extreme political views.

Features: Milhouse, Principal Skinner, Grampa, Jasper.

Couch: None. The opening sequence crashes straight from the school and into the episode.

And introducing: Nelson Muntz, Herman.

Trivia: Lisa refers to her teacher as Mrs (rather than Miss) Hoover, but we don't see her. Herman's store claims to have a pair of Hitler's teeth in a display case. There's a poster of Krusty in Bart's room although we still haven't seen him. There's a first mention of Kwik-E-Mart (spelt Quick-E-Mart) and squishees, but no sign of Apu.

Homage: There are lines taken wholesale from *Patton* (Franklin Schnaffner, 1970), and some vague nods in the marching sequences to *Full Metal Jacket* (Stanley Kubrick, 1986).

Mmmmm: . . . cupcakes.

Notes: Some good lines and setpieces aside – we love Bart's fantasy of death at Nelson's hands – this episode nevertheless feels a bit unsure of itself, particularly towards the end.

6
7G06:
'Moaning Lisa'

Written by Al Jean and Mike Reiss
Directed by Wesley Archer
Also starring: Susan Blu, Miriam Flynn, Pamela Hayden, Ron Taylor

Premise: Overlooked middle child Lisa Simpson is racked by angst, with only her sax for solace. Is the world really such a dreadful, hopeless place? Can jazz legend Bleedin' Gums Murphy use his straight-blowin' sound to help? Meanwhile, Homer and Bart are playing the SUPER SLUGFEST video game. Homer makes a horrifying discovery – Bart's smarter than him.

Features: Mr Largo, Janey, Moe.

Couch: Maggie pops up but is caught safely by Marge.

And introducing: Bleedin' Gums Murphy, Mrs Bouvier.

Trivia: Lisa's brushing with Glum toothpaste. We hear about the Springfield Jazz Hole, the Symphony Hall, the Museum of Natural History, the Springfield Arts Center, and Barney's Bowlerama. This episode also contains the first appearance of Homer's all-time favourite greasy snack, Pork Rinds Lite.

Notes for Brits: Robert Goulet is an American crooner. See also '$pringfield'.

Look out for: the scene in which Bart and Lisa urge Maggie to 'run to the one who loves you best'.

Hello, can I speak to: Jock Strapp.

Notes: Certain scenes of this, the most syrupy of *Simpsons* episodes, have sent viewers raised on the later seasons scurrying to the bathroom. Yes, the final moments may give you goosepimples, and are a world away from the anti-schmaltz normally associated with the series, but there is still much to recommend here. In fact, the Homer/Bart subplot is more successful than the main storyline; Homer's nightmare about their relationship is genuinely disturbing. This episode also contains the celebrated 'Maggie, run to the one you love best' scene.

7

7G09:
'Call of the Simpsons'

Written by John Swartzwelder
Directed by Wesley Archer
Additional cast: Albert Brooks (as Cowboy Bob)

Premise: In an attempt to keep up with the Flanderses, Homer purchases an RV and the Simpsons set off for the wild. Where bears, bees, rabbits and curious naturalists with camcorders await.

Features: Tod Flanders, Ned Flanders, Dr Marvin Monroe.

Couch: The Simpsons just sit down.

Trivia: Flanders has bought a Behemoth RV. Homer peruses the Ultimate Behemoth, which comes complete with its own satellite, Van-Sat 1. Homer makes the front page of the *Springfield Weekly* and the *National Informer* (several times).

Homage: The incidental score tips a hat to *Swallows and Amazons*, and the TV anchorman's order to 'Get those bears out of here' sounds suspiciously like Mr Peebley's weekly order to Botch in Hanna-Barbera's 'The Hair Bear Bunch'.

Notes: This was not to be the only appearance of bears in the series. As with a lot of the first season this episode is a bit less than the sum of its parts. The early stuff at the RV Round-Up is much better than the main camping story, although there's some nice Marge–Lisa bonding, and who could resist Maggie and the bears?

8

7G07:

'The Tell-Tale Head'

Written by Al Jean, Mike Reiss, Sam Simon, Matt Groening
Directed by Rich Moore
Additional cast: Marcia Wallace, Pamela Hayden,
Tress MacNeille

Premise: Homer and Bart sneak through the streets of Springfield by night, only to be met by a bloodthirsty mob. But what events led to this grim confrontation – and how are they connected with the statue of town founder Jebediah Obadiah Zachariah Jedadiah Springfield?

Features: Principal Skinner, Ms Krabappel, Mr Burns, Smithers, Grampa, Moe, Barney, Janey, Wiggum. The mob also contains Dr Marvin Monroe, Patty and Selma, Otto, Ned Flanders, Mr and Mrs Winfield, Milhouse, Jasper, the two barflies.

Couch: The Simpsons rush into the living room with such force that Bart is squeezed out and thrown into the air.

And introducing: Rev. Lovejoy, Krusty, Jimbo Jones, Kearney, Dolph, Apu. Lovejoy and Krusty are given their first few lines as part of the mob. And Sideshow Bob, as Krusty's silent stooge. Not a hint of the terrors to come. And his hair is in curls rather than dreads.

Trivia: Jimbo has a copy of *Playdude* magazine, which appears in several subsequent episodes. Four squishees comes to $4.52. Homer flips through the *Bowl Earth Catalog* to select a new bowling ball, and likes the look of the Stealth Bowler. Jebediah Springfield built the town's first hospital in 1848, and is said to have killed a bear with his bare hands. KBBL runs a show called *Mambo in the Morning*.

Homage: The title refers to Edgar Allan Poe's short story 'The Tell-Tale Heart', published in 1843 (and thus a close contemporary of Jebediah) and a staple text in American public education. (Poe's influence is felt again in 'Treehouse of Horror' and 'Lisa's Rival'.)

Notes: This episode is one of only two to bear an on-screen title (Christmas and Hallowe'en specials aside). This is a lot more like it, with the Simpsons grossly dysfunctional in church, Homer dispensing terrible advice, and a real moral dilemma for Bart.

9

7G11:

'Jacques To Be Wild'
(aka 'Life in the Fast Lane')

Written by John Swartzwelder
Directed by David Silverman
Additional cast: Albert Brooks (as Jacques), Maggie Roswell

Premise: Homer's birthday gift to Marge drives her into the arms of the romantic Frenchman Jacques. Will she be swayed away from the family by his continental charms?

Features: Patty and Selma, Mr and Mrs Winfield, Mr Burns, Smithers.

Couch: None. The titles crash straight in from the school to the episode.

And introducing: Helen Lovejoy, Lenny.

Trivia: Homer and Marge dine at The Singing Sirloin – Home of Ballads and Salads, having considered Chez Pierre and the Rusty Barnacle. Marge meets Jacques at Barney's New Bowlarama (rebuilt since the fire referred to in 'Moaning Lisa'), and takes brunch with him at Shorty's coffee shop. She is 34 and wears size 13AA shoes. He lives at Fiesta Terrace, a luxury block designed for 'single living'.

Homage: Marge's romantic dream pays respect to the surreal dance numbers of thirties Hollywood, in particular *The Gay Divorcee* (Mark Sandrich, 1934). The plot's resolution recalls *An Officer and a Gentleman* (Taylor Hackford, 1982), complete with a rendition (nearly) of its Oscar-winning theme 'Up Where We Belong'.

Look out for: Take a good look at the full moon when Jacques drops Marge home in his car.

Notes: Marge's dilemma is made especially memorable by the contrast between husband and suitor. Homer's attempt to pay her a compliment about her peanut butter sandwich making ability is a touching moment. A very good, very assured episode that has seen some viewers (particularly female ones) tearing out their hair at the conclusion.

10

7G10:

'Homer's Night Out'

Written by Jon Vitti   **Directed by** Rich Moore
Also starring: JoAnn Harris, Pamela Hayden,
Maggie Roswell
Special guest voice: Sam McMurray (as Gulliver Dark)

Premise: Bart's new mail-order spy camera (as used by the CIA, cost $1.50) snaps Homer mid-belly dance with the exotic Princess Kashmir (real name Shawna Tifton). Only by teaching Bart that women are not sex objects can Homer appease the wrath of Marge.

Features: Lenny, Martin, Milhouse, Lewis, Rev. Lovejoy, Smithers, Mr Burns, Apu, Moe, Barney.

Couch: It collapses.

And introducing: Carl.

Trivia: Homer weighs 239 lbs, and once had an assistant at work, Eugene Fisk. Marge attends an exercise class.

Notes for the Uneducated: Diane Arbus (1923–71) was a photographer who specialised in portraits of grotesque or eccentric individuals. So Martin's friend's comparison of Bart's work to hers is quite valid.

That's Homer Simpson, sir: 'a low-level employee in Sector 7G'.

Notes: It's odd to see Smithers out with a chick (although, to be fair, he's double-dating with Mr Burns). And Mr Burns recognises Homer at the Sapphire Lounge (although, to be fair, his memory had to be jogged earlier in the episode).

11
7G13:
'The Crepes of Wrath'

Written by George Meyer, Sam Simon,
John Swartzwelder, Jon Vitti
Directed by Wesley Archer, Milton Gray
Also starring: Pamela Hayden, Christian Coffinet,
Tress MacNeille

Premise: Bart's bad behaviour forces Principal Skinner to enrol him in a foreign exchange programme. While the Simpson family welcome Albanian Adil, Bart becomes the grape-treading slave of two sinister Frenchmen.

Features: Principal Skinner, Milhouse, Lewis, Richard, Lenny.

Couch: Homer pops out on to the floor.

And introducing: Mrs Skinner.

Trivia: This is the first appearance of Bart's talking Krusty doll.

Homage: Cesar and Ugolin are lifted directly from *L'eau des Collines* by Marcel Pagnol, a two-part classic of French literature filmed as *Jean de Florette* (Claude Berri, 1986) and *Manon des Sources* (Claude Berri, 1986), which tells of two unscrupulous peasant farmers. Maggie's gift from France is a nod to *Le Ballon Rouge* (Albert Lamorrisse, 1956), a short French children's film.

Notes for the Uneducated: When Bart arrives in France, Cesar cycles him through several famous French paintings.

Notes: The first *Simpsons* episode devoted to jibes at a whole nation, and where better than France to start? A *tour de force*, perhaps the first episode to make the viewer's jaw drop at the audacity and invention of the series' makers. By now Homer has lost what little fatherly dignity he had at the season's start, and has become the guzzling, lazy dimwit that is the lynchpin of the show's success.

12
7G12:
'Krusty Gets Busted'

Written by Jay Kogen and Wallace Wolodarsky
Directed by Brad Bird
Also starring: Pamela Hayden
Special guest voice: Kelsey Grammer (as Sideshow Bob)
'Itchy and Scratchy Theme' by Sam Simon
'Ev'ry Time We Say Goodbye' written by Cole Porter

Premise: 'Comedy, thy name is Krusty.' Krusty the Klown, TV hero of Springfield's children, is tried for the armed robbery of the Kwik-E-Mart. Bart and Lisa investigate, convinced that Krusty has been framed. How does Krusty's unusually literate sidekick Sideshow Bob fit into the picture?

Features: Krusty, Sideshow Bob, Patty and Selma, Apu, Eddie and Lou, Wiggum, Rev. Lovejoy.

Couch: Maggie pops up and is fielded by Marge.

And introducing: Scott Christian, Kent Brockman.

Trivia: Krusty began his career as a street mime in Tupelo, Mississippi, and had a heart attack in 1986. His child literacy posters read 'Give A Hoot – Read A Book!', and we see an excerpt from an old show where Sideshow Bob hands him J. D. Salinger's loss-of-childhood classic *The Catcher in the Rye* from the Bucket o' Books.

Homage: The opening of Act II, with Krusty's face zooming up only to be slammed behind bars, looks very much like the closing credit motif of the British sixties spy TV series *The Prisoner*. The incidental music almost breaks into the theme of *Mission: Impossible* at one point, and there's a reference to *Scooby Doo* that we aren't going to spoil by spelling out here.

Notes for the Uneducated: *The Man in the Iron Mask* is a swashbuckling epic novel by Alexandre Dumas. The theme tune of Sideshow Bob's show is Mozart's 'Eine Kleine Nachtmusik'. Stoicism is a school of philosophy, started in ancient Greece, which held that all reality is material but there must be a distinction drawn between physical matter and the animating principle of life. In his dressing-room Sideshow Bob has a poster for a production of Verdi's tragic opera *Don Carlos*. Gore Vidal is an American intellectual and commentator. Susan Sontag is an academic in the field of popular culture.

Itchy and Scratchy in: 'Burning Love'.

Notes: The invention of the Simpsons' arch enemy as a lugubrious yet psychotic Englishman in dreadlocks succeeds wonderfully in this super-fast, super-funny episode that works by constantly reversing the audience's expectations (we love the rapt child audience listening to Sideshow Bob's reading). Bart and Lisa adopt the investigative role that is to crop up in every successive Bob episode. Also memorable for Patty and Selma's Mexican odyssey eight-carousel slide show ('here's Selma with a Mexican delicacy – a taco platter').

13
7G01:
'Some Enchanted Evening'

Written by Matt Groening and Sam Simon
Directed by David Silverman, Kent Butterworth
Also starring: Christopher Collins (as TV host),
June Foray (as receptionist), Paul Willson
Special guest voice: Penny Marshall (as Miss Botz)

Premise: Despairing of Homer, Marge calls Dr Marvin Monroe's KBBL agony phone-in 'K-Babble'. His advice: a romantic night out. Bart, Lisa and Maggie are left in the hands of the mysterious babysitter Miss Lucille Botz, and sit down to watch *America's Most Armed and Dangerous*.

Features: Dr Marvin Monroe, Moe, Barney, the two barflies.

Couch: The Simpsons rush in – and just sit down.

And introducing: Arnie Pie, Bill from KBBL.

Trivia: Miss Botz's services are obtained through the Rubber Baby Buggy Bumper Babysitting service. K-Babble's phone number is 555 PAIN. Dr Monroe's assistant holds up two notes: LINE 1 – MARGE, ANOTHER UNAPPRECIATED WIFE and LINE 2 – PAUL HSI, NAILBITER (NOT HIS OWN). Springfield has the flower store 'Howard's Flowers'.

America's Most Armed and Dangerous's telephone number is 1-800-USQUEAL.

Homage: Miss Botz's pursuit of Bart into the cellar is reminiscent of Robert Mitchum's pursuit of a young boy in *Night of the Hunter* (Charles Laughton, 1955). In Moe's Tavern we hear 'The Man That Got Away', from *A Star Is Born* (George Cukor, 1954).

Hello, can I speak to: Al Coholic, Oliver Clothesoff.

Notes: It's quite a shock to discover that this confident, fully rounded episode was the first to be made. The perfect template.

Second Season

1990–1991
22 Episodes

14
7F03:
'Bart Gets an F'

Written by David M. Stern
Directed by David Silverman
Also starring: JoAnn Harris, Pamela Hayden,
Russi Taylor
Special guest voice: Marcia Wallace (as Ms Krabappel)

Premise: Bart has failed yet again and faces the prospect of sitting the fourth grade for another year. His attempts to befriend Martin only lead to Martin becoming cool. Even a deal with God can't get Bart out of this one – especially when it leads to Mayor Quimby declaring 'Snow Day' – 'The Funnest Day in the History of Springfield'.

Features: Ms Krabappel, Martin Prince, Milhouse, Wendell, Lewis, Richard, Otto, Sherri and Terri, Principal Skinner, Nelson Muntz, Mr Burns, Smithers, Chief Wiggum, Krusty the Klown, Rev. Lovejoy, Helen Lovejoy, Grampa, Sideshow Bob, Apu, Patty, Selma.

Couch: The Simpsons rush in – and the sofa falls through the floor.

And introducing: Mayor Quimby, Jasper.

Trivia: Homer makes Bart watch *Gorilla the Conqueror*. We get to see Bart playing the video game 'Escape From Grandma's House'.

Itchy and Scratchy in: 'Let Them Eat Scratchy'.

Notes: Edna Krabappel comes into her own here, dreading getting stuck with Bart and yet relishing his failures. Of course, seven years on, and they're all still in the fourth grade, but that's cartoons. A cracking opener to the second season – especially memorable for the sequence in which Bart prays for school to be cancelled the following day only to find himself exiled from the ensuing winter wonderland.

15

7F02:

'Simpson and Delilah'

Written by Jon Vitti **Directed by** Rich Moore
Also starring: Pamela Hayden
Special guest voice: Harvey Fierstein (as Karl)

Premise: Homer's attempts to grow more hair increase his confidence. He's aided by a new secretary, the passionate Karl. All Karl needs to do now is prove to Homer that his success is a result of self-confidence and genuine hard work, not new hair. And then there's a vengeful Smithers to deal with . . .

Features: Patty, Selma, Carl, Lenny, Moe, Barney, the Winfields, Rev. Lovejoy, Mr Burns, Smithers, Milhouse, Lewis.

Couch: The Simpsons rush in – and break into an Egyptian dance.

Trivia: Karl takes Homer to the ROYAL MAJESTY MENS-WEAR STORE – FOR THE OBESE OR GANGLY MAN. Among the hair tonics in Homer's cabinet are U Wanna B

Hair E, Hair Chow, Bald Buster, Hair Master and Gorilla Man Scalp Blaster. Mr Burns is 81.

Homage: Homer runs out into the streets to spread the news of his hair's return in a lifted scene from *It's a Wonderful Life* (Frank Capra, 1946). His entry into the executive washroom closely parallels a scene in *Will Success Spoil Rock Hunter?* (Frank Tashlin, 1957).

Notes for Brits: Karl's line 'Don't Judge Me, Love Me' is a slogan of the American gay rights movement. Mr Burns refers to Du Mont TV, a short-lived US TV network from the 1950s.

Look out for: The reading of Karl's letter – an obvious gag, but a good one.

Notes: Brought to life by the superb character of Karl, helped no doubt by Harvey Fierstein's unique vocal drawl. Sadly Homer loses out at the end, but for a brief moment, he achieves glory. The glory of Mr Burns' executive washroom is another highlight.

16

7F04:

'The Simpsons Hallowe'en Special'
(aka 'Treehouse of Horror')

Written by Jay Kogen, Wallace Wolodarsky,
John Swartzwelder, Edgar Allan Poe and Sam Simon
Directed by Wes Archer, Rich Moore, David Silverman
Special guest voice: James Earl Jones
(as the Narrator, the Mover, and Serak the Preparer)

Premise: It's Hallowe'en – and in Bart's treehouse it's time to share tales of terror. In 'Bad Dream House' the Simpsons move into a haunted house. In 'Hungry are The Damned' they are abducted by ravenous aliens. And in 'The Raven' Homer mourns the loss of his beloved Lenore.

And introducing: Kodos, Kang.

Tombstones: Ishmael Simpson, Ezekiel Simpson, Cornelius V. Simpson (all three of these are American politicians or historical figures), Garfield, The Grateful Dead, Casper The Friendly Boy, Elvis, Your Name Here, Paul McCartney, Disco.

Homage: The haunted house segment owes a lot to *The Exorcist* (William Friedkin, 1973) (Maggie's revolving head), *Poltergeist* (Tobe Hooper, 1982) (the reference to the house being built on the site of an Indian burial ground), and *The Amityville Horror* (Stuart Rosenberg, 1979) (the bleeding walls), while the Rigellian plan for humanity recalls the *Twilight Zone* episode 'To Serve Man'. 'The Raven' is an almost direct transcription of Edgar Allan Poe's poem of lost love and ghastly redemption.

Notes: The first two segments work better than the third, but this is a marvellous episode, and set a high standard for the Hallowe'en specials to come.

17

7F01:

'Two Cars in Every Garage, Three Eyes on Every Fish'

Written by Sam Simon and John Swartzwelder
Directed by Wes Archer
Also starring: Maggie Roswell

Premise: Mr Burns wants to run for Governor against model politician and liberal Mary Bailey. But to win the hearts of the residents of Springfield, he must prove that it isn't his plant that's mutating the fish in the lake into three-eyed radioactive monsters.

Features: Lenny, Mr Burns, Smithers, Grampa, Jasper, Barney, Moe, the two barflies, Scott Christian.

Couch: The Simpsons rush in – and get snappered up by the sofabed.

Trivia: Bart has a cutting in his scrapbook relating to the events of 'The Tell-Tale Head'.

Homage: Mr Burns' initial address before a huge poster of himself is a steal from *Citizen Kane* (Orson Welles, 1941). It may be a coincidence, but the character played by Donna Reed in *It's a Wonderful Life*, the movie perhaps most referenced in *The Simpsons*, was called Mary Bailey.

Notes: A superb example of political satire, demonstrating the lengths people will go to to win votes. Marge, of course, sees straight through Burns and uses Blinky the three-eyed fish to demonstrate his lack of conviction. Poor Blinky – although three-eyed fish are seen again, notably in 'Lisa's Wedding'.

18
7F05:
'Dancin' Homer'

Written by Ken Levine and David Isaacs
Directed by Mark Kirkland
Also starring: Pamela Hayden
Special guest voices: Ken Levine (as Dan Horde),
Daryl L. Coley, Tony Bennett (as themselves),
Tom Poston (as Capital City Goofball)

Premise: Homer becomes a baseball mascot for a local team, thanks to his butt-swinging dance to 'The Baby Elephant

Walk'. The team's subsequent high scores bring him to the attention of the major league head hunters and big commmmercial sponsors. But will success spoil Homer?

Features: Barney, Moe, Otto, Mr Burns, Smithers, Bleedin' Gums Murphy, Helen Lovejoy, Ned Flanders, Milhouse, Janey, Patty and Selma, the two barflies.

Couch: The Simpsons, minus Maggie, rush in and sit down – and Maggie peeks out of Marge's hair.

Trivia: The Duff Brewery appears to be in Capital City which is some 220 miles away from Springfield.

Song: 'Capital City' sung by Tony Bennett.

Notes: Understanding baseball isn't really a requirement for this episode, as the humour doesn't come from the games so much as the personalities. Tony Bennett's cameo is great, and Homer's dance has rightly become legendary.

19

7F08:

'Dead Putting Society'

Written by Jeff Martin   **Directed by** Rich Moore
Also starring: Maggie Roswell

Premise: The friction between neighbours Flanders and Simpson reaches boiling point. So Ned and Homer enter their sons in a miniature golf game. There'll be no loser – but the father of the boy 'that doesn't win' will have to mow the other's lawn, wearing his wife's best Sunday dress.

Features: The Flanderses, Rev. Lovejoy, Helen Lovejoy, Ralph, Jimbo Jones, Dolph, Kearney, Krusty, Principal Skinner, Ms Krabappel.

Couch: The Simpsons rush in – followed by Snowball II and Santa's Little Helper.

Trivia: Maud Flanders' nickname for Ned is Spongecake.

Look out for: Maggie's solo exploration of Sir Putt-A-Lot's.

Notes: Apart from the memorable lawn mowing sequence at the end, this episode is notable for our first viewing of the gaudy, gadget-filled, God-fearing splendour that is the Flanderses' home.

20
7F07:
'Bart vs. Thanksgiving'

Written by George Meyer   **Directed by** David Silverman
  Also starring: Greg Berg (as the bum), Maggie Roswell

Premise: It's Thanksgiving, and Lisa has made a marvellous centrepiece for the table – which Bart accidentally throws on the fire. Unwilling to apologise, Bart and Santa's Little Helper run away to join the down and outs in Downtown Springfield.

Features: Patty, Selma, Jackie Bouvier, Grampa, Mr Burns, Smithers, Kent Brockman, Eddie, Lou.

Couch: Grampa is asleep on the sofa but wakes up with a start when the family dash in.

And introducing: Bill and Marty at KBBL.

Trivia: Homer's favourite football team are the Dallas Cowboys. The music to accompany the break in the Thanksgiving Parade is 'Get Dancing', a 1974 hit by Disco-Tex and the Sex-O-Lettes.

Notes for the Uneducated: Lisa's angst-ridden poem – 'My soul carved in slices/ By spiky-haired demons' is very close to Allen Ginsberg's poem 'Howl'. Mr Burns' mansion is at the crossroads of Croesus and Mammon, both of whom are mythological figures of greed.

Look out for: Homer telling the family that the Thanksgiving Parade only features old cartoon characters. And the sexless sanitised pop group Hooray For Everything.

Notes: Marge's mother Jackie is particularly nightmarish in her first real appearance. The final sequence on the rooftop with Lisa and Bart is lovely, and Homer's comment to Marge is a magical wrap-up to a good show.

21
7F06:
'Bart the Daredevil'

Written by Jay Kogen and Wallace Wolodarsky
Directed by Wesley Meyer Archer
Also starring: Pamela Hayden, Maggie Roswell

Premise: Springfield's Speedway plays host to daredevil Captain Lance Murdoch and Truck-o-Saurus, America's biggest monster truck. It's setting the local kids a very bad example. Especially Bart.

Features: Milhouse, Lewis, Richard, Nelson, Barney, Principal Skinner, Mr Largo, Ned Flanders, Tod, Otto.

Couch: The Simpsons rush in – but Homer's weight proves too much for the sofa.

And introducing: Dr Hibbert.

Notes: This is the episode with the sequence everyone remembers, as Homer falls down the gorge. He's getting much stupider by this point.

22

7F09:

'Itchy and Scratchy and Marge'

Written by John Swartzwelder   **Directed by** Jim Reardon
Additional cast: Pamela Hayden, Maggie Roswell
Special guest voice: Alex Rocco (as Roger Myers)

Premise: After watching an Itchy and Scratchy cartoon Maggie strikes Homer with a mallet. Horrified, Marge vows to put a stop to violence on children's television. But when the ball of censorship starts to roll, where will it all end?

Features: Krusty, Kent Brockman, the Flanderses.

Couch: The Simpsons rush in – but the sofa's not there.

Homage: The idyllic scene of happy children at play in a world without TV violence recalls the Beethoven's '6th Symphony' sequence from Walt Disney's *Fantasia* (1940). Best of all, and one of the first and best detailed movie spoofs in the series, is Maggie's attack on Homer – complete with rended tablecloth, gory red paint and eyeball close-up, which is lifted directly from *Psycho* (Alfred Hitchcock, 1960).

Itchy and Scratchy in: 'Hold That Feline', 'Kitchen Cut-Ups', and the sanitised, Marge-approved 'Porch Pals'.

Look out for: The Marge-approved version of Itchy and Scratchy: 'They love, they share . . .'

Notes: Homer's doomed attempt to build a spice rack is only the start of another great episode, which works as a superb debate about television violence and politically inspired censorship. The ending is especially poignant, as the peda-gogues of Springfield swoop on Michelangelo's David as an example of filth and degradation.

23

7F10:

'Bart Gets Hit By a Car'

Written by John Swartzwelder
Directed by Mark Kirkland
Also starring: Doris Grau
Special guest voice: Phil Hartman (as Lionel Hutz)

Premise: Bart is knocked off his skateboard by Mr Burns in his car. After a brief trip to Heaven, and a slightly less brief visit to Hell, he falls to Earth. With the help of dodgy lawyer Lionel Hutz, Homer tries to sue Burns for a million dollars. And Marge and Lisa discover there are many ways that you can arrive at the truth.

Features: Smithers, Mr Burns, Ned Flanders, Todd Flanders, Dr Hibbert, Larry, Carl, Charlie, Herman, Moe, Barney.

Couch: Homer wriggles until he forces the others on to the floor.

And introducing: Springfield DA, Lionel Hutz, Dr Nick Riviera.

Trivia: This episode has an on-screen title – 'preceded by Episode 23' – which, indeed, it is. Hutz's card reads 'Lionel Hutz Attorney at Law as seen on TV KLondike 5-LAWW. Clogging up our courts since 1976.' Satan (who bears an uncanny resemblance to Ned Flanders) realises Bart is ahead of schedule during his brief trip to Hell, telling Bart he's not, in fact, due to go to hell until the Yankees next win the Pennant – in about a century. Dr Nick Riviera's credentials are Mayo Clinic Correspondence School; Female Body Inspector; Club Med School and I Went to Medical School for Four Years and all I got was this Lousy Diploma.

Homage: Bart's revival mirrors the return of Dorothy to Earth in *The Wizard of Oz* (Victor Fleming, 1939). The Devil's first line is, appropriately enough, the first line of the Rolling Stones' 'Sympathy for the Devil'.

Notes for the Uneducated: Hell as seen in this episode is taken from Hieronymous Bosch's painting 'The Garden of Earthly Delights'.

Look out for: The differing flashbacks to the car accident given by Bart and Mr Burns.

Notes: An interesting episode in that we begin to see the very dark side of Burns that will develop later, although Smithers is still just a toady. A good introduction for Lionel Hutz and a nice look at Hell, Heaven and the original Snowball.

24

7F11:

'One Fish, Two Fish, Blowfish, Blue Fish'

Written by Nell Scovell **Directed by** Wesley M. Archer
Also starring: Joey Miyashima (as Toshiro),
Diana Tanaka (as the hostess), Sab Shimono (as Master Chef)
Special guest voices: Larry King (as himself),
George Takei (as Akira)

Premise: Lisa convinces the family to try a new Sushi restaurant, the Happy Sumo. A menu mix-up leads to Homer eating a poisoned blowfish. Dr Hibbert gives him twenty-four hours to live. He sets about placing his affairs in order.

Features: Mr Burns, Smithers, Moe, Barney, the two barflies, Grampa, Ned Flanders, Dr Hibbert, Eddie, Lou.

Couch: The sofa tips over backwards and only Maggie crawls back up again.

Trivia: Homer lists thirteen things to do before he dies. These are: (1) Make list (2) Eat hearty breakfast (3) Make videotape for Maggie (4) Have man-to-man with Bart (5) Listen to Lisa play her sax (6) Make funeral arrangements (7) Make peace with Dad (8) Beer with the boys at the bar (9) Tell off boss (10) Go hang gliding (11) Plant a tree (12) A final dinner with my beloved family (13) Be intimate with Marge.

Homage: The Happy Sumo's karaoke machine plays host to Japanese businessman Richie Sakai (a reference to the *Simpsons* producer of the same name), who sings 'Gypsies, Tramps and Thieves', a 1971 hit for Cher, and Lisa and Bart, who duet on Isaac Hayes' '71 'Theme From Shaft'. The scene where Homer hammers on the car window calling Marge's name is a lift from *The Graduate* (Mike Nichols, 1967).

Hello, can I speak to: Seymour Butz.

That's Homer Simpson, sir: 'One of the schmoos from Sector 7G'.

Notes: Again, a playful dig at racial stereotypes. Homer comes over as a reasonable man who wants to live his last day in style, and the closing twist is easily as good as the farewells leading up to it.

25

7F12:

'The Way We Was'

Written by Al Jean, Mike Reiss and Sam Simon
Directed by David Silverman
Also starring: Tress MacNeille, Maggie Roswell,
Jon Lovitz (as Artie Ziff)

Premise: When the television breaks down, Lisa and Bart are forced to listen to Marge and Homer explaining how they met, at Springfield High in 1974.

Features: Dr Hibbert, Barney, Grampa, Jackie Bouvier, Patty, Selma.

Couch: The Simpsons rush in – and the sofa falls through the floor.

And introducing: McBain (as played by Rainier Wolfcastle).

Trivia: We see the TV film review show *Yakkin' About Movies*. McBain stars in *Today We Kill, Tomorrow We Die*.

Homage: Marge's date Artie Ziff sings the Carpenters 1970 hit '(They Long To Be) Close To You'. Homer much prefers the Steve Miller Band's 1973 single 'The Joker' and Barry White's 1974 hit 'You're The First, The Last, My Everything'. We also hear Van McCoy's 'The Hustle'.

Look out for: Homer trying to work out which guidance counsellor he needs to see by going through the alphabet.

Notes: A superb episode. Some colourful background for Homer and Marge (and a glimpse of Homer and Barney's schooldays) plus our introduction to the world of the McBain movies. Excellent.

26
7F13:
'Homer vs. Lisa and the 8th Commandment'

Written by Steve Pepoon **Directed by** Rich Moore
Also starring: Pamela Hayden, Tress MacNeille
Special guest voice: Phil Hartman (as Troy McClure)

Premise: Homer gets hooked up to cable TV for $50 – '1600 hours of quality programming every day!' Lisa's not happy – will cable piracy send the Simpsons to hell?

Features: Ned Flanders, Rev. Lovejoy, Miss Allbright, Milhouse, Martin, Dr Nick Riviera, Lenny, Carl, Smithers, Mr Burns, Barney, Moe, the two barflies, Lou and Eddie.

Couch: The Simpsons perform a shimmying dance number.

And introducing: Troy McClure.

Trivia: Cable delights include 'Hear Me Roar', the network for women, pro-wrestling from Mexico, reruns of *Jaws*, *Die Hard* and *Police Academy*, Congress, World Series of Cockfighting, 'I Can't Believe They Invented It!', The Blockbuster Channel, and Top Hat Adult Entertainment (titles including 'Stardust Mammaries' and 'Broadcast Nudes').

Hi, I'm Troy McClure, you may remember me from: such movies as *Cry Yuma* and *Here Comes the Coastguard*.

Notes for Brits: Tatum and Watson are close cousins of Mike Tyson and James 'Buster' Douglas respectively (Douglas, like Watson, was in the habit of dedicating matches to unlikely people).

Notes for the Uneducated: Lisa's non-violent protest is reminiscent of Mahatma Gandhi's protests against the British occupation of India, during which, just like Lisa, he would drink only lemonade. 'Gentleman Jim' Corbett (1866–1933) was the first heavyweight boxing champion under the Queensberry Rules. The fight remembered by Mr Burns took place in 1897! 'Hear Me Roar' is a reference to a line in the chorus of Helen Reddy's hit 'I Am Woman'.

That's Homer Simpson, sir: 'one of your drones from sector 7G'.

Notes: A skilful demonstration of a moral dilemma that must have plagued millions since the inception of cable TV.

27

7F15:

'Principal Charming'

Written by David Stern   **Directed by** Mark Kirkland
Also starring: Pamela Hayden, Maggie Roswell
Special guest voice: Marcia Wallace (as Ms Krabappel)

Premise: Selma must find a husband. Homer thinks he's found the perfect match – Principal Skinner. But Skinner falls for Patty – who comes to realise that her life of celibacy might have been an error.

Features: Barney, Mrs Winfield, Krusty, Otto, Apu, Hans Moleman, Principal Skinner, Stanley, Richard, Milhouse, Lewis, Chief Wiggum, Sherri and Terri, Moe, the two barflies.

Couch: The Simpsons rush in – and get caught in the sofabed.

And introducing: Groundskeeper Willie.

Trivia: The rotating restaurant in Springfield is the Sit-n-Rotate Room. Patty and Selma are 40, and live in apartment 1599. Patty and Skinner see *Space Mutants V: The Land Down Under*. 'Gee, Your Lip Looks Hairless' is a kind of beauty product. Seymour has extensive files on Bart's tardiness, rudeness and vandalism amongst others. Homer's work number is KLondike 5.6832, home is KLondike 5.6754 and Moe's Tavern is KLondike 5.1239. Happy Hour at Moe's lasts thirty minutes (naturally), between 5 and 5.30 p.m. Selma sings 'Brandy', a 1971 hit for Scott English.

Homage: There's a scene recreated from *Vertigo* (Alfred Hitchcock, 1958), as Principal Skinner climbs the school tower. Homer's attempts to locate a suitable man for Patty include a computer-enhanced overlay on his vision that closely resembles that used by *The Terminator* (James

Cameron, 1984). And Principal Skinner's final return to the school is straight out of *Gone With the Wind*.

Hello, can I speak to: Homer Sexual.

Notes: Good fun, with both Patty and Selma gaining a degree of humanity. Bart makes very good use of his new-found freedom as Skinner's pseudo-in-law, much to the annoyance of Groundskeeper Willie, making his first appearance.

28

7F16:

'Oh Brother, Where Art Thou?'

Written by Jeff Martin   **Directed by** Wes Archer
Also starring: Pamela Hayden, Maggie Roswell
Special guest voice: Danny DeVito (as Herb)

Premise: Homer tracks down his long-lost half brother, Herb Powell. Herb is a millionaire car manufacturer, a success that Homer certainly isn't. Convinced that Homer's common touch can give him the edge over his competitors, Herb allows Homer to design a car for the average guy.

Features: Wolfcastle (as McBain), Jasper, Grampa, Dr Hibbert.

Couch: The Simpsons, minus Maggie, rush in and sit down – and Maggie peeks out of Marge's hair.

Trivia: We see the best McBain movie – and learn that he'll be back in *You Have the Right to Remain Dead*. The orphanage director has a long-lost twin brother – and he bears more than a passing resemblance to Dr Julius Hibbert, in which case they may have another brother, Bleedin' Gums Murphy (see 'Round Springfield').

Homage: The line 'As far as I'm concerned, I have no brother' comes from *The Godfather* (Francis Ford Coppola, 1973).

Itchy and Scratchy in: 'Sundae Bloody Sundae'.

Notes: Although it's inevitable that Homer's car will be a disaster, the joy of this episode is anticipating exactly what sort of disaster. Herb Powell returns in 'Brother, Can You Spare Two Dimes'.

29

7F14:

'Bart's Dog Gets an F'

Written by Jon Vitti   **Directed by** Jim Reardon
Also starring: Frank Welker
Special guest voices: Phil Hartman (as Troy McClure),
Tracey Ullman (as Miss Winthropp)

Premise: Santa's Little Helper is getting restless and destructive, so Bart takes him to obedience school. However, he doesn't learn very much and so Homer threatens to get rid of him if he doesn't improve.

Features: Dr Hibbert, Sylvia Hibbert, Mrs Winfield, Ned Flanders, Lenny, Newspaper vendor, Kent Brockman, Krusty, Troy McClure, Martin Prince.

Couch: The Simpsons rush in – and are joined by Santa's Little Helper and Snowball II.

Trivia: There is a brief shot of Miss Botz from 'Some Enchanted Evening' on Kent's show. Other dogs at Miss Winthropp's class include Buddy and Lao-Tzu. The magazines Homer buys for Lisa are *Teen Scream*, *Teen Screen* and *Teen Steam*. Other mags on sale include *Teen Team*, *Teen Dream*, *Teen Spleen* and *Non-Threatening Boys*. Tracey Ullman's Miss

Winthropp clearly seems to be based on the late TV dog trainer, Barbara Woodhouse.

Homage: The shots of Santa's Little Helper's point of view are a lift from *Predator* (John McTiernan, 1987). Dr Hibbert's home and his family rather resemble Bill Cosby's home and family in *The Cosby Show*, which was running against this season of *The Simpsons* at the time.

Notes: An enjoyable episode this, heightened by both Tracey Ullman's Miss Winthropp and Frank Welker's muted dog noises.

30
7F17:
'Old Money'

Written by Jay Kogen and Wallace Wolodarsky
Directed by David Silverman
Also starring: Maggie Roswell
Special guest voices: Phil Hartman (as Lionel Hutz),
Audrey Meadows (as Beatrice),
Marcia Wallace (as Ms Krabappel)

Premise: Grampa's dating glamorous Beatrice Simmons. When she passes away, Grampa is left $106,000 to spend as he wishes and so he heads for the casino – pursued by Homer.

Features: Grampa, Jasper, Herman, Dr Hibbert, Rev. Lovejoy, Lionel Hutz, Moe, Barney, Otto, Mr Burns, Smithers, Dr John Frink, Dr Marvin Monroe, Kent Brockman, Apu, Ms Krabappel, Mr Largo, Krusty, Nelson Muntz, Sideshow Mel, Helen Lovejoy, Ned Flanders, Maude Flanders, Principal Skinner.

Couch: The Simpsons rush in – and surprise slumbering Grampa.

Trivia: Homer's list of places to take Grampa include Pony Rides, The Glassblower in Old Springfield Town, the Museum of Barnyard Oddities and the Springfield Mystery Spot. Grampa considers visiting Club Mod, going paragliding and heading to Diz-Nee-Land ('not affiliated with Disneyland, DisneyWorld or anything else from the Walt Disney Company').

Homage: Grampa's passionate pill-popping with Beatrice is a rather cruel adaptation of the erotic food scene from *Tom Jones* (Tony Richardson, 1963).

Notes: A wonderful episode, very sad but ultimately uplifting, with great one-liners (particularly from Grampa). The closing credits (for no readily apparent reason) list the roles played by the six members of the regular cast.

31

7F18:

'Brush with Greatness'

Written by Brian K. Roberts   **Directed by** Jim Reardon
Also starring: Maggie Roswell
Special guest voices: Jon Lovitz (as Lombardo),
Ringo Starr (as himself)

Premise: After the Simpsons take a trip to Mount Splashmore Water Park, Homer decides to lose weight. Decades after her creative spirit was crushed by the education system and an unanswered letter to Ringo Starr, frustrated Marge takes up art classes. She's commissioned to paint a portrait of Mr Burns – and catches him in an extremely unflattering light.

Features: Krusty, Sideshow Mel, Kent Brockman, Apu, Carl, Barney, Moe, Dr Hibbert, Miss Hoover.

Couch: The sofa tips sideways but Maggie ends up safe on a cushion.

Trivia: Mount Splashmore offers a whole two hours' free parking and nose plug rental, and has a post-ride trauma centre on the premises. The unveiling of Marge's painting of Burns is to mark the opening of the Burns Wing of the Springfield Palace of Fine Art.

Homage: Krusty wipes his make-up from his face in a very similar way to Jack Nicholson as the Joker in *Batman* (Tim Burton, 1989). Homer limbers up just like Sylvester Stallone in *Rocky* (John G. Avildsen, 1976), and the animated Ringo Starr hasn't changed much since *Yellow Submarine* (George Dunning, 1968).

Look out for: The very clever blocking of Burns' genitals in Marge's portrait.

Song: 'Take Me to Mount Splashmore' sung by Krusty.

Notes: A superb episode, with Marge rightfully centre stage. Despite his general unpleasantness, Mr Burns' gratitude to Marge is both welcome and unexpected. And the dig at Water Parks is spot on.

32
7F19:
'Lisa's Substitute'

Written by Jon Vitti   **Directed by** Rich Moore
Also starring: Pamela Hayden, Maggie Roswell,
JoAnn Harris, Russi Taylor
Special guest voices: Marcia Wallace (as Ms Krabappel),
Sam Etic (a pseudonym for Dustin Hoffman –
as Mr Bergstrom)

Premise: When Miss Hoover falls ill, Lisa's class gets a substitute teacher – rugged liberal Mr Bergstrom. Lisa's instantly smitten, and a special relationship develops. But what will happen when Mr Bergstrom has to go?

Features: Janey, Miss Hoover, Principal Skinner, Ralph, Sherri and Terri, Martin Prince, Wendell, Edna Krabappel, Lewis, Richard, Milhouse, Nelson Muntz.

Couch: The Simpsons rush in – but the sofa's gone missing.

Trivia: Other guests at The Happy Gypsy include I. Kamerman, J. Vitti and P. Hogan.

Homage: Ms Krabappel's attempted seduction of Mr Bergstrom is lifted from Dustin Hoffman's similar situation in *The Graduate* (Mike Nichols, 1967).

Notes for the Uneducated: Mr Bergstrom reads E. B. White's children's classic *Charlotte's Web* to Lisa's class.

Look out for: Ms Krabappel's sheer delight at the result of the school election.

Notes: Despite a scene-stealing performance from Ms Krabappel, this is Lisa's show. Mr Bergstrom's last message for Lisa is a delightful touch and adds the finishing touch to a wonderful episode.

33

7F20:

'War of the Simpsons'

Written by John Swartzwelder
Directed by Mark Kirkland
Also starring: Pamela Hayden, Maggie Roswell

Premise: Following a disastrous party, the Simpsons' marriage takes a turn for the worse. Marge and Homer head for Rev. Lovejoy's retreat for unhappy couples. Homer, however, would rather go fishing for the legendary trout known as General

Sherman. Back home, Bart and Lisa make mischief with Grampa.

Features: Ned Flanders, Maude Flanders, Moe, Dr Hibbert, Mrs Hibbert, Barney, Selma, Patty, Rev. Lovejoy, Helen Lovejoy, Grampa, Rainier Wolfcastle, Milhouse, Otto, Snake, Wendell, Sherri and Terri, Janey, Nelson, Lewis, Richard, Jimbo Jones, Dolph, Kearney.

Couch: Homer wiggles about so much that the others are squeezed on to the floor.

Homage: The trip taken by Grampa and the kids to the safari is a lift from *The Omen* (Richard Donner, 1976), and some of Marge and Homer's arguments are taken from *Who's Afraid Of Virginia Woolf?* (Mike Nichols, 1966). Among the music heard in this episode is Homer's rendition of 'We Are the Champions', a 1977 hit for Queen. Tom Jones' 'It's Not Unusual' (1965), Dusty Springfield's 'The Look of Love' (1967) and KC and the Sunshine Band's 'That's the Way (I Like It)' (1975) are also heard.

Notes for the Uneducated: Homer's recollection of the party – as an evening of witty ripostes and sophisticated rivalry – suggests the activities of the 1930s New York literary circle known as the Algonquin Round Table.

Notes: The Homer vs. Marge plot is good on its own, but this is also Grampa's big moment. His final revelation to Bart and Lisa is inspired.

34

7F21:

'Three Men and a Comic Book'

Written by Jeff Martin   **Directed by** Wes Archer
Also starring: Pamela Hayden, Russi Taylor

Special guest voices: Daniel Stern (as *The Wonder Years'* narrator), Cloris Leachman (as Mrs Glick)

Premise: Bart must have Issue One of *Radioactive Man* ($100) but even after working hard for Mrs Glick, he hasn't enough cash until he teams up with Milhouse and Martin, and they buy it jointly to share on schooldays. But who will keep it at weekends?

Features: Nelson Muntz, Otto, Milhouse, Barney, Lou and Eddie, Patty and Selma, Apu.

Couch: The sofa falls over backwards, but Maggie gets up.

And introducing: The Android's Dungeon Guy.

Trivia: It is the twelfth annual 'Close Encounter of the Comic Book Kind' Convention. Lisa collects 'Casper the Friendly Ghost' comics. Some attendees are dressed up for the occasion; costumes include Krusty the Klown, Bug Man and Radioactive Man. Bart, of course, is Bartman. Patty and Selma are fans of Frankie Avalon. Buddy Hodges has just finished a run in *Cats*.

Homage: There's a great sequence parodying *The Wonder Years* – Bart stares into the distance and his voice is heard saying 'I didn't realise it at the time, but a little piece of my childhood had slipped away for ever that day . . .'

Notes: Unless you have a passing understanding of comic books and their buyers' behaviour, some of this will pass you by. Believe every cruel word.

35
7F22:
'Blood Feud'

Written by George Meyer   **Directed by** David Silverman
Also starring: Maggie Roswell

Premise: When Mr Burns fails to turn up at the unveiling of the new Springfield nuclear emergency warning sign, Smithers discovers him dying. A search for a blood donor goes out and Bart saves the day. With help from ghostwriter Roman Mr Burns starts to pen his autobiography. But things go wrong when Homer, expecting a hefty reward, is palmed off with a thank-you card.

Features: Mr Burns, Smithers, Mayor Quimby, Chief Wiggum, Dr Hibbert, Barney, Moe, Otto, Lenny, Carl, the FeMail Man.

Couch: The sofa falls through the floor.

Trivia: Mr Burns' biography is called *Will There Ever Be A Rainbow?* Other books Roman has ghostwritten include *Like Hell I Can't!*, *Up From The Muck* and *The Unsinkable Sedrorovin Murghurobag*. Burns' and Bart's blood type is OO– while Homer's is A+. Lisa's shoe size is 4B, Bart has 16 permanent and 8 baby teeth and is allergic to butterscotch, imitation butterscotch and Glo-in-the-Dark Monster Make-Up.

Notes for the Uneducated: The Springfield Post Office has an amusing variant on Michelangelo's 1511 painting 'The Creation of Adam'.

Look out for: The end sequence where the family discuss the moral implications of the episode.

Hello, can I speak to: Mike Rotch.

Notes: One of those shows that people always talk about when discussing *The Simpsons* – and rightfully so. Homer's transformation from angry parent to sensible, calm husband (and his comment about understanding why wives are called 'the better half') is excellent, as is his reaction to Bart posting his angry letter. Their attempts to retrieve the letter (Homer telling the postal clerk he's Mr Burns) and Burns' eventual reaction are fabulous.

Third Season

1991–1992
23 Episodes

36

7F24:
'Stark Raving Dad'

Written by Al Jean and Mike Reiss
Directed by Rich Moore
Additional cast: Pamela Hayden, Kipp Lennon
Special guest voice: John Jay Smith (pseudonym for
Michael Jackson – as Leon Kompowsky)

Premise: A mixed wash accident leads to Homer's incarceration in a mental institution – where he encounters Michael Jackson. Sort of. Back home, it's Lisa's birthday – and Bart's forgotten to buy her a present.

Features: Mr Burns, Smithers, Lenny, Carl, Dr Marvin Monroe, Milhouse, Kearney, Otto, Krusty, Snake, Grampa, Barney, Dr Hibbert, Selma, Mrs Winfield, Moe, Bill and Marty from KBBL, Apu, Quimby, Kent Brockman. There are so many cameos outside the Simpsons' house at the end we could be here all day – but notables include Princess Kashmir and the twins dated by Mr Burns and Smithers, both from 'Homer's Night Out'.

Couch: The Simpsons hit the sofa with such force that it topples backwards and smashes through the wall.

Homage: Many scenes and lines are taken from *One Flew Over the Cuckoo's Nest* (Milos Forman, 1975). Floyd, the 'idiot savant' at the rest home, comes from *Rain Man* (Barry Levinson, 1988).

Notes for Brits: The guy in the crowd with the rainbow Afro wig and the 'John 3:16' placard is 'the Rainbow Man', a born-again Christian who in the late seventies and early eighties attempted to appear on television as often as possible, often showing up at big televised events.

Itchy and Scratchy in: 'Bang the Cat Slowly'.

That's Homer Simpson, sir: 'one of your boobs from sector 7G.'

Notes: This episode was held over to start the third season with a real kick. Startling in its audacity towards Michael Jackson, whose agreement to provide the voice of Leon in this episode proves either that he's got a more developed sense of his own ridiculousness than you might expect, or that he just didn't understand what the writers were saying about him.

37

7F23:

'When Flanders Failed'

Written by Jon Vitti   **Directed by** Jim Reardon
Also starring: Pamela Hayden, Maggie Roswell,
Tress MacNeille

Premise: Ned Flanders gives up his office job and opens up the Leftorium, a gift shop for southpaws (that's left-handed people) in Springfield Mall. But before long, the business fails and the Flanderses lose everything. Only Homer can come to their rescue.

Features: The Flanderses, Jasper, Jimbo Jones, Kearney, Dolph, Barney, Moe, Mr Burns, Smithers, Ms Krabappel, Apu,

Otto, Lionel Hutz, Sideshow Mel, Kent Brockman, Principal Skinner, Dr Nick, Dr Marvin Monroe, Chief Wiggum, Helen Lovejoy, Lenny, Mayor Quimby, Eddie and Lou.

Couch: The Simpsons rush in – and break into an Egyptian dance.

Trivia: The Springfield Martial Arts Academy is next door to Shakespeare's Fried Chicken. Among the production credits on Itchy and Scratchy are Mobile Medical Unit Trauma Staff on Call, Arson Control, Bomb Squad, Fire Prevention Team, Catering for the Director (Fine French Cuisine), Catering for Staff (Krusty Burgers), Production Supervisors in Charge of Coffee, Miscellaneous Dirty Work Staff and, of course, Assistants to the Assistants.

Homage: Several sequences are lifted from *It's a Wonderful Life*.

Notes for the Uneducated: *The Art of War* by Sun Tzu is a genuine ancient text.

Itchy and Scratchy in: 'O Solo Meow'.

Mmmmm: . . . barbecue.

Look out for: Mr Burns and his white cat.

Notes: A clever episode – very conveniently for Flanders, it seems that everyone except the Rev. Lovejoy, the Simpsons and Hans Moleman are left-handed.

38
8F01:
'Mr Lisa Goes to Washington'

Written by George Meyer   **Directed by** Wes Archer
Also starring: JoAnn Harris, Pamela Hayden,
Tress MacNeille, Maggie Roswell
Special guest voice: Lona Williams

Premise: Lisa wins a speech competition run by the Reading Digest – 'The Patriots of Tomorrow' – and heads for Washington. When she uncovers corruption at the highest levels of the Capitol, she alters her speech to reflect her disgust – and stirs trouble.

Features: Nelson, Lenny, Carl, Jasper, Barney, Moe.

Couch: The family rush in – and sit on Santa's Little Helper.

Trivia: The Simpson address is given here as 94 Evergreen Terrace, Springfield, TA 192005. There's a film poster advertising *Creature with a Shovel* featuring Troy McClure. Homer reads the articles 'Can We Trust Bermuda?', 'They Call Me Dr Soybeans' and 'Motoring Mishaps' in Reading Digest. We see the Springfield state seal for the first time in this episode.

Homage: Lisa's exposure of corruption mirrors the events of *Mr Smith Goes to Washington* (Frank Capra, 1939).

Notes: One of the best Lisa-centric episodes, with her talk with Jefferson and her nightmare vision of politicians as pigs especially worthy of note.

39

8F03:

'Bart the Murderer'

Written by John Swartzwelder   **Directed by** Rich Moore
Additional cast: JoAnn Harris, Pamela Hayden
Special guest voices: Joe Mantegna (as Don Tony),
Phil Hartman (as Lionel Hutz), Neil Patrick Harris (as himself),
Marcia Wallace (as Ms Krabappel)

Premise: Bart's having a bad day – but it gets even worse, and then much better when he finds himself at the Legitimate Businessman's Social Club, home of Don Tony's mob. The gang can grant Bart his greatest desire – the death of Principal Skinner.

Features: Ms Krabappel, Ralph Wiggum, Nelson, Richard, Lewis, Principal Skinner, Miss Hoover, Milhouse, Troy McClure, Chief Wiggum, Groundskeeper Willie, Rev. Lovejoy, Lionel Hutz, Smithers, Mr Burns, Eddie.

Couch: The family form a pyramid, with Maggie on top.

Homage: Principally *GoodFellas* (Martin Scorsese, 1990), in which a young boy is employed by the Mob as their messenger (the sequence when Bart falls down the steps into the cellar club is very similar) – but also *The Godfather* (Francis Ford Coppola, 1972). Bart sings Frank Sinatra's 'Witchcraft' in the kitchen.

Hi, I'm Troy McClure, you may remember me from: such films as *The Revenge of Abe Lincoln* and *The Wackiest Covered Wagon in the West.*

Itchy and Scratchy in: 'The Sounds of Silencers'.

Notes: This episode contains what may be Principal Skinner's finest hour, as he explains away his apparent death to a stunned courtroom.

40

8F04:

'Homer Defined'

Written by Howard Gewirtz   **Directed by** Mark Kirkland
Also starring: Maggie Roswell, Pamela Hayden, Russi Taylor
Special guest voices: Jon Lovitz (as Aristotle Amadopolis),
Earvin 'Magic' Johnson Jnr, Chick Hearn (as themselves)

Premise: Homer becomes a celebrity when he stops two nuclear meltdowns, much to the delight of Mr Burns and

Lisa. But can Homer continue the rise to stardom without his mediocrity showing through? Bart's also got problems – Milhouse has been forbidden to associate with him.

Features: Otto, Milhouse, Sherri and Terri, Martin Prince, Richard, Mr Burns, Smithers, Lenny, Carl, Apu, Kent Brockman, Barney, Moe, Jasper, Grampa, Dr John Frink, Principal Skinner, Mrs van Houten, Scott Christian, Chief Wiggum, Snake.

Couch: As the Simpsons run in, an alien escapes through a trapdoor.

Trivia: Smithers' Yorkshire Terrier is called Hercules. Smithers also tells us that Homer was employed under Project: Bootstrap, for which Mr Burns blames ex-President Gerald Ford.

Homage: The calm female voice in the nuclear plant counting the seconds to meltdown comes from *The Andromeda Strain* (Robert Wise, 1970).

Itchy and Scratchy in: 'My Dinner with Itchy'.

Mmmmm: . . . custard . . . purple.

Notes: An excellent episode, with Marge trying to convince Mrs van Houten that Bart should be allowed to play with Milhouse adding another layer. Lisa's faith in her heroic father makes a nice change, and the resolution, as Homer earns a place in the dictionary, is most satisfying.

41
8F05:
'Like Father, Like Clown'

Written by Jay Kogen and Wallace Wolodarsky
Directed by Jeffrey Lynch with Brad Bird
Also starring: Pamela Hayden, Doris Grau, Tress MacNeille

Special guest voices:
Jackie Mason (as Rabbi Hyman Krustofski)

Premise: Disowned by his father Rabbi Krustofski, Krusty sinks into a spiral of drink and depression. Can Bart and Lisa find a way to convince Rabbi Krustofski to accept his estranged son?

Features: Krusty, Sideshow Mel, Apu, Milhouse, Rev. Lovejoy, Moe, Barney.

Couch: Bart runs on late and lies across the rest of the family.

Trivia: Bart is Krusty Buddy # 13602. The Springfield X cinema is showing: *For Your Thighs Only*, *Crocodile Done Me* and *Doctor Strangepants*. Among the magazines on sale in the shop are: *Ballooning Monthly*, *Cooking With Coconut Magazine*, *Fabergé Egg Owner*, *Ballpoint Pen Digest* and *Modern Jewish Father*. The KBBL religious radio show featuring Rabbi Krustofski and Rev. Lovejoy is called *Gabbin' About God*. Lisa's research into the Jewish people leads her to the books *The Big Book of the Church People*, *Jewishness Revisited* and *Views on Jews*.

Homage: This episode draws heavily on *The Jazz Singer* (Richard Fleischer, 1980) for its main theme of a Jewish father disowning his son for going into showbusiness. The song played at the end is 'O Mein Papa', a 1952 hit for Eddie Fisher.

Itchy and Scratchy in: 'Field of Screams'.

Notes: A magnificent show, with Jackie Mason wonderfully over the top as Krusty's long-lost pa, and Lois Pennycandy giving Krusty a good talking to about Bart. The shared directors' credit is presumably because a lot of footage from 'Krusty Gets Busted' is included, and that episode was directed by Brad Bird.

42

8F02:

'The Simpsons Hallowe'en Special II'
(aka 'Treehouse of Horror II')

Written by Al Jean and Mike Reiss, Jeff Martin,
George Meyer, Sam Simon, John Swartzwelder
Directed by Jim Reardon
Additional cast: Maggie Roswell
Special guest voice: Marcia Wallace (as Ms Krabappel)

Premise: Homer, Lisa and Bart ignore Marge's warnings, and consume a haul of candy obtained from trick-or-treating. Three nightmares commence . . . Lisa dreams of the Monkey's Paw, which grants its owners four wishes; Bart dreams of possessing awesome mental powers; and Homer dreams of being replaced by a robot with his own brain.

Features: Kent Brockman, Jimbo, Kearney, Otto, Helen Lovejoy, Moe, Krusty, Kodos and Kang, Quimby, Apu, Jasper, Principal Skinner, Ms Krabappel, Barney, the two barflies, Dr Marvin Monroe, Smithers, Mr Burns, Lenny, Carl, Groundskeeper Willie.

Tombstones: Bambi's Mom, Jim Morrison, Cajun Cooking, Walt Disney, Lose Weight Now Ask Me How.

Trivia: Homer tries to smuggle a HONK IF YOU'RE MOROCCAN bumper sticker through customs. Simpsons merchandise in Lisa's nightmare includes the album 'The Simpsons Go Calypso!' (available on CD and 8-track cartridge), a Bart T-shirt (price $18), and Bart's 'Get a Mammogram, Man' public health campaign. It looks like the head of Jebediah Springfield's statue wasn't very well glued back on after 'The Tell-Tale Head'.

Homage: The horse's head in Lisa's bed is similar to *The Godfather* (Francis Ford Coppola, 1972). Marge's hair recalls *Bride of Frankenstein* (James Whale, 1932). The big influence is *The Twilight Zone* TV series; the episodes 'A Small Talent for War' and 'It's a Good Life' form the basis for Lisa's and Bart's dreams respectively. 'It's a Good Life' was remade as part of *Twilight Zone – The Movie* (Various, 1983). There are also references to the seventies *Charlie Brown* TV cartoons (the crowd of trick-or-treaters at the start of the episode), and *The Wizard of Oz* (Victor Fleming, 1939) (Mr Burns' scolding of his robot creation). Homer's attempt to smuggle the Monkey's Paw into America by taping it to his body and his discovery by customs guards, recalls the attempt to smuggle drugs out of Turkey in *Midnight Express* (Alan Parker, 1978). We draw a blank on the identity of the baker in Lisa's nightmare.

Mmmmm: . . . sprinkles.

Hello, can I speak to: I'm A Stupid Moron With An Ugly Face And A Big Butt And My Butt Smells And I Like To Kiss My Own Butt.

Moe's secrets: He carries a sawn-off shotgun.

Notes: A marked improvement on the first, uneven Hallowe'en special. All three tales succeed, with Bart's nightmare of gaining awesome powers being perhaps the most successful.

43

8F06:

'Lisa's Pony'

Written by Al Jean and Mike Reiss
Directed by Carlos Baeza
Also starring: Doris Grau, Pamela Hayden,
Tress MacNeille, Frank Welker
Special guest voice: Marcia Wallace (as Ms Krabappel)

Premise: Homer embarrasses Lisa horribly at a school concert. To make it up to her, he buys her Princess, a pony – but he has to take a second job, at the Kwik-E-Mart, to pay for its upkeep.

Features: Principal Skinner, Grampa, Jasper, Moe, Groundskeeper Willie, Milhouse, Ms Krabappel, Lunchlady Doris, Bleedin' Gums Murphy, Sherri and Terri, Nelson Muntz, Ned Flanders, Maude Flanders, Smithers, Mr Burns, Apu, Ralph.

Couch: The Simpsons rush in – and sit on Homer.

Trivia: Princess is bought from the Grateful Gelding Stables.

Homage: When Lisa was taking her first steps, Homer was busy watching the cheesy seventies TV series *Fantasy Island*. There's a nod to *2001: A Space Odyssey* (Stanley Kubrick, 1969) which we aren't going to spoil by explaining here. *National Velvet* (Clarence Brown, 1945) also supplies a reference.

Notes for Brits: The sequence in which Homer's sleeping self drifts away is inspired by the US cartoon strip 'Little Nemo in Slumberland', which dates from the beginning of the twentieth century.

Mmmmm: . . . beer.

Look out for: Lisa waking up with Princess in her bed.

Notes: In which Lisa has to face up to her responsibilities as the only level-headed member of the family. We get some nice flashbacks to Lisa as a baby (but not as cute as those in 'Lisa on Ice'). Good stuff.

44

8F07:
'Saturdays of Thunder'

Written by Ken Levene and David Issacs
Directed by Jim Reardon

Also starring: JoAnn Harris, Pamela Hayden, Russi Taylor
Special guest voices: Phil Hartman (as Troy McClure),
Larry McKay

Premise: After realising he's a very bad father, Homer tries to get involved with Bart's attempts to win the local Soapbox Derby. However, once Bart adopts the injured Martin Prince's vehicle, Homer feels redundant and excluded. In desperation, he turns to Ned Flanders for help.

Features: Troy McClure, Dr Nick Riviera, Patty, Selma, McBain, Milhouse, Lewis, Richard, Martin Prince, Wendell, Nelson Muntz, Dr Hibbert, Ned Flanders, Barney, Moe, Mayor Quimby.

Couch: The sofa collapses in on itself, leaving the Simpsons' legs in the air.

Trivia: Videos for hire at Video Village include in the foreign section *Da Da Da*, *Border Siesta* and in the sports section *The Bad Football*, *Speedboat Bloopers*, *Frisbee 1991*, *Super Jock III*, *Go Fight – A Cheerleader's Story*, *Death by Knockout*, *Bench Clearing Brawls*, *Blood on the Ice* and *Football's Greatest Injuries*. At the hairdressers, Patty reads *Idle Chatter* magazine, while Selma pores over *Peephole*.

Homage: The McBain movie seen at the start of the episode, with its scenario of the retiring cop being shot, is drawn from *Lethal Weapon* (Richard Donner, 1987). The race recalls the chariot scenes from *Ben-Hur* (William Wyler, 1959) and *Days of Thunder* (Tony Scott, 1990). The closing song is 'Wind Beneath My Wings', a hit for Bette Midler in 1985, used as the theme to *Days of Thunder*.

Hi, I'm Troy McClure, you may remember me from: such TV series as *Buck Henderson, Union Buster* and *Troy and Company's Summertime Smile Factory*.

Look out for: Homer's Foam Dome hat. Martin Prince steals the show with his impassioned bed scene and the scene where he burns up and is ignored by a team of firefighters.

Notes: 'Men-do-za!' The best McBain clip is only one highlight of this fine episode, which is centred around Homer's fractured relationship with Bart.

45

8F08:

'Flaming Moe's'

Written by Robert Cohen
Directed by Rich Moore and Alain Smart
Also starring: JoAnn Harris, Russi Taylor
Special guest voices: Phil Hartman (as Lionel Hutz),
Marcia Wallace (as Ms Krabappel),
Catherine O'Hara (as Colette), Aerosmith (as themselves)

Premise: 'It's like there's a party in my mouth, and everyone's invited!' Homer accidentally invents a marvellous cocktail. Moe proceeds to take the credit, turning his bar into Springfield's hottest nightspot and attracting the attentions of Harv Bannister, Vice President of Tipsy McStagger's Good Time Drinking and Eating Emporium. Moe's success drives Homer insane with jealousy.

Features: Kent Brockman, Moe, Patty and Selma, Barney, Martin Prince, Ms Krabappel, Nelson, Krusty, Mayor Quimby, Otto, Lenny, Carl, Jasper, Lou and Eddie, Dr John Frink, Lionel Hutz, Chief Wiggum, Dr Marvin Monroe.

Couch: The Simpsons rush in – to find the sofa's been stolen.

Trivia: Moe's Tavern is on Walnut Street.

Homage: Aerosmith and Moe perform 'Walk This Way', the 1986 hit single they performed with Run DMC. Aerosmith perform the closing track 'Young Lust'. There's a brilliant tribute to the *Cheers* title sequence, as Moe's Tavern becomes Flaming Moe's. The notion of a brewery buying out a bar for one drink is a nod to *Cocktail* (Roger Donaldson, 1988), while Homer plummeting from the rafters recalls *The Phantom of the Opera*. The sequence in which Frink analyses a Flaming Moe comes from *The Nutty Professor* (Jerry Lewis, 1963).

Notes for Brits: A Flaming Mo is American slang for a camp homosexual. Just thought you should know.

Hello, can I speak to: Hugh Jass. (This is one of the most satisfying prank calls in the series – watch the episode to see what we mean.)

Notes: 'He's squashed Aerosmith!' Possibly the best *Simpsons* episode, with a constant stream of gags, inspired animation (in particular the sequence when Homer begins to see and hear Moe everywhere, from Maggie's gurgles to the leaves on the trees), and a superb plot that twists about in every direction but the one you might expect.

46

8F09:

'Burns Verkaufen der Kraftwerk'

Written by Jon Vitti   **Directed by** Mark Kirkland
Special guest voice: Phil Hartman (as Lionel Hutz)

Premise: Or 'Burns Sells the Power Plant'. To some Germans, who have a highly developed work ethic. Bad news for Homer.

Features: Smithers, Mr Burns, Carl, Lenny, Grampa, Jasper, Moe, Barney, Lionel Hutz.

Couch: The Simpsons rush in – and back off as Santa's Little Helper rears up menacingly.

Trivia: Homer owns a 5000-piece Battlestar Galactica jigsaw ('Based on the hit TV show!').

Notes for the Uneducated: 'Come here, I want you' were the first words spoken by Alexander Graham Bell on his invention, the telephone. Mr Burns quotes from the poem 'Barefoot Boy (With Cheek of Tan)' by John Greenleaf Whittier.

Hello, can I speak to: Bea O'Problem.

That's Homer Simpson, sir: 'one of your workers from sector sieven-gruber.'

Notes: Homer in the land of chocolate and Smithers counselling Mr Burns with the aid of his sock-puppet friend, Mr Snappy the Alligator, are the highlights of this episode.

47

8F10:
'I Married Marge'

Written by Jeff Martin   **Director** not credited
Additional cast: Doris Grau, Maggie Roswell

Premise: Marge takes a pregnancy test, prompting Homer to reminisce about the events surrounding the birth of Bart – and his hurried marriage to Marge.

Features: Patty and Selma, Mrs Bouvier, Barney, Dr Hibbert, Grampa, Smithers, Mr Burns.

Couch: The Simpsons cartwheel into the living room wearing fixed grins and adopt a cheesy showbiz pose on the sofa.

Trivia: At the nuclear plant, doughnuts are delivered by Rolling Donuts, and one of Homer's keen co-interviewees is reading *Fission Illustrated* magazine. Homer works briefly at Ye Olde Candle Shoppe, as a door-to-door salesman for Slash-Co Knives, and as a target at the Pitiless Pup Attack Dog School, before ending up at the Gulp 'n' Blow Drive-thru. And a poster announces that the first *Space Mutants* movie is coming soon to the Springfield Aztec cinema.

Homage: Homer and Barney are watching seventies glamour crime series *Charlie's Angels* when Marge phones with news of her pregnancy. Homer's encounter with the doughnut delivery man at the gates of the nuclear plant recalls *Willie Wonka and the Chocolate Factory* (Mel Stuart, 1971).

Notes for Brits: The episode's title is a reference to the US sitcom *I Married Joan*. John Anderson ran alongside Ronald Reagan and Jimmy Carter in the 1980 US Presidential election.

Notes: A very moving episode with plenty of great setpieces.

48

8F11:

'Radio Bart'

Written by Jon Vitti   **Directed by** Carlos Beaza
Also starring: Pamela Hayden, Russi Taylor,
Maggie Roswell
Special guest voices: Sting (as himself),
Marcia Wallace (as Ms Krabappel)

Premise: Bart gets a voice-throwing microphone for his birthday. His pranks begin harmlessly enough – but things get serious when he pretends to be Timmy O'Toole, a boy trapped down a well. Serious enough to encourage Sting to lead a host of celebrities in 'We're Sending Our Love Down the Well'.

Features: Krusty, Sideshow Mel, Grampa, Patty and Selma, Martin, Milhouse, Ms Krabappel, the Flanderses, Principal Skinner, Kent Brockman, Dr Frink, Rainier Wolfcastle, Chief Wiggum, Lou and Eddie.

Couch: The Simpsons rush in and sit down – and start to bounce about.

Trivia: Video games seen at Chuck E. Cheez include 'Coffee Fiend' and 'Comic Shop'.

Homage: A man called Quint suggests using chocolate attached to a fish-hook to save Timmy – he's straight out of *Jaws* (Steven Spielberg, 1976). Funky-See, Funky-Do with their hit 'I Do Believe We're Naked' resemble late-eighties lip-sync fraudsters Milli Vanilli.

Notes: The Police had a song called 'Canary Down the Mine', and Sting had made a point of campaigning for good causes, which explains why he was singled out in this sharp critique of celebrity posturing and media panic.

49

8F12:

'Lisa the Greek'

Written by Jay Kogen and Wallace Wolodarsky   **Directed by** Rich Moore
Also starring: Maggie Roswell
Special guest voice: Phil Hartman (as Troy McClure)

Premise: Determined to get Homer's attention, Lisa joins him watching the ball game and predicts the winners, making Homer very rich. However, when Lisa realises her father's sudden affection for her is based solely on her predictions, she forces him to choose between her love and her precognition skills.

Features: Moe, Chief Wiggum, John Frink, Krusty the Klown, Sideshow Mel, Sherri and Terri, Kearney, Dolph, Jimbo Jones, Barney Gumble, Herman, Ralph, Miss Hoover, Rev. Lovejoy, Troy McClure.

Couch: The Simpsons rush in – and sit on Santa's Little Helper.

Trivia: Springfield's children's clothing store is called 'Wee Monsieur'. Lisa's favourite song is 'The Broken Neck Blues'.

Hi, I'm Troy McClure, you may remember me from: *Handle With Care.*

Notes for Brits: The title is a reference to US baseball pundit Jimmy 'the Greek' Snyder.

Mmmmm: . . . crunched-up cookie things.

Look out for: Marge, knowing her son well, is able to recognise Bart's expression even behind the pile of clothes she has made him hold.

Notes: Homer's very fortunate that the right team wins at the end of this episode. It's nice to see him and Lisa getting along so well for once.

50

8F14:

'Homer Alone'

Written by David Stern **Directed by** Mark Kirkland
Also starring: Maggie Roswell
Special guest voice: Phil Hartman (as Troy McClure)

Premise: The pressure of her family's constant moaning, questions and reliance takes its toll on Marge and she flips out on the freeway. The cure – a solitary pampering holiday at Rancho Relaxo. This leaves Bart and Lisa stranded with Patty and Selma while Homer 'looks after' Maggie.

Features: Patty, Selma, Krusty the Klown, Barney, Troy McClure, Chief Wiggum, Kent Brockman, Eddie, Lou, Otto, Lenny, Carl, Nelson, Mayor Quimby, Arnie Pie.

Couch: The Simpsons land on all fours in a pyramid fashion, with Marge and Homer at the bottom, Lisa and Bart in the middle and Maggie at the summit.

Trivia: Patty and Selma live in apartment 1597. There is a beauty salon in Springfield called Le Pamperie and a jewellers called The Family Jewel, as well as an English-themed garage known as Buckingham Palace, complete with a cockney-accented, busby-wearing guard. Maggie falls asleep atop the Phineas Q Butterfats ice-cream parlour. Rancho Relaxo is Springfield's only Health Spa (although Marge takes nearly an hour's train journey to get there). Marge's hair tops six feet, and her criminal number is 50763. Movies available at Rancho Relaxo are *Thelma and Louise* (which Marge selects), *The Happy Elves Meet Fuzzy Snuggle-duck* and *The Erotic Awakening of S*. The activities in which she takes part are bungee jumping, kayaking, calligraphy, cigar making and hula dancing.

Homage: The episode starts with a pastiche of Warner Bros' *Roadrunner/Wile E. Coyote* cartoons as Homer chases Bart around the house. In freeze-frame, we learn that Bart is Brat'us Don'thaveacow'us whilst Homer is Homo Neanderthal'us. The music Homer gets on the phone while trying to find Maggie is 'Baby Come Back', a 1968 hit for The Equals. This is the first time we discover Patty and Selma's devotion to *McGyver*, a rather banal American series starring Richard Dean Anderson as a survivalist problem-solver and crimebuster who used 'brilliant improvisation' to win the day.

Hi, I'm Troy McClure, you may remember me from: *Today We Kill, Tomorrow We Die, Gladys the Groovy Mule*, and *Calling All Quakers*.

Mmmmm: . . . strained peas.

Look out for: Homer's disastrous attempt to look after Maggie supplies many great moments, including his pathetic puppet show.

Notes: After the first few minutes, this episode becomes less about Marge than the family's reliance on her. Bart and Lisa's torturous time at Patty and Selma's is wonderful ('Richard Dean Anderson is gonna be in my dreams tonight!' says Selma of McGyver), but it's Homer losing Maggie, and working out what to tell Marge upon her return, that provides the best jokes.

51

8F16:

'Bart the Lover'

Written by Jon Vitti   **Directed by** Carlos Baeza
Also starring: Maggie Roswell, Pamela Hayden
Special guest voice: Marcia Wallace (as Ms Krabappel)

Premise: Inspired by a visiting team of yo-yo spinners, Bart learns the art of double loops, spins and backflips – and gets a week in detention. Rummaging through Ms Krabappel's drawer, he realises she has placed a Lonely Hearts ad. A cruel plan forms in his mind – and he assumes the persona of Woody to woo her – epistolarily.

Features: Ms Krabappel, Principal Skinner, Groundskeeper Willie, Miss Hoover, Milhouse, Nelson Muntz, Jasper, Apu, Ned Flanders, Maude Flanders, Todd Flanders, Rod Flanders, Jimbo Jones, Rev. and Helen Lovejoy, Martin Prince, Sherri and Terri, Otto, Wendell, Ralph.

Couch: The Simpsons rush in – and the alien watching TV on the sofa escapes through a trapdoor.

Trivia: Ms Krabappel eats Chef Lonely Heart's Soup For One on a regular basis, it seems. Her choice this time is for Chicken Noodle. The restaurant chosen by Bart for Edna to meet Woody is The Gilded Truffle, while he nips next door to the cinema to see *Ernest Needs a Kidney*, which he finds very amusing. Marge only ever received one love letter from Homer, a drunken message scrawled on a postcard from the Duff Beer factory, site of the world's largest pull-tab. The Simpsons appear to live at 94 Evergreen Terrace in this episode.

Notes for Brits: Woody's name is adapted from that of ex-President Woodrow Wilson, although the picture Bart selects to accompany his letter is of National Hockey League player Gordie Howe.

Look out for: Homer determined not to swear, despite receiving some appalling injuries trying to build the dog house. Rev. Lovejoy's reaction to receiving (what is presumably one in a long line) a phone call from Ned Flanders.

Notes: Bart sees his pranks backfire, for once. We love Homer's suggestion for a good kiss-off letter ('Dear Edna, Welcome to Dumpsville, Population: You. PS I am gay.') .

52

8F13:

'Homer at the Bat'

Written by John Swartzwelder
Directed by Jim Reardon
Also starring: Maggie Roswell
Special guest voices: Terry Cashman, Jose Canseco, Mike Scioscia, Ozzie Smith, Don Mattingly, Steve Sax, Roger Clemens, Wade Boggs, Ken Griffey Jnr and Darryl Strawberry (all as themselves), Jon Lovitz (as Aristotle Amadopolis)

Premise: Homer's on a winning streak as captain of the power-plant baseball team, the Springfield Atoms. Mr Burns becomes greedy for victory (and a million-dollar bet against a business rival) and replaces the team with star players. But fate has a way of interfering with the best-laid plans, despite the odds against all nine players meeting bizarre accidents . . .

Features: Lenny, Carl, Charlie, Chief Wiggum, Eddie, Apu, Otto, Miss Hoover, Principal Skinner, Mrs Skinner, Mr Burns, Smithers, Ralph, Wendell, Richard, Lewis, Milhouse, Dr Hibbert, Barney, Moe.

Couch: The Simpsons crash into each other, leaving them senseless apart from Maggie.

Trivia: The SNPP poster advertising safety at work shows how the Heimlich Manoeuvre works – and shows a man coughing up an entire lobster.

Homage: The lucky baseball bat that was struck by lightning comes from *The Natural* (Barry Levinson, 1984).

Notes for Brits: Mr Burns suggests baseball players Honus Wagner, Cap Anson and 3-Finger Brown for his team – all of whom are long dead.

Mmmmm: . . . doughnuts . . . potato chips.

Look out for: Mr Burns, who is on top form as a very unlikely baseball coach. His explanation to Homer of the hand signals he intends to give the team from the bench ('If I tap my belt buckle, not once, twice, but thrice . . .') is one of his finest moments in the entire series.

Song: 'Talkin' Baseball' sung over the end credits.

Notes: You need a degree in baseball rules and in-jokes to get most of this (or a good grounding in contemporary baseball politics, at least) but despite that, this is a great episode because the accidents that befall the pro players are so funny. And Homer wins out, a rare but invigorating event.

53
8F15:
'Separate Vocations'

Written by George Meyer   **Directed by** Jeffrey Lynch
Also starring: Pamela Hayden, Maggie Roswell,
Russi Taylor, Tress MacNeille
Special guest voice: Marcia Wallace (as Ms Krabappel),
Steve Allen (as the Alternate Bart)

Premise: The students of Springfield Elementary sit the Career Aptitude Normalising Test – or CANT. A mix-up in the results sends Bart on a run with the Springfield Police, and dooms Lisa to the life of a home-maker. Bart discovers that a man in uniform can get away with anything, while Lisa becomes a cosmetics-abusing, gum-chewing rebel without a cause.

Features: Ms Krabappel, Sherri and Terri, Milhouse, Miss Hoover, Janey, Richard, Lewis, Wendell, Martin Prince, Ralph, Lou, Eddie, Mrs Winfield, Mayor Quimby, Sideshow Mel, Apu, Snake, Chief Wiggum, Patty, Selma, Principal Skinner, Groundskeeper Willie, Jimbo Jones, Kearney, Dolph, Mr Largo.

Couch: Bart jumps across the other Simpsons.

Trivia: CANT results predict that Janey is to be an architect, Milhouse a military strongman, and Martin a systems analyst – his dream job.

Homage: After the first ad break in this episode, a caption comes up, proclaiming ACT II – DEATH DRIVES A STICK, in homage to the TV series *The Streets of San Francisco* and numerous other Quinn Martin-produced crime shows. The car chase comes straight from the classic *Bullitt* (Peter Yates, 1968). *The Wild One* (Laslo Benedek, 1954) supplies Lisa's answer to Miss Hoover's question 'What are you rebelling against?'

Look out for: The heavily loaded questions in the CANT test.

Notes: *The Simpsons* at its best – not only hilarious but daringly outspoken on a whole range of issues – the failures of the education system, police abuses of power, the stifling of children's creativity . . .

54
8F17:
'Dog of Death'

Written by John Swartzwelder
Directed by Jim Reardon
Also starring: Maggie Roswell, Frank Welker

Premise: Lottery fever grips Springfield. When Homer blows a large amount of cash on duplicate tickets the Simpsons are left penniless after financing a life-saving operation performed on Santa's Little Helper. He runs away – and becomes one of Mr Burns' slavering hounds.

Features: Patty, Selma, Jackie Bouvier, Grampa, Mr Burns, Smithers, Ned Flanders, Moe, Barney, Kent Brockman, Apu, Sanjay, Ms Krabappel, Principal Skinner, Elizabeth Hoover, Chief Wiggum, Lou, Eddie, Lenny, Otto Mans, Krusty the Klown, Sideshow Mel.

Couch: The Simpsons rush in – and the others sit on Homer.

Trivia: Marge's regular lottery numbers are 3, 6, 17, 18, 2 and 29. The eldest of Burns' hounds is called Crippler.

Homage: Santa's Little Helper's odyssey recalls *The Incredible Journey* (Fletcher Markle, 1963), while his aversion therapy at the hands of Mr Burns and Smithers owes a lot to *A Clockwork Orange* (Stanley Kubrick, 1971), complete with eye-opening clamps, distressing film footage, and Beethoven's 9th Symphony. There are nods to the *Lassie* film series in his rescuing of a child from a burning house. Shirley Jackson's novel *The Lottery* has no clues on winning the lottery at all but is in fact a chilling tale of conformity gone mad.

Notes for Brits: The medic seen at the beginning of this episode is very similar to Ben Casey, the central character in a US TV medical show of the same name.

Mmmmm: . . . snouts.

Notes: Great things about 'Dog of Death' – Homer's dream of winning the lottery, the list of dogs in Doggie Heaven and Hell, Mr Burns' anti-niceness therapy on Santa's Little Helper. And the closing caveat that NO DOGS WERE HARMED IN THE FILMING OF THIS EPISODE. A CAT GOT SICK AND SOMEONE SHOT A DUCK, BUT THAT'S IT.

55

8F19:

'Colonel Homer'

Written by Matt Groening   **Directed by** Mark Kirkland
Special guest voice: Beverly D'Angelo (as Lurleen)

Premise: After a row with Marge, Homer spends the night at a dodgy Country and Western bar in remote Hicksville. There he discovers singing sensation Lurleen Lumpkin. He becomes her manager and her career spirals upwards – as Homer's family life begins to spiral downwards.

Features: Patty, Lenny, Carl, Krusty, Sideshow Mel, Snake.

Couch: The sofa collapses in on itself.

Trivia: The local beer in Hicksville is Fudd. The radio station that promotes Lurleen is KUDD. Lurleen lives in the Spittle County Royal King Trailer Park which, on Homer's first visit has not had a tornado for fourteen days. On his next visit, it's become two days!

Homage: Lenny sings 'There's a Kind of Hush (All Over the World)', a 1976 hit for The Carpenters.

Songs: Lurleen's songs include 'I'm Basting a Turkey with My Tears', 'Stand By Your Manager', 'Don't Look Up My Dress Unless You Mean It' and 'I'm Sick of Your Lyin' Lips and False Teeth'.

Notes: A good example of *The Simpsons* fixing itself on a target (in this case, Country & Western music) and extracting every possible gag. Lurleen's songs are all marvellous.

56

8F20:

'Black Widower'

Written by Jon Vitti
(from a story by Thomas Chastain and Sam Simon)
Directed by David Silverman
Special guest voice: Kelsey Grammer (as Sideshow Bob)

Premise: A reformed Sideshow Bob has been released from jail and proposed marriage to Selma. Only Bart sees through Bob – but can he convince everyone else that Selma's luxury honeymoon could lead to her gory death?

Features: Patty, Selma, Sideshow Bob, Krusty, Sideshow Mel, Barney, Moe, Grampa, Jackie Bouvier, Eddie, Lou, Chief Wiggum, Apu, Snake, Rev. Lovejoy, Helen Lovejoy.

Couch: The Simpsons rush in – to find the sofa being stolen.

Trivia: Working in prison, Sideshow Bob makes number plates for cars, producing ones that read DIE BART, RIP BART, BART DOA, and IH8 BART. Krusty's telethon has raised $385,382.35. Sideshow Bob wins the Best Supporting Performer in a Children's Show Emmy. His co-nominees are Droopy Drawers, Colonel Coward, Pepito the Biggest Cat in the World, and Suck-Up, the vacuum.

Homage: *Black Widow* (Bob Rafelson, 1987) provides some of the main plot elements, particularly nobody believing Bart's pleas that Sideshow Bob is dangerous. Sideshow Bob's prisoner number is 24601, the same as Jean Valjean's in Victor Hugo's novel *Les Miserables*. At the Happy Sumo karaoke, Sideshow Bob and Selma sing 'Somethin' Stupid', a 1967 hit for Frank and Nancy Sinatra.

Mmmmm: . . . appetisers.

Look out for: Lisa's reaction to the screening of an episode of US cartoon series 'Dinosaurs' – and Bart trying to convince Homer of Bob's evil plan.

Notes: A terrific show, with Kelsey Grammer back in full force as Sideshow Bob Terwilliger. Additional touches, such as the dinosaurs gag and Bob's reaction to McGyver, make the whole thing great fun.

57
8F21:
'Otto Show'

Written by Jeff Martin   **Directed by** Wes Archer
Also starring: Pamela Hayden, Russi Taylor
Special guest voices:
Michael McKean, Christopher Guest (as Spinal Tap)

Premise: 'Otto – there's one palindrome you won't be hearing for a while.' Otto loses his job, his home and everything else and comes to live with the Simpsons, while Bart, having enjoyed his first rock concert, decides to become a guitarist.

Features: Patty, Selma, Milhouse, Bill and Marty at KBBL, Otto, Snake, Kent Brockman, Martin Prince, Sherri and Terri, Chief Wiggum, Janey, Lou, Eddie, Principal Skinner, Ralph, Apu, Lewis, Richard.

Couch: The Simpsons rush in – to find an aggressive, snarling Santa's Little Helper on the sofa.

Trivia: Spinal Tap's world tour has taken in London, Paris, Munich and Springfield. (There's a possible reference in that list to the chorus of M's 1979 hit 'Pop Muzik'.) Otto's driving licence gives his details as 'Ht 5'10 wt 150 DOB 01-18-63'.

Homage: Principally *This Is Spinal Tap* (Rob Reiner, 1984). There's also mention of *Happy Days*. We hear Homer singing a vocal version of Herb Alpert's 1965 hit 'Spanish Flea', and Otto practises the guitar solo of Lynyrd Skynyrd's 'Free Bird'. Otto's father's occupation – an admiral – and their estranged relationship suggest a parallel with Jim Morrison of the Doors.

Look out for: Spinal Tap's doomed laser light show and inept stage effects ('We salute you, our half-inflated Dark Lord!').

Notes: A nice episode for Otto and some great moments for Skinner as he tries to drive the bus, but especially memorable for Homer's moment of forgetfulness after the concert. Michael McKean, Christopher Guest and Harry Shearer reprise their roles from *This Is Spinal Tap* perfectly.

58

8F22:
'Bart's Friend Falls in Love'

Written by Jay Kogen and Wallace Wolodarsky
Directed by Jim Reardon
Also starring: Maggie Roswell, Pamela Hayden,
Russi Taylor
Special guest voices:
Kimmy Robertson (as Samantha Stanky),
Phil Hartman (as Troy McClure),
Marcia Wallace (as Ms Krabappel)

Premise: What could come between Bart and Milhouse? Samantha Stanky could. She's the new girl at Springfield Elementary. Meanwhile, Homer's trying to lose weight using a subliminal tape to make him eat less. But it's the wrong tape – and instead, his vocabulary starts to improve dramatically.

Features: Milhouse, Principal Skinner, Ms Krabappel, Troy McClure, Otto, Kent Brockman, Dr Marvin Monroe, Martin.

Couch: The Simpsons rush in – and the sofa topples backwards.

Trivia: Samantha is keen on the Doomed Romance series of comics, including the adventures of 'Bonnie Crane: Girl Attorney'.

Homage: The opening sequence, as Homer steals Bart's money, is a direct lift from *Raiders of the Lost Ark* (Steven Spielberg, 1981) – and the closing sequence is a direct lift from *Casablanca* (Michael Curtiz, 1942). We see a singing nun singing 'Dominique', the Singing Nun's hit from 1965. Lisa's reading a magazine with the headline THE YEAR 2525 – WERE ZAGER & EVANS RIGHT? Zager and Evans were behind the song 'In the Year 2525'.

Hi, I'm Troy McClure, you may remember me from: such educational films as *Lead Paint, Delicious But Deadly* and *Here Comes the Metric System*.

Notes: One for everybody's top 10, and a fitting end to a season that had seen *The Simpsons* consolidate its success and become even more daring and intelligent.

Fourth Season

1992–1993
23 Episodes

59
8F23:
'Brother Can You Spare Two Dimes?'

Written by John Swartzwelder   **Directed by** Rich Moore
Also starring: Maggie Roswell
Special guest voices: Joe Frasier (as himself),
Danny DeVito (as Herb)

Premise: The ruined Herb Powell returns to Homer's life. This time he's trying to patent a unique baby-deciphering device. He badly needs cash – and Homer's just won $2000.

Features: Lenny, Mr Burns, Smithers, Dr John Frink, Herb Powell, Rev. Lovejoy, Helen Lovejoy, Ned Flanders, Maude Flanders, Todd Flanders, Rod Flanders, Carl, Apu, Principal Skinner, Moe, Barney.

Couch: The Simpsons cartwheel on to the sofa.

Trivia: Homer wins the First Annual Montgomery Burns Award for Outstanding Achievement in the Field of Excellence. There are flashbacks to 'Oh Brother, Where Art Thou'.

Homage: Homer's TV memories include Kristen shooting JR from *Dallas*, the Berlin Wall coming down in 1989, the Hands Across America event of 1985, and the sitcom *Welcome Back, Kotter*. His 'trip' on the vibro-chair references the climax of *2001: A Space Odyssey* (Stanley Kubrick, 1969).

Notes for the Uneducated: The novel *Less Than Zero* by Brett Easton Ellis is a tale of contemporary youth's angst.

Look out for: Bart and Lisa avoiding the blame for the destruction of the sofa.

That's Homer Simpson, sir: 'one of your cabbage heads from Sector 7G.'

Notes: We love the drinking bird, the development of Homer's fixation for mechanically aided chairs, and Maggie talking through Herb's translator device.

60

8F24:

'Kamp Krusty'

Written by David M. Stern   **Directed by** Mark Kirkland
Also starring: Pamela Hayden, Tress MacNeille,
Maggie Roswell, Russi Taylor
Special guest voice: Marcia Wallace (as Ms Krabappel)

Premise: School's out – and Bart and Lisa enrol at Kamp Krusty, site of summer thrills – 'archery, wallet-making, the whole magilla'. But Krusty's not there – and in his place is the sinister Mr Black.

Features: Ms Krabappel, Principal Skinner, Miss Hoover, Nelson, Sherri and Terri, Lewis, Janey Wendell, Grounds-keeper Willie, Otto, Krusty, Dr Hibbert, Martin Prince, Mr Prince, Milhouse, Dolph, Jimbo, Kearney, Barney, Ralph, Kent Brockman.

Couch: The Simpsons rush in – to find the sofa occupied by Fred Flintstone – together with Pebbles and Wilma.

Trivia: Lisa's letter home is addressed to 430 Spalding Way, not 742 Evergreen Terrace.

Homage: 'School's Out' by Alice Cooper was a Number One in the US and UK in 1972. The episode plays out with Frank Sinatra's 'South of the Border'. Lisa's mistrust of the postal system and robed moonlight flit to a waiting rider are a nod to many nineteenth-century novels, but most particularly Wilkie Collins' *The Woman in White*. There's also a reference to Allan Sherman's 1963 summer camp hit 'Hello Muddah, Hello Faddah'.

Song: 'Hail to Thee, Kamp Krusty' sung by the campers.

Notes: A bit baffling to non-Americans unfamiliar with the summer camp system. But top grade stuff nonetheless. Anyone who's worked as a counsellor in such a place can testify to this episode's authenticity.

61

8F18:

'A Streetcar Named Marge'

Written by Jeff Martin   **Directed by** Rich Moore
Also starring: Maggie Roswell, Lona Williams
Special guest voices: Jon Lovitz (as Llewellyn Sinclair),
Phil Hartman (as Lionel Hutz and Troy McClure)

Premise: Bored, Marge auditions for a part in *Oh, Streetcar!*, a musical version of Tennessee Williams' *A Streetcar Named Desire* directed by the eccentric Llewellyn Sinclair. Maggie meanwhile is enrolled at the Ayn Rand School for Tots, where her pacifier is confiscated.

Features: Patty, Selma, Grampa, Barney Gumble, Apu, Moe, Lionel Hutz, Ned Flanders, Helen Lovejoy, Otto Mans, Jasper, Chief Wiggum, Troy McClure, Herman.

Couch: The Simpsons rush in – to be gobbled up by a monstrous sofa.

Trivia: The pageant judges are skin-care consultant Rowena, Syndicated Columnist William F. George, Token Black Panelist Dreaderick Tatum, and Mr Foswell, the Man Behind Those Infamous 'Worst Dressed' Lists. The pageant is sponsored by Meryl Streep's perfume Versatility – 'Smell Like Streep, For Cheap!'

Homage: The musical production of Tennessee Williams' *A Streetcar Named Desire* resembles many others of its genre – but the title refers to the sixties revue *Oh, Calcutta*. There are sequences paying respect to *The Italian Job* (Peter Collinson, 1969), and in a spectacular fashion, Maggie re-creates the break-out from *The Great Escape* (John Sturges, 1963). Best of all is the sequence with the room filled with eerily silent babies sucking on their pacifiers which parodies, music and all, *The Birds* (Alfred Hitchcock, 1963) – and is immediately followed by a cameo from its director. When Homer fans a shredded theatre programme he's copying a character from *Citizen Kane*. We also hear the first few lines of Janis Ian's angsty 1971 hit 'At Seventeen'. Bart's cry of 'a pain in me gulliver' is yet another line from A *Clockwork Orange*.

Notes for Brits: The Ayn Rand Foundation is an American right-wing thinktank.

Look out for: Homer opening a tin of dessert – and our first sight of Ned Flanders' body.

Songs: *Oh, Streetcar!* contains such gems as 'New Orleans!', 'Simple Paperboy' and 'The Kindness of Strangers'.

Notes: A great episode, in which Marge can neither sing nor act but once stimulated by Homer's crass stupidity, learns at least to emote. Llewellyn Sinclair bears a strong resemblance to Jon Lovitz's character in the cartoon series 'The Critic'. The ending is wonderful – just when you think Homer has let Marge down again, he comes up trumps.

62
9F01:
'Homer the Heretic'

Written by George Meyer **Directed by** Jim Reardon
Also starring: Maggie Roswell

Premise: Homer elects to avoid church, much to Marge's consternation. But then he receives a message from God in his dream – it's OK to skip church! Could this be the start of a new religion?

Features: Rev. Lovejoy, Ned Flanders, Maude Flanders, Todd Flanders, Rod Flanders, Helen Lovejoy, Grampa, Groundskeeper Willie, Moe, Krusty, Apu, Dolph, Kearney, Jimbo Jones, Mrs van Houten, Chief Wiggum, Barney, Kent Brockman, Otto, Mr van Houten.

Couch: The sofa swivels round into the wall, and an empty sofa assumes its place.

Homage: Homer sings 'Delilah', a 1968 hit for Tom Jones and 'Short Shorts' a hit for the Royal Teens in 1958. His underwear dance around the empty house recalls Tom Cruise in *Risky Business* (William J. Cassidy, 1983).

Itchy and Scratchy in: 'Flay Me to the Moon' – one of the very goriest.

Mmmmm: . . . fattening.

Notes: A brilliant episode, underlining everything that *The Simpsons* is about. Homer hates church (his argument to God makes a lot of sense, really), Marge wants the kids to see Homer as an example, and everyone pulls together in the end. Good stuff, and if God really is like that, he's a groovy kind of guy.

63

9F02:

'Lisa the Beauty Queen'

Written by Jeff Martin   **Directed by** Mark Kirkland
Also starring: Pamela Hayden, JoAnn Harris, Doris Grau,
Lona Williams
Special guest voice: Bob Hope (as himself)

Premise: Lisa has a caricature sketched – and its exaggeration of her unusual features convinces her of her ugliness. To boost her confidence, Homer enters her for the local beauty pageant. But can Lisa hope to compete with a Shirley Temple lookalike who has had eyelash implants in Paraguay? And will her social conscience allow her to compete in a contest that uses the slogan GOD BLESS MUMMY AND DADDY AND LARAMIE CIGARETTES?

Features: Principal Skinner, Chief Wiggum, Groundskeeper Willie, Mayor Quimby, Martin Prince, Nelson Muntz, Otto, Milhouse, Jimbo Jones, Kearney, Dolph, Dr Hibbert, Ned Flanders, Maude Flanders, Todd Flanders, Rod Flanders, Grampa, Moe, Apu, Sanjay, Barney, Krusty.

Couch: Maggie is seated but the others run off the film strip, into nothingness and then back to the sofa.

Trivia: Lisa's tryout hairstyles include a Princess Leia look, as well as a miniature Marge-look. The Springfield Waxworks' Chamber of Horrors contains Mr T, Ronald Reagan and Dr Ruth.

Homage: The escape from Fort Springfield is taken detail-for-detail from *Apocalypse Now* (Francis Ford Coppola, 1979). The song 'Blimpy Boy' is a close cousin to the Seekers' 1966 smash 'Georgie Girl'. Kent Brockman's cry of 'Oh, the humanity . . .' recalls the commentary of the Hindenberg airship crash disaster.

Mmmmm: (no food named, but Homer is polishing off a jar of petroleum jelly!)

Notes: Krusty gets some of his best lines in a few brief appearances. Another top-notch episode.

64

9F04:

'Treehouse of Horror III'

Written by Al Jean, Mike Reiss, Jay Kogen,
Wallace Wolodarsky, Sam Simon and Jon Vitti
Directed by Carlos Baeza

Premise: Another trio of Hallowe'en tales. In 'Clown Without Pity', Homer is pursued by a cursed Krusty doll; 'King Homer' sees Marge joining up for an expedition to the tropics; and 'Dial Z for Zombies' depicts a Springfield overrun by the living dead.

Couch: The Simpsons have become skeletons.

Tombstones: Drexel's Class, I'm With Stupid, R. Buckminster Fuller, Slapstick, American Workmanship Fish Police, Capitol Critters, Family Dog.

Homage: 'Clown Without Pity' is a nod to the *Twilight Zone* episode 'Living Doll', 'King Homer' is an obvious homage to *King Kong*, and 'Dial Z . . .' recalls George Romero's zombie pictures in general and *Night of the Living Dead* in particular.

Notes for Brits: *Fish Police* and *Capitol Critters* were flop US TV series that attempted to cash in on the success of *The Simpsons*. *Drexel's Class* was another Fox show that also flopped.

Notes: Another seasonal treat. 'Night of the Living Dead' is particularly impressive ('Dad, you killed the zombie Flanders!' 'He was a zombie?').

65

9F03:

'Itchy & Scratchy: The Movie'

Written by John Swartzwelder   **Directed by** Rich Moore
Additional cast: Pamela Hayden, Maggie Roswell
Special guest voice: Marcia Wallace (as Ms Krabappel)

Premise: Bart's behaving very badly. After some prompting from fretful Marge, Homer comes up with the ultimate punishment – Bart can never see *Itchy & Scratchy: The Movie* (53% original footage), the animated movie that will be the defining moment for his generation.

Features: Grampa, Groundskeeper Willie, Miss Hoover, Ms Krabappel, Jasper, Krusty, Bumblebee Man, Kent Brockman, Chief Wiggum, Snake, Milhouse, Nelson, Lou and Eddie, Ned and Rod Flanders, Otto, Lewis, Wendell.

Couch: The Simpsons rush in – and the sofa deflates.

Trivia: Homer chooses a seventies' style Fab lolly from the ice-cream van. In Marge's nightmare of Bart's future, Sherri and Terri are among the audience at the strip show. According to Lisa, the *Itchy & Scratchy Movie* features voice cameos by Dustin Hoffman and Michael Jackson ('they didn't use their real names but you could tell it was them'). The future cinema still has a photo of young Bart inside the ticket booth.

Homage: The *Star Trek* movie series (we get to see the start of *Star Trek XII – So Very Tired*). Scratchy's première appearance owes much to Mickey Mouse's debut, *Steamboat Willie* (1928). 'Yummy Yummy Yummy' was a hit for Ohio Express in 1968. *Soylent Green* (Richard Fleischer, 1973) tells the story of a futuristic foodstuff made from human bodies.

Itchy and Scratchy in: Scratchy's first appearance was solo in 1928's *That Happy Cat*. Their first cartoon together was 1929's *Steamboat Itchy*. During the war they teamed up against Hitler in an unnamed cartoon.

Mmmmm: . . . Burger. (As in ex-Chief Justice of the Supreme Court Warren Burger.) And . . . soylent green.

Notes: There's some defining dumb Homer stuff in this superb episode – his suggestion for punishing Bart's misbehaviour is to give him a present, and his trick for avoiding jury duty is 'to say you're prejudiced against all races'.

66

9F05:

'Marge Gets a Job'

Written by Bill Oakley and Josh Weinstein
Directed by Jeff Lynch
Special guest voices:
Phil Hartman (as Troy McClure and Lionel Hutz),
Tom Jones (as himself),
Marcia Wallace (as Ms Krabappel)

Premise: The Simpsons' house is sinking. To pay for repairs, Marge gets a job – at Sector 7G of the Springfield Nuclear Power Plant. Mr Burns is smitten – and secures the services of Tom Jones to woo her.

Features: Ned Flanders, Nelson, Troy McClure, Kent Brockman, Mr Burns, Smithers, Grampa, Ms Krabappel, Lenny, Carl, Krusty, Chief Wiggum, Groundskeeper Willie, Lionel Hutz, Janey, Martin, Charlie, Eddie.

Couch: The Simpsons rush in – and have to swap their heads about to match their bodies.

Trivia: Smithers finds Tom Jones working a Vegas-style club called The Copper Slipper (tonight – TOM JONES (and double jackpot slots)).

Homage: We hear the Empire theme from *The Empire Strikes Back* (Irvin Kirshner, 1980). Smithers' song recalls the tribute to Kane in *Citizen Kane* (Orson Welles, 1941). The sequence of the papers travelling through the chute is culled directly from *Stolen Kisses* (François Truffaut, 1968), which depicts a letter travelling through underground pipes in Paris. Krustylu Studios seems to be a reference to Paramount's Desilu Studios (which produced the sixties sitcom *I Love Lucy*).

Hi, I'm Troy McClure, you may remember me from: such instructional videos as *Mothballing Your Battleship* and *Dig Your Own Grave – And Save!*

Song: 'He's Mr Burns' sung by Smithers.

Notes: We like Bart's fantasy of the radioactive Marie and Pierre Curie, and Smithers' fantasy of his loved one flying through the window. A collection of wonderful set pieces rather than a story, which fizzles out without any real attempt at an ending. Some people's favourite episode.

67

9F06:

'New Kid on the Block'

Written by Conan O'Brien   **Directed by** Wes Archer
Also starring: Pamela Hayden, Maggie Roswell
Special guest voices: Sara Gilbert (as Laura Powers),
Pamela Reed (as Ruth Powers),
Phil Hartman (as Lionel Hutz)

Premise: The Winfields move away and the Powers move in. Bart is attracted to Laura Powers immediately, while Marge befriends single mum Ruth. Bart believes that a romance is blooming, until Laura meets Jimbo Jones and the young Simpson learns how green jealousy can get.

Features: Mrs Winfield, Captain McCallister, Kearney, Dolph, Dutchman Waiter, Apu, Lionel Hutz, Grampa, Jimbo Jones, Principal Skinner, Judge, Springfield DA, Moe, Barney, the two barflies.

Couch: The sofa falls through the floor.

Trivia: The company the Powers' employ to move are 'Clumsy Student Movers'. Bart and Laura play 'Escape from Death Row' at the amusement arcade. The Simpsons' address is given here as 1094 Evergreen Terrace.

Mmmmm: . . . shrimps.

Look out for: Homer's useless attempts to talk to Bart about women, comparing them to refrigerators and beer. The fate of Abby, Bart's original babysitter.

Hello, can I speak to: Amanda Huggenkiss, Ivana Tinkle.

Notes: A fun episode, introducing the Powers family (Ruth is the star of 'Marge on the Lam'). This is the last appearance of the Winfields, and only Mrs Winfield is seen.

68
9F07:
'Mr Plow'

Written by Jon Vitti   **Directed by** Jim Reardon
Additional cast: Pamela Hayden
Special guest voices: Phil Hartman (as Troy McClure),
Linda Ronstadt (as herself), Adam West (as himself)

Premise: Springfield's buried under snow – and only Homer's new business, Mr Plow (call KL5–3226) can rescue the citizens' driveways. Until the Plow King (proprietor Barney Gumble) appears.

Features: Troy McClure, Moe, Krusty, Bumblebee Man, Bill and Marty at KBBL, Barney, Rev. Lovejoy, Captain McCallister, Grampa, Apu, Principal Skinner, Groundskeeper Willie, Nelson, Mayor Quimby, Carl, Ned Flanders, Kent Brockman, Arnie Pie, God.

Couch: The Simpsons rush in – but the sofa isn't there. Doesn't stop them sitting down, though.

Trivia: Barney's working as 'Big Baby' for Lullaby$ nappy store. Captain MacAllister's chanteys are available on a three CD set (bonus CD 'Hornpipe Fever' available for quick orderers). The free T-shirt given away to Mr Plow's customers reads STOCKDALE FOR VEEP. Springfield has a weather blackspot called Widow's Peak. Kent Brockman's opinion slot MY TWO CENTS appears for the first time.

Homage: The sixties *Batman* TV series (during the Adam West sequences the camera starts tilting). The sequence in which the snowmen's faces melt recalls the fate of the Nazis in *Raiders of the Lost Ark* (Steven Spielberg, 1981). The McMahon & Tate Agency was the ad agency Darren worked for in the sixties TV series *Bewitched*.

Hi, my name's Troy McClure, you may remember me from: such films as *The Erotic Adventures of Hercules* and *Dial M for Murderousness*.

Notes for Brits: *Carnival of Stars* is a thinly veiled version of the US series, in which celebrities do their party pieces.

Songs: 'Call Mr Plow' sung by Homer. 'Call The Plow King' sung by Barney and Linda Ronstadt. The 'Mr Plow Rap' rapped by Homer. 'Señor Plow' sung by Linda Ronstadt.

Notes: A good one. The highlights; the TV show *Carnival of Stars*, featuring Angela Lansbury walking on hot coals

('Excitement, she wrote!'), Homer's flashback to all he's done for Barney, and best of all, the McMahon & Tate ad agency's arty commercial for Mr Plow.

69
9F08:
'Lisa's First Word'

Written by Jeff Martin **Directed by** Mark Kirkland
Also starring: Pamela Hayden
Special guest voice: Elizabeth Taylor (as Maggie)

Premise: The Simpsons are trying to get Maggie to talk. Homer and Marge are thrown into a fit of reminiscence, and recall the growing pains of Bart and Lisa.

Features: Patty and Selma, Captain McCallister, Dr Hibbert, the Flanderses, Krusty, Grampa, and, in a very brief cameo, Sideshow Bob.

Couch: The Simpsons rush in – to form part of a high-kicking showbiz circus extravaganza.

Homage: 'Girls Just Wanna Have Fun' by Cyndi Lauper was a US No 1 hit in 1983.

Notes for Brits: Democrat presidential candidate Walter Mondale taunted a rival with the phrase 'Where's the beef?' at an election rally in early 1984. The phrase originates for a slogan for the Wendy's hamburger chain. Dr Hibbert refers to Mary-Lou Retton, an American Olympic medallist.

Mmmmm: . . . hog fat.

Song: 'We Welcome You' sung to the Simpsons upon their arrival in Evergreen Terrace by the Flanderses.

Notes: A convincing portrait of young marriage and hardship in the days of Reaganomics – and the biggest name to guest voice gets the littlest, but the most significant, to say.

70

9F09:

'Homer's Triple Bypass'

Written by Gary Apple and Michael Carrington
Directed by David Silverman
Also starring: Maggie Roswell

Premise: All Homer's years of bacon-gorging have caught up with him. A massive heart attack will mean massively expensive surgery – unless he goes to Dr Nick Riviera. His special offer – $129.95 for an operation. Any operation.

Features: Chief Wiggum, Lou and Eddie, Rev. Lovejoy, Snake, Mr Burns, Smithers, Patty and Selma, Grampa, Rabbi Krustofsky, Dr Nick, Ned Flanders, Miss Allbright, Krusty, Lenny, Carl, Barney, Moe, Apu, Jasper, Hans Moleman.

Couch: The Simpsons rush in – but they've been miniaturized.

Homage: Homer quotes the German philosopher Nietzsche: 'Whatever does not kill me can only make me stronger.' 'Cops in Springfield', featuring Chief Wiggum and his bungling deputies, is homage to the US camcorder police documentary series *Cops*. Homer performs a sock-puppet show to Bart and Lisa using puppets of Akbar and Jeff from Matt Groening's 'Life in Hell' cartoon strip.

Mmmmm: . . . ham.

Notes: 'Cloud goes up, cloud goes down . . .' A cautionary tale that gives Dr Nick his biggest chance to shine.

71

9F10:

'Marge vs. the Monorail'

Written by Conan O' Brien   **Directed by** Rich Moore
Also starring: Doris Grau, Maggie Roswell
Special guest voices: Phil Hartman (as Lyle Lanley),
Leonard Nimoy (as himself)

Premise: Springfield's Town Council comes into a few million dollars. Should the citizens spend the cash on widening Main Street, thus attracting more trade to the city, reducing accidents, and improving public health – or give it all to travelling salesman Lyle Lanley in exchange for his monorail?

Features: Carl, Lenny, Smithers, Mr Burns, Judge, Miss Hoover, Principal Skinner, Snake, Mayor Quimby, Apu, Rev. Lovejoy, Grampa, Chief Wiggum, Maude Flanders, Lou, Eddie, Barney, Jasper, Ned Flanders, Mr Largo, the van Houtens, Patty, Selma, Dr Marvin Monroe, Herman, Dr Hibbert, Otto, Krusty, Ralph, Kent Brockman, Captain McCallister.

Couch: The Simpsons are joined on the sofa by Selma, Patty, Apu, Krusty, Grampa, Herman, Eddie, Smithers, Burns, Edna, Seymour, Elizabeth, Princess Kashmir, Jasper, Jackie, Wiggum, Ned, Maude, Barney, Moe, Dr Hibbert, Kent Brockman, Otto, Nelson, Milhouse and Martin.

Trivia: Lyle Lanley has sold monorails to Brockway, Ogdenville and North Haverbrook – North Haverbrook seems nearest of these to Springfield. The three other follies that Springfield has invested in previously include the popsicle-stick skyscraper, the giant magnifying glass and the escalator to nowhere.

Homage: The opening moments re-create the title sequence of *The Flintstones* ('Simpson, Homer Simpson . . .'). There are nods to *Silence of the Lambs* (Jonathan Demme, 1990) (Mr Burns is wheeled in wearing Hannibal Lecter's mask at his court appearance), and *Them!* (Gordon Douglas, 1984) (the giant creatures). But the main influence is *The Music Man* (Morton da Costa, 1962), the story of a trickster who persuades a smalltown council to finance a dodgy scheme (in that case it was a showband rather than a monorail).

Mmmmm: . . . chicken.

Look out for: The irradiated squirrel and the return of Lurleen Lumpkin (here voiced by Doris Grau).

Song: 'Monorail', sung by the people of Springfield.

Notes: An unsurpassed episode. It's hard to know where to start dishing out the praise – Leonard Nimoy's guest appearance, the Monorail song, Marge's narration, the truck full of popcorn . . .

72
9F11:
'Selma's Choice'

Written by David Stern   **Directed by** Carlos Baeza
Also starring: Pamela Hayden, Doris Grau
Special guest voice: Phil Hartman (as Lionel Hutz)

Premise: After the death of Gladys Bouvier, Selma begins to hanker after having children. When Homer falls ill – he's been eating a week-old foot-long hoagie – she tests her suitability as a family woman by taking Bart, Lisa and Maggie to Duff Gardens – where Bart is nearly decapitated and Lisa falls under the spell of a dangerous narcotic.

Features: Patty, Selma, Jackie Bouvier, Lionel Hutz, Grounds-keeper Willie, Hans Moleman, Eddie, Lou, Jimbo Jones, Dolph, Kearney, Barney Gumble, Carl.

Couch: The Simpsons rush in – and are netted.

Trivia: The Springfield Sperm Bank was established in 1858.

Homage: Marge is aware how ill Homer has become when he says he actually wants to watch *Yentl* (Barbra Streisand, 1983). Marge's flashback to an idyllic family swim recalls *Prince of Tides* (Barbra Streisand, 1991). Lisa's drug-induced behaviour at Duff Gardens ('I Am the Lizard Queen!') recalls Jim Morrison of the Doors, who claimed to be 'Lizard King'. The episode plays out with Carole King's 'Natural Woman'.

Look out for: Maggie's reaction when Selma announces she wants a baby. Bart's beer glasses.

Song: Lou Reed's 1972 hit 'Walk on the Wild Side' sung by sanitised teensters Hooray For Everything.

Notes: 'The legend of the dog-faced woman!' A nice episode for Selma and good for Marge and Homer as well. But it's the kids who provide the highlights in this one, with their antics at Duff Gardens.

73
9F12:
'Brother from the Same Planet'

Written by Jon Vitti   **Directed by** Jeff Lynch
Also starring: Pamela Hayden, Tress MacNeille,
Russi Taylor
Special guest voices: Marcia Wallace (as Ms Krabappel),
Phil Hartman (as Lionel Hutz)

Premise: Bart feels neglected by Homer, and applies to the Bigger Brothers agency for a replacement role model. He gets the strapping, action-loving Tom. Vengeful Homer joins Bigger Brothers and gets himself a little brother, Pepe. Meanwhile, Lisa's got hooked to non-threatening boy Corey Masterson's phone hotline.

Features: Nelson, Milhouse, Ms Krabappel, Krusty, Martin, Principal Skinner, Lionel Hutz, Grampa, Kent Brockman.

Couch: The Simpsons rush in, sit down – and the wall rotates, leaving an identical empty sofa.

Trivia: Lisa reads *Non-Threatening Boys* magazine.

Homage: Homer's female double is singing Helen Reddy's 1974 hit 'I Am Woman'. Tom and Bart watch a very faithfully recreated episode of Ren and Stimpy. Homer's accusation of Bart is a re-creation of Richard Burton's accusation of Elizabeth Taylor in *Who's Afraid of Virginia Woolf?* (Mike Nichols, 1966), and Milhouse's garbled reception of Bart's psychic message recalls *The Shining* (Stanley Kubrick, 1980). The flying nun glimpsed by Bart outside the football ground is a reference to a 1960s US sitcom *The Flying Nun* about, er, a flying nun.

Notes for Brits: Bobby Sherman was a minor pop star of the mid-sixties.

Notes: We love Homer sitting at home trying to remember to pick up Bart – he's watching a TV show about a baseball star called Bart, with pictures of Bart on all sides, and even Maggie seems to be calling her brother's name.

74

9F13:

'I Love Lisa'

Written by Frank Mula   **Directed by** Wes Archer

Also starring: Michael Carrington (as Rex), Doris Grau, Pamela Hayden, Maggie Roswell

Premise: It's Valentine's Day. Out of pity, Lisa sends Ralph Wiggum a Valentine. She'd love to forget him – but he's got tickets for Krusty's 29th anniversary show, and then he's cast as George Washington opposite her Martha in the school's President's Day pageant.

Features: Bill and Marty at KBBL, Grampa, Jasper, Moe, Barney, Ned Flanders, Maud Flanders, Apu, Janey, Miss Hoover, Ralph, Principal Skinner, Milhouse, Lunchlady Doris, Sherri and Terri, Sideshow Mel, Chief Wiggum, Lou and Eddie, Groundskeeper Willie, Rod Flanders, Patty and Selma, Jimbo Jones, Kearney, Dolph.

Couch: The Simpsons rush in – to form part of a high-kicking circus showbiz extravaganza.

Trivia: Bart's such a big Krusty fan he owns the Krusty Home Pregnancy Test.

Homage: 'Monster Mash' by Bobby 'Boris' Pickett and the Crypt-Kickers was a graveyard smash in the late sixties. Itchy and Scratchy's adventure unfolds to an orchestral version of Tony Bennett's 'Stranger in Paradise'. Homer's conscience speaks with the voice of Droopy. The clips from Krusty's 29 years of TV pay homage to seminal moments in the history of American television. 'Break on Thru (To the Other Side)' was the first single released by the Doors in 1966.

Notes for Brits: Oral Roberts is an American televangelist.

Itchy and Scratchy in: 'My Bloody Valentine'.

Songs: 'Do You Think I'm Cuddly?' sung by Ned Flanders to Maud as a Valentine's offering. 'We are the Mediocre Presidents' sung by the boys of Springfield Elementary.

Notes: Things to love about 'I Love Lisa': Chief Wiggum chasing a duck to get his badge back. Principal Skinner's flashback to Valentine's Day in 'Nam. Bart and Milhouse as John Wilkes Booth and Lincoln. And these are just the icing on the cake of the main plot.

75

9F14:

'Duffless'

Written by David McStern   **Directed by** Jim Reardon
Also starring: Pamela Hayden, Maggie Roswell
Special guest voices: Phil Hartman (as Troy McClure),
Marcia Wallace (as Ms Krabappel)

Premise: Lisa and Bart enter projects in the school science exhibition. When Bart destroys Lisa's hothouse tomato, she vows vengeance, and begins a series of tests to compare his intelligence to a hamster's. Meanwhile, Homer is caught and breathalysed after visiting the Duff beer factory. Marge convinces him to give up beer for a month.

Features: Patty, Selma, Principal Skinner, Ms Krabappel, Miss Hoover, Mr Largo, Lewis, Richard, Martin Prince, Ralph Wiggum, Milhouse van Houten, Nelson, Barney, the two barflies, Moe, Troy McClure, Mrs Wiggum, Jasper, Rev. Lovejoy, Helen Lovejoy, Ned Flanders, Maude Flanders, Otto, Hans Moleman, Chief Wiggum, Eddie, Lou, Lionel Hutz.

Couch: Maggie is seated but the others run off the film strip, into nothingness and then back to the sofa.

Trivia: Hans Moleman claims to be only 31. Lisa's first science project is a massive tomato grown using steroids to alleviate world starvation. The replacement involves a hamster called J. D. McGregor. Nelson Muntz's project is Wasting Squirrels with BB Guns, while Martin Prince investigates travel via hot air balloon. Milhouse discovers gravity via a useless Slinky and Ralph Wiggum learns about alcohol-fuelled cars. Homer's Class C driving licence is C4043243, expiring on 05.12.95, having been issued on 07/27/92. According to this, he lives at 742 Evergreen Terrace, Springfield, NT 49007. He was born 05.12.56, he is 6', no hair with blue eyes. The fake ID with which Homer bought his first Duff beer belonged to Brian McGee, age 26, born 08.2.48.

Homage: Bart's inability to grasp a pair of cherry-topped cupcakes from a high shelf nods to *A Clockwork Orange* (Stanley Kubrick, 1970). Homer used to listen to Queen, which going from the poster on his wall is probably around the 'Day at the Races/A Night at the Opera' era.

Hi, I'm Troy McClure, you may remember me from: Driving information films such as *Alice's Adventures Through the Windshield Glass* and *The Decapitation of Larry Leadfoot*.

Notes for the Uneducated: Lisa refers to her experiment on Bart as 'half P. T. Barnum, half B. F. Skinner'. Barnum was a nineteenth-century circus impresario; Skinner was a behavioural psychologist whose most famous experiments were in the solitary confinement of human beings.

Mmmmm: . . . gummi beers.

Look out for: Jub-Jub finding Selma frightening with Supperware on her head. Barney mistaking a pile of rags for Princess Diana. Duff, Duff Lite and Duff Dry all coming from the same pipe. Homer's fruitless discussions with his brain.

Notes: A superb episode with a sincere message. Homer is excellent throughout, but it is the cameos by Principal Skinner and Edna Krabappel that steal the show, especially the latter's reaction to Milhouse's Slinky.

76
9F15:
'Last Exit to Springfield'

Written by Jay Kogen and Wallace Wolodarsky
Directed by Mark Kirkland
Special guest voice: Dr Joyce Brothers (as herself)

Premise: Lisa needs braces – but Mr Burns has withdrawn the dental plan from his workers' rights. Homer becomes leader of the union to win it back. But can he come out on top in negotiations with Mr Burns?

Features: Mr Burns, Smithers, Ralph, Lenny, Carl, Bumblebee Man, Principal Skinner, Grampa, Jasper, Kent Brockman.

Couch: The Simpsons rush in – but the sofa has turned into a monster.

Homage: Lisa's given gas, and ends up in the Yellow Submarine alongside the Beatles – her dream ends with the final chord of their song 'A Day in the Life'. Mr Burns' monkeys are working on *A Tale of Two Cities*. Lisa's reaction to the first sight of her brace in the mirror recalls the Joker's reaction to his deformed face in *Batman* (Tim Burton, 1989).

Mmmmm: . . . organised crime.

Song: Lisa sings a folk protest song, 'They Have the Plant But We Have the Power'.

That's Homer Simpson, sir: 'He thwarted your campaign for governor, you ran over his son, he saved the plant from meltdown, and his wife painted you in the nude.'

Notes: This fine episode contains several of our favourite sequences – Mr Burns' fantasy of he and Smithers running the plant for themselves, Homer's fantasy of becoming Mafia boss Don Homer, Lisa's fantasy flight with the Beatles. And one of our favourite one-off characters – the dentist who bays

'Liar!' at his patients and relaxes them by explaining the function of his tools ('This is the gouger, which I'll be using to hack out teeth from your jaw'). A classic, and the series' most marked expedition into the surreal – up to this point.

77

9F17:

'So It's Come to This: A Simpsons Clip Show'

Written by Jon Vitti   **Directed by** Carlos Baeza
Also starring: Maggie Roswell

Premise: A can of beer shook up by Bart as an April Fool's joke sends Homer into a coma. Perhaps clips from previous episodes might jog his slumbering consciousness.

Features: The Flanderses, Captain McCallister, Chief Wiggum, Lou and Eddie, Dr Hibbert, Barney, Moe, Grampa, Dr Nick, Dr John Frink.

Couch: The Simpsons rush in, sit down – but their heads are on the wrong bodies.

And introducing: Bumblebee Man.

Homage: Barney's reaction to Homer's hospitalisation – pulling a water fountain off the wall – comes from *One Flew Over the Cuckoo's Nest* (Milos Forman, 1975). Dr Frink's suggestion to miniaturise a submarine and inject it into Homer's body mirrors the plot of *Fantastic Voyage* (Richard Fleischer, 1966).

Mmmmm: ... beer ... chocolate.

Notes: About as good as a clip show ever gets, and as the title suggests, refreshingly upfront about itself.

78

9F16:
'The Front'

Written by Adam I. Lapidus   **Directed by** Rich Moore
Also starring: Doris Grau, Maggie Roswell
Special guest voice: Brooke Shields (as herself)

Premise: After a really dull Itchy and Scratchy cartoon, Bart and Lisa try to sell a script for a better one but aren't taken seriously as they're just kids. So they use Grampa's name and as a result, he gets hired as a writer.

Features: Krusty, Grampa, Principal Skinner, Barney, Side-show Mel.

Couch: The Simpsons rush in – to form part of a circus showbiz extravaganza.

Trivia: Grampa claims to have spent forty years as a night watchman at a cranberry silo. The Itchy and Scratchy writers are caricatures of some *Simpsons* writers, notably Al Jean, Jeff Martin, George Meyer, Mike Reiss, Sam Simon, John Swartzwelder and Jon Vitti. Artie Ziff and Principal Dondelinger previously appeared in 'The Way We Was'. The other nominees for Best Writing in a Cartoon Series are: Strondaar – 'The Wedding' episode; Action Figure Man – The 'How to Buy Action Figure Man' episode; and Ren & Stimpy – The Season Premiere (Clip Not Done Yet).

Homage: Artie Ziff's suggestion to Homer about Marge recalls the central plot of *Indecent Proposal* (Adrian Lyne, 1993).

Itchy and Scratchy in: 'Little Barbershop of Horrors', 'Dazed and Confused' and 'Screams from a Mall'.

Look out for: Lisa walking down the corridors of the animation studio. Itchy and Scratchy's anti-drugs message.

Notes: An ironic look at the animation industry, with a higher than average Itchy and Scratchy count. The episode proper is followed by 'The Adventures of Ned Flanders' in 'Love That God', starring Ned, Rod and Todd, with its own, rather wonderful, theme tune.

79

9F18:

'Whacking Day'

Written by John Swartzwelder   **Directed by** Jeff Lynch
Also starring: Doris Grau, Pamela Hayden
Special guest voice: Barry White (as himself)

Premise: It's time for Springfield's annual Whacking Day – the traditional day for the whacking of snakes. Socially conscious Lisa objects. Can soul legend Barry White help her save her slithery reptilian chums?

Features: Principal Skinner, Ms Krabappel, Jimbo Jones, Nelson, Milhouse, Groundskeeper Willie, Superintendent Chalmers, Kearney, Dolph, Ralph, Janey, Lunchlady Doris, Kent Brockman, Grampa, Barney, Spotty Boy, Apu, Chief Wiggum, Lou and Eddie, Rev. Lovejoy, Mayor Quimby, Mr Largo.

Couch: The Simpsons rush in – but there's a child's chair where the sofa should be.

Trivia: Bart's cockney fixation makes an appearance – he would like to be a nineteenth-century cockney bootblack.

Itchy and Scratchy in: A short JFK-like picture – guest director Oliver Stone.

Mmmmm: . . . beer.

Songs: 'Won't You Come Home, Franz Brauder?' sung by Grampa in his alias as a German cabaret artist during WWII. 'O Whacking day, O Whacking Day' sung by the Springfield Boys Choir.

Notes: Lisa gives cruel traditions a good drubbing, and there are some good scenes as Bart is expelled from school. Superintendent Chalmers and Skinner cement their edgy relationship (Skinner has strung a banner reading WE LOVE CHALMIE on the school wall).

80
9F20:
'Marge in Chains'

Written by Bill Oakley and Josh Weinstein
Directed by Jim Reardon
Also starring: Pamela Hayden, Tress MacNeille,
Maggie Roswell
Special guest voices: David Crosby (as himself),
Phil Hartman (as Troy McClure, Lionel Hutz)

Premise: The dreaded Osaka flu hits Springfield. In all the confusion, Marge accidentally pockets a bottle of Colonel Kwik-E-Mart's Kentucky Bourbon, and ends up on trial accused of the Kennedy assassination.

Features: Troy McClure, Dr Nick, Principal Skinner, Mother Skinner, Patty and Selma, Chief Wiggum, Kent Brockman, Arnie Pie, Otto, Quimby, Mr Burns, Smithers, Dr Hibbert, the Flanderses, Grampa, Apu, Helen Lovejoy, Lionel Hutz, Miss Hoover, Rev. Lovejoy, the Springfield DA, Dr Frink, Snake, Milhouse, Nelson, Lou, Barney.

Couch: The Simpsons rush in – but they've shrunk.

Trivia: The Osaka flu speaks with the voice of Snake. Quimby's motto is CORRUPTUS IN EXTREMIS.

Homage: Flanders laughs sinfully at an episode of US sitcom *Married With Children*.

Hi, I'm Troy McClure, you may remember me from: such films as *P Is For Psycho* and *The President's Neck Is Missing*.

Itchy and Scratchy in: 'Germs of Endearment'.

Mmmmm: . . . pi.

Notes: 'Can you imagine a world without lawyers?' We like Bart's plan to rescue Marge from prison by becoming the glamorous Bartina, and Lionel Hutz is supremely inept – 'I move for a bad court thingy,' he tells the judge.

81

9F19:

'Krusty Gets Kancelled'

Written by John Swartzwelder
Directed by David Silverman
Also starring: Pamela Hayden
Special guest voices: Marcia Wallace (as Ms Krabappel), Luke Perry, Barry White, Johnny Carson, Hugh Heffner, Bette Midler, Elizabeth Taylor and The Red Hot Chili Peppers (as themselves)

Premise: 'Gabbo is coming . . .' When a ventriloquist's act takes Krusty out of the Nielsons and into cancellation, Bart and Lisa set up a great comeback event featuring many of Krusty's best showbiz friends.

Features: Kent Brockman, Rainier Wolfcastle, Troy McClure, Mr Burns, Smithers, Rev. Lovejoy, Jasper, Grampa, Krusty,

Lois Pennycandy, Bumblebee Man, Milhouse van Houten, Nelson Muntz, Mayor Quimby, Sideshow Mel, Moe, Barney, Chief Wiggum, Dr Hibbert.

Couch: The Simpsons rush in – and get netted.

Trivia: Wolfcastle is making two new McBain movies – *McBain* and *Help, My Son Is a Nerd*.

Homage: Krusty sings 'Send in the Clowns', a Steven Sondheim song made famous by Judy Collins in 1975. Bette Midler sings her 1985 hit 'Wind Beneath My Wings' while Johnny Carson hums music from Puccini's *Madame Butterfly*. Gabbo, the malevolent ventriloquist's dummy, has his roots in a similar creature in *Magic* (Richard Attenborough, 1978).

Mmmmm: . . . delicious.

Look out for: 'Worker & Parasite', the Russian version of Itchy and Scratchy.

Notes: Lots of great guest stars for the season's finale. Elizabeth Taylor's self-mocking cameo is the highlight, although Bette Midler's anti-litter attacks come close.

Fifth Season

1993–1994
22 Episodes

82
9F21:
'Homer's Barbershop Quartet'

Written by Jeff Martin   **Directed by** Mark Kirkland
Also starring: Pamela Hayden
Special guest voices: George Harrison (as himself),
David Crosby (as himself)
Additional vocals by The Dapper Dans (as the singing
voices of the Be Sharps)

Premise: At Springfield's swap-meet, Bart discovers a record apparently made by Homer. Homer recalls his brief pop stardom as a member of barbershop quartet, the Be Sharps – a Grammy, a concealed marriage, a Japanese conceptual artist . . .

Features: Mayor Quimby, Moe, Nelson, Milhouse, Flanders, Principal Skinner, Herman, Chief Wiggum, Apu, Barney, Grampa, Snake, Rev. Lovejoy, Groundskeeper Willie, Jasper, Captain McCallister, Lou and Eddie.

Couch: The Simpsons rush in – and explode.

Trivia: At Moe's Cavern in 1985 there's a sign reading 'For a Good Time Call Edna Krabappel'. The new name given to Apu by Nigel – Apu du Beaumarchais – means Apu of the Beautiful Market.

Homage: At the swap-meet, Moe is trying to make his oysters do impressions of comedienne Lucille Ball. Grampa and Jasper tune in by accident to a radio skit on the recently deceased (in 1985) right-winger Ray Cohn. There are many, many music references, mostly to the Beatles (Moe's 'Cavern', Barney's Japanese girlfriend, the rooftop concert, Homer's final remark 'I hope we passed the audition', which is from their movie *Let It Be*) and Elvis (he bought his mother a pink Cadillac, and the line 'I didn't pay any girls to scream' comes from one of his movies). Krusty's LP ''Swonderful, 'Smarvellous, 'SKrusty' refers to an album with a similar title by Ray Conniff, while 'Melvin & the Squirrels' are close relations of US kiddie cartoon pop group, Alvin & the Chipmunks. At the Grammy ceremony you can see Spinal Tap, Leon Kompowski from the episode 'Stark Raving Dad', and somebody we think is MC Hammer.

Note for Brits: It's rather saddening to hear Dexy's Midnight Runners referred to in jest ('you haven't heard the last of them!') by Homer. Their only US hit was 'Come On Eileen' in 1983. They fared rather better in the UK, of course.

Notes: This blasts the new season off to a fantastic start. Epic in its scale and its total disregard of the series' continuity – but who cares?

83

9F22:

'Cape Feare (Not Affiliated with the Film "Cape Fear")'

Written by Jon Vitti   **Directed by** Rich Moore
Also starring: Pamela Hayden
Special guest voice: Kelsey Grammer (as Sideshow Bob)

Premise: 'Die, Bart, die!' Sideshow Bob gets parole – and he's out for revenge on this century's Dennis the Menace. The Simpsons must flee from Springfield to Terror Lake – and become the Thompsons – if Bart's going to stand a chance . . .

Features: Wolfcastle, Milhouse, Nelson, Marty at KBBL, Sideshow Bob, Ned Flanders, Ms Krabappel, Martin, Chief Wiggum, Lou and Eddie, Moe, Snake, Patty and Selma, Grampa, Jasper.

Couch: The Simpsons rush in – and form part of a chorus line.

Homage: Principally *Cape Fear* (J. Lee Thompson, 1962) and its remake (Martin Scorsese, 1991). Several scenes are recycled wholesale, in particular Bob stalking the Simpsons in the cinema and hiding himself under the 'Thompsons' car. Homer surprising Bart with his new hockey mask recalls *Friday 13th Part II* (Steve Miner, 1981).

Notes for Brits: Sideshow Bob is writing to a column in the American *Reader's Digest* called 'Life In These United States'.

Moe's secrets: He has a secret cache of pandas behind the tavern.

Notes: One of the very best, well remembered for the alternative opening sequence to 'The Thompsons', the luckless Sideshow Bob's encounter with seventeen (count 'em) rakes, and Homer's FBI WITNESS RELOCATION PROGRAM T-shirt and baseball cap.

84
1F01:
'Rosebud'

Written by John Swartzwelder   **Directed by** Wes Archer

Also starring: Pamela Hayden
Special guest voices: The Ramones (as themselves)

Premise: It's Mr Burns' birthday and no matter how big or grand the party that is thrown for him, he wants to be reunited with his lost teddy bear, Bobo, which he abandoned when he was adopted. The bear is now loved by Maggie and Homer has to choose between Burns' happiness (and a lot of money) or Maggie's favourite toy.

Features: Mr Burns, Smithers, Ned Flanders, Dr Hibbert, Moe, Jasper, Groundskeeper Willie, Ms Krabappel, Otto, Grampa, Bumblebee Man, Lenny, Carl, John Frink, Mr and Mrs van Houten, Apu, Principal Skinner, Barney, Nelson, Jimbo Jones, Dolph, Kearney, Kent Brockman, Martin Prince.

Couch: The Simpsons dash into the living room only to find a Simpson family of clones already seated there.

Trivia: The Ramones sing 'Happy Birthday to Burnsie' which results in the old man demanding the execution of the Rolling Stones. Among the gifts presented to Burns are a first draft of the American constitution, containing the word 'suckers', Excalibur, and a picture of Mark Twain naked.

Homage: Principally, *Citizen Kane* – the snowbound farewell to Kane's sleigh is re-created using young Mr Burns, Bobo and NEV-R-BREAK SNOW GLOBES. Also *The Wizard of Oz* (Burns' guards); *Mission: Impossible* as Burns and Smithers try to steal Bobo; *The Honeymooners* as Smithers and Burns create a sitcom on television; and *Planet of the Apes* supplies the superb and surreal epilogue.

That's Homer Simpson, sir: 'one of the carbon blobs from Sector 7G.'

Mmmmm: . . . 64 slices of American cheese.

Look out for: Smithers' ideal birthday desire; the slide show of Burns' life with his head sellotaped over famous pictures, including Marilyn Monroe's famous pic standing over the updraft; best of all, the revelation that Burns' brother is comedian George Burns.

Notes: A great story, as Homer comes good against Mr Burns' total evil. Until Maggie (almost) melts Mr Burns' heart – a hint of what was yet to come between these two, perhaps?

85

1F02:
'Homer Goes to College'

Written by Conan O'Brien   **Directed by** Jim Reardon
Also starring: Maggie Roswell

Premise: The Nuclear Plant is investigated and Homer is found to be deficient in his understanding of nuclear physics. He's packed off to college – where he tries to turn three 'nerds' into 'jocks'.

Features: Mr Burns, Smithers, Krusty the Klown, Dr Hibbert, Lenny, 'Diamond' Joe Quimby, Snake, Grampa.

Couch: The Simpsons are squashed beneath a Monty Python-animated foot.

Trivia: Springfield University was established in 1952. We get to see Lisa's idol Corey Masterson in his college caper *School of Hard Knockers*.

Homage: Just about every corny American high-school film ever made. Also, *The Maltese Falcon* (John Huston, 1941) (Mr Burns' line about the search for the jade monkey). Lisa lists some famous nerds, including popcorn magnate Orville Redenbacher, Talking Heads singer David Byrne and Supreme Court Justice David Souter. The song played over the end credits is 'Louie Louie', a hit for the Kingsmen in 1964.

Itchy and Scratchy in: 'Burning Down the Mouse'.

Look out for: Mr Burns' attempt to send the Inspectors through a trapdoor. Homer turning into a monster until he remembers to eat. Homer chasing the squirrels. The Nerds' Monty Python routine.

Notes: Homer at his most excruciatingly stupid in another superb episode – his attitude to the college's 'stuffy old dean' (who was, in fact, bassist for the Pretenders) is a joy.

86
1F03:
'Marge on the Lam'

Written by Bill Canterbury   **Directed by** Mark Kirkland
Also starring: Pamela Hayden, Maggie Roswell,
Russi Taylor
Special guest voices: Phil Hartman (as Troy McClure and
Lionel Hutz), George Fenneman (as the narrator),
Pamela Reed (as Ruth Powers)

Premise: Marge decides to spend some time with her new neighbour, Ruth. She hadn't bargained for going on the run across country in a stolen car.

Features: Troy McClure, Ruth Powers, Carl, Lenny, Patty, Selma, Ned Flanders, Maude Flanders, Rev. Lovejoy, Helen Lovejoy, Mr Burns, Smithers, Barney, Lionel Hutz, Grounds-keeper Willie, Kent Brockman, Kearney, Moe, Otto, Mayor Quimby, Apu, Chief Wiggum.

Couch: The Simpsons rush in – and crash through the wall.

Trivia: Lionel Hutz's alternative identities are Miguel Sanchez and Dr Nguyen van Falk. Ruth Powers was introduced in 'New Kid on the Block'. Marge and Ruth visit a Country and Western dirt bar called The Sh*tkickers and a punk club called The Hate Box.

Homage: The episode's very clearly based on *Thelma and Louise* (Ridley Scott, 1991). Both Ruth and Chief Wiggum have tapes of Lesley Gore's 1964 hit 'Sunshine, Lollipops and Rainbows'. Ruth also has a Guns 'n' Roses cassette, featuring their first single, 1987's 'Welcome to the Jungle'. The closing theme is played in the style of the theme of *Dragnet*.

Hi, I'm Troy McClure, you may remember me from: such telethons as 'Out With Gout '88' and 'Let's Save Tony Orlando's House'.

Notes for the Uneducated: Garrison Keillor, parodied in the opening sequence of the episode, is an American author and intellectual.

Mmmmm: . . . invisible Cola . . . candy.

Look out for: Chief Wiggum's rationale of 'ghost cars'. Homer hitting the television set and demanding that it be more funny.

Notes: Marge getting to let her hair down is always a treat, and in Ruth Powers she seems to have a real friend. A pity we don't see more of her.

87

1F04:
'Treehouse of Horror IV'

Written by Conan O'Brien, Bill Oakley, Josh Weinstein, Greg Daniels, Dan McGrath and Bill Canterbury
Directed by David Silverman
Additional cast: Pamela Hayden, Russi Taylor, Frank Welker
Special guest voices: Phil Hartman (as Lionel Hutz)

Premise: In 'The Devil and Homer Simpson', Homer makes a pact with the Devil – his soul for a doughnut. 'Nightmare at

5 ft' sees Bart's schoolbus menaced by a monster. 'Dracula' features a vampiric Mr Burns out for blood.

Tombstones: Elvis – Accept It, A Balanced Budget, Subtle Political Satire and TV Violence.

Homage: *The Twilight Zone* again, although this time there are also nods to *Night Gallery*, with Bart in the role of its host Rod Serling. The closing sequence is a reference to *Merry Christmas, Charlie Brown*, another seasonal cartoon special.

Mmmmm: . . . forbidden donut.

Look out for: Hell's Jury, including Blackbeard and Richard Nixon.

Notes: Probably the best of the Treehouses of Horror, with many notable sequences. We're particularly fond of Hell's Dept of Ironic Punishments and Chief Wiggum's attempts to deal with Dracula.

88

1F05:

'Bart's Inner Child'

Written by George Meyer   **Directed by** Bob Anderson
Also starring: Russi Taylor, Albert Brooks
(as Brad Goodman), Pamela Hayden
Special guest voices: Phil Hartman (as Troy McClure and
Lionel Hutz), Marcia Wallace (as Ms Krabappel),
James Brown (as himself)

Premise: Homer decides to invest in a trampoline, while Marge is busy discovering the message of Brad Goodman and his self-awareness seminars.

Features: Krusty, Otto, Milhouse, Martin Prince, Sherri and Terri, Lewis, Richard, Nelson, Janey, Dolph, Kearney, Todd

Flanders, Rod Flanders, Ralph Wiggum, Snake, Jimbo Jones, Ned Flanders, Patty, Selma, Troy McClure, Dr Hibbert, Hans Moleman, Sideshow Mel, Ms Krabappel, Miss Hoover, Mayor Quimby, Mr Burns, Smithers, Apu, Lenny, Moe, Maude Flanders, Principal Skinner, Mrs Skinner, Barney, Jasper, Grampa, Kent Brockman, Rev. Lovejoy, Groundskeeper Willie, Dr Marvin Monroe, Carl, Chief Wiggum, Captain McCallister, Sanjay, Helen Lovejoy, Snake, Lionel Hutz.

Couch: The family rush in – to find the sofa occupied by a very fat man.

Homage: James Brown sings 'I Got You', his 1966 hit. Rev. Lovejoy plays Scott Joplin's 'The Entertainer' on the church organ.

Hi, I'm Troy McClure, you may remember me from: such self-help videos as *Smoke Yourself Thin* and *Get Confident, Stupid!*

Notes for Brits: Brad Goodman is a parody of American self-help guru John Bradshaw. Many of their methods are similar – Bradshaw uses diagrams on a blackboard to explain simplistic points.

Look out for: Homer trying to get rid of the trampoline off a cliff and the subsequent Looney Toons-style sight gags.

Notes: A very bizarre episode in which everyone just has a good time. Bart might think Brad Goodman is a bit of a fraud, but nevertheless, he doesn't do any real harm.

89

1F06:

'Boy Scoutz 'n the Hood'

Written by Dan McGrath   **Directed by** Jeffrey Lynch

Also starring: Pamela Hayden, Maggie Roswell,
Russi Taylor
Special guest voices: Marcia Wallace (as Ms Krabappel),
Ernest Borgnine (as himself)

Premise: After getting tanked up on a Squishee, Bart discovers that he joined the Scouts whilst under the influence of the sugar. Homer joins him, Ned and Todd Flanders for a weekend rafting expedition.

Features: Martin Prince, Jimbo Jones, Dolph, Kearney, Milhouse, Apu, Snake, Barney, Principal Skinner, Nelson, Ms Krabappel, Jasper, Ned Flanders, Todd Flanders, Moe, Han Moleman, Dr Hibbert, Captain McCallister, Chief Wiggum, Patty, Selma, Lou, Eddie, Krusty.

Couch: The family's eyes rush in – followed by their bodies.

Homage: In Homer's dream, he's singing 'Sugar Sugar', a 1969 hit for cartoon pop group The Archies. Hans Moleman's cry of 'This is a knife' comes from *Crocodile Dundee* (Peter Faiman, 1986).

Itchy and Scratchy in: 'Aaaahhhhh Wilderness'.

Mmmmm: . . . pressed peanut sweepings . . . pretty goo . . . apple . . . hamburgers.

Look out for: One of the best jokes of the series – the dolphins warbling 'You're going to die' to trapped Homer and company.

Notes: A terrific episode, with Homer so stupid it isn't true, yet still saving the day. Seeing Ned Flanders get it wrong (and slapped about for the trouble) is great but show-stealer is a toss-up between Ernest Borgnine's great self-deprecating role, the ironic seagull and the dolphins.

90

1F07:

'The Last Temptation of Homer'

Written by Frank Mula   **Directed by** Carlos Baeza
Also starring: Pamela Hayden, Maggie Roswell,
Russi Taylor
Special guest voices: Phil Hartman (as Lionel Hutz), Werner
Klempere (as Colonel Klink), Michelle Pfeiffer (as Mindy
Simmons), Marcia Wallace (as Ms Krabappel)

Premise: When the power plant's Dangerous Emissions Officer is accidentally transported to an Arabian table-dancing establishment, Mr Burns hires the beautiful Mindy Simmons – a woman obsessed with doughnuts, beer, and TV. And Homer. Meanwhile, Bart's become a nerd.

Features: Milhouse, Principal Skinner, Ms Krabappel, Martin, Lenny, Carl, Charlie, Mr Burns, Smithers, Dr Hibbert, Sherri and Terri, Nelson, Dolph, Jimbo, Kearney, Moe, Barney, Grampa, Kent Brockman, Ned Flanders, Lionel Hutz, Rod and Todd Flanders, Hans Moleman.

Couch: The Simpsons rush in – and find themselves guests on *Late Night With Letterman*.

Trivia: Homer and Mindy are selling copies of 'Will There Ever Be a Rainbow' at the energy convention.

Homage: Homer's unsexy thoughts include Barney acting out the title sequence of sixties sitcom *I Dream of Jeannie*. Homer flicks past what looks like a BBC wildlife documentary. His guardian angel appears to him in the form of Colonel Klink from the 1960s sitcom *Hogan's Heroes*, in a sequence that draws heavily from *It's A Wonderful Life* and Dickens' *A Christmas Carol*. Homer sings a rough approximation of Barry Manilow's 1977 hit 'Mandy'. Mr Burns' attempt to deal with employees charging room service to the company is reminiscent of the Wicked Witch of the West's attempts to deal with Dorothy in *The Wizard of Oz*.

Notes for Brits: Roger Ebert, referred to by Homer, is a renowned film critic and sometime screenwriter.

Notes for the Uneducated: Homer's garbled message to Mindy includes 'nam myoho renge kyo', the common chant of Nichiren Daishonin Buddhism.

Mmmmm: . . . foot-long chilli dog . . . Marge.

Notes: 'Desserts aren't always right.' 'But they're so sweet.' Homer gets the chance to cheat on Marge in this wonderfully scripted episode.

91

1F08:

'$pringfield (or How I Learnt to Stop Worrying and Love Legalized Gambling)'

Written by Bill Oakley and Josh Weinstein
Directed by Wes Archer
Also starring: Pamela Hayden
Special guest voices: Gerry Cooney (as himself),
Robert Goulet (as himself)

Premise: 'Once something's been approved by the government it's no longer immoral!' To raise cash for Springfield's beleagured public finances, Mayor Quimby legalises gambling, Mr Burns opens a casino, and Marge develops a problem with a one-armed bandit.

Features: Grampa, Jasper, Mr Burns, Smithers, Scott Christian, Kent Brockman, Barney, Mayor Quimby, Principal Skinner, Patty and Selma, Rev. Lovejoy, Captain McCallister, Otto, Spotty Boy, Krusty.

Couch: The Simpsons rush in – and collide and shatter.

Notes for Brits: *The Gong Show* (briefly screened on Channel 4 in the late eighties in the UK) was a seventies talent show.

Homage: Mr Burns' distressing condition is inspired by the eccentric millionaire recluse Howard Hughes, who had a similar dread of germs and built a (more workable) plane called the Spruce Goose. His bed looks similar to the one occupied by Keir Dullea in the final shots of *2001* (Stanley Kubrick, 1969). Dustin Hoffman and Tom Cruise appear at the casino to reprise their roles from *Rain Man* (Barry Levinson, 1988). And Krusty's midnight casino show for adults only mirrors a similar show recorded by Bill Cosby.

Notes: There's a lovely nod to the earlier episodes in which Marge protests the citizenry's hare-brained ideas at council meetings. A series of bizarre moments rather than a story – we're especially fond of Homer's photographic memory and Mr Burns' descent into insanity – but great fun.

92

1F09:

'Homer the Vigilante'

Written by John Swartzwelder
Directed by Jim Reardon
Also starring: Pamela Hayden
Special guest voice: Sam Neill (as Malloy)

Premise: 'YOU HAVE JUST BEEN ROBBED BY THE SPRINGFIELD CAT BURGLAR – EST. 1957.' The calling card of the criminal genius who has robbed Lisa of her saxophone, Flanders of his Shroud of Turin beach towels and Principal Skinner of his Stormin' Norman commemorative plates. Can the vigilante posse led by Homer stop him? Or will they just throw their weight around?

Features: Nelson, Ned Flanders, Principal Skinner, Barney, Chief Wiggum, Lou and Eddie, Kent Brockman, Dr John Frink, Otto, Jimbo, Jasper, Kearney, Dolph, Grampa, Apu, Ruth Powers, Moe, Lenny, Captain MacAllister, Herman, Selma, Mayor Quimby, Ruth Powers, Mrs van Houten, Carl, Patty, Ms Krabappel, Milhouse, Lionel Hutz, Miss Hoover, Dr Hibbert, Dr Nick Riviera, Groundskeeper Willie.

Couch: The Simpsons rush in – and explode.

Homage: *It's a Mad, Mad, Mad, Mad World* (Stanley Kramer, 1963) provides the frenetic ending (in the movie the search was for a giant W – you can see it behind the giant T in this episode). The *Pink Panther* movies provide the music for the cat burglaries. The character of Malloy comes from David Niven's performance as *Raffles* (Sam Wood, 1939), and Homer re-creates Slim Pickens' role from the climax of *Dr Strangelove* (Stanley Kubrick, 1963) in his fantasy of hippie-bombing. Homer and Skinner's nods outside the museum recall *Dragnet*.

Notes: 'So, Professor, would you say it's time for everyone to panic?' 'Yes, I would, Kent.' A bit lacking in focus, this episode nevertheless contains a number of satisfying set-pieces – we like Frink's walking house security system – and displays Wiggum at his all time most useless.

93

1F10:

'Homer and Apu'

Written by Greg Daniels   **Directed by** Mark Kirkland
Also starring: Michael Carrington, Pamela Hayden
Special guest voice: James Woods (as himself)

Premise: Homer uses Kent Brockman's consumer programme *Bark Back* to expose Apu's practice of selling rotten meat. It looks like Apu will have to hand in his pricing gun for good. Perhaps a trip to India, and the head of the Kwik-E-Mart organisation, can help resolve things.

Features: Apu, Martin, Dr Hibbert, Patty and Selma, Kent Brockman, Barney, Spotty Boy, Grampa, Jimbo Jones.

Couch: The Simpsons are hiding in terror behind the sofa.

Homage: The subplot involving James Woods mirrors the plot of his movie *The Hard Way* (John Badham, 1991), in which Michael J. Fox plays an actor who's prepared to do any amount of research to prepare for a role. Homer's speech to Kent Brockman 'No way, man, get yourself another patsy!' is from *JFK* (Oliver Stone, 1993).

Song: 'Who Needs the Kwik-E-Mart?' sung by Apu and the Simpsons.

Notes: 'Are we in India yet?' One of the very best, with the gags coming thick and fast. We particularly like the spy camera concealed in Homer's massive stetson, Apu and Marge's trip to the Monster Mart (Apu's advice on supermarket queue-jumping is worth heeding), and 'Who Needs the Kwik-E-Mart?', possibly the cleverest song in the series. And the Christians harassing people at the Indian airport, and Homer's wastage of three questions, and James Woods' parting words to the Simpsons, and the footage of Apu doing a hummingbird impression . . .

94

1F11:

'Bart Gets Famous'

Written by John Swartzwelder   **Directed by** Susie Dietter

Also starring: Marcia Wallace, Pamela Hayden, Maggie
Roswell, Russi Taylor
Special guest voice: Conan O'Brien (as himself)

Premise: The Springfield Elementary 4th Grade field trip is
to the local box factory, so Bart slips away and finds work at
Channel 6, initially as Krusty's PA. However, after Sideshow
Mel is poisoned, Bart takes part in a sketch, destroys the set
and says 'I didn't do it', which immediately makes him a
star.

Features: Mr Burns, Principal Skinner, Edna Krabappel,
Martin Prince, Lewis, Richard, Sherri and Terri, Wendell,
Nelson Muntz, Milhouse, Otto, Ned Flanders, Grampa,
Barney Gumble, Kent Brockman, 'Diamond' Joe Quimby,
Selma, Patty, Snake, Apu, Sideshow Mel, Bumblebee Man.

Couch: The Simpsons rush in, meld, and become an amor-
phous glob.

Trivia: Bart's popularity really takes off in a sketch known as
'The "I Didn't Do It" Boy in the Ming Vase and a Ladder
Sketch'. Sideshow Mel is allergic to cheese. Krusty, much to
Bart's sadness, does not remember him as the boy who saved
him from jail or who reunited him with his father. Bart does
indeed appear to be credited on Krusty's show under Assistants to the Producers, but it's not entirely clear and the other
kids' readings of the name could be just as likely.

Homage: Bart's first single is a cover of MC Hammer's 1990
hit 'U Can't Touch This', and his other showbiz chums
include Billy Crystal, Farrah Fawcett Majors, Laurie Anderson, Spike Lee and Kitty Carlisle. *Planet of the Apes* is
referenced (again) as Homer thinks Bart has been turned into
a box. Bart guests on Conan O'Brien's chat show – in real
life, O'Brien is the writer of several *Simpsons* episodes.

Notes: Even without that final sequence, this would still
be one of the best episodes, with Bart at his very best.
The scenes in the box factory are superb, as is Martin and

Skinner's joyful singing and, once again, Edna and Bart's enforced team-up.

95

1F12:

'Lisa vs. Malibu Stacy'

Written by Bill Oakley and Josh Weinstein
Directed by Jeffrey Lynch
Also starring: Maggie Roswell, Pamela Hayden,
Special guest voice: Kathleen Turner (as Stacy Lovell)

Premise: Lisa buys a talking Malibu Stacy, only to discover it's saying things like 'Don't ask me, I'm just a girl' and 'I wish they taught shopping at school'. After tracking down Malibu Stacy's creator, she creates a radical rival – Lisa Lionheart. But when it's big business versus a little girl, guess who'll win. . .

Features: Grampa, Dr Hibbert, Mrs Hibbert, Jasper, Smithers, Krusty, Kent Brockman, Hans Moleman.

Couch: The Simpsons are crushed by a Monty Python foot.

Trivia: Stacy Lovell's list of husbands is fabulously surreal, featuring Ken, Johnny, GI Joe, Doctor Colossus and Steve Austin. Among the Malibu Stacys available to buy are: Achy-Breaky Stacy, Live from the Improv Stacy, Talking Malibu Stacy and Malibu Stacy with a New Hat!

Notes for the Uneducated: Gertrude Stein was a feminist intellectual and author in the 1930s. Lisa's other inspirations include feminist cartoonist Cathy Guisewite.

Look out for: Lisa's comments about how awful she'd feel if people put out bad merchandise with her name on it.

Notes: Lisa at her crusading best, Homer at his stupidest and Grampa getting all the best lines again, especially at Krusty Burgers. Kathleen Turner's spot as the real Malibu Stacy is superb.

96

1F13:

'Deep Space Homer'

Written by David Mirkin   **Directed by** Carlos Baeza
Also starring: Maggie Roswell, Pamela Hayden
Special guest voices: James Taylor, Buzz Aldrin (as themselves)

Premise: NASA decide they need to rekindle public awareness of the space programme by sending an average guy into space. Homer is chosen.

Features: Lenny, Carl, Smithers, Mr Burns, Barney, Grampa, Patty, Selma, Kent Brockman.

Couch: A very fat man occupies the sofa.

Homage: Among the shows received by NASA from space are alien versions of *Married, With Children* and *Home Improvement*. Homer's chip-crunching in zero gravity to the strains of the 'Blue Danube' is another take on *2001*. The astronaut-testing sequence comes from *The Right Stuff* (Geoffrey Kirkland, 1983). Homer and Barney's fight is lifted from the *Star Trek* episode 'The Gamesters of Triskelion', and comes complete with that series' stock fight music.

Itchy and Scratchy in: 'Scar Trek: The Next Laceration'.

Mmmmm: . . . medicine.

Look out for: The violence warning after the Itchy and Scratchy cartoon has aired. Homer's sudden understanding of the climax to *Planet of the Apes*.

Notes: More of a handful of gags than a story – but very memorable for the chip-crunching sequence and Kent Brockman's reaction to a feared ant invasion.

97

1F14:

'Homer Loves Flanders'

Written by David Richardson   **Directed by** Wes Archer
Also starring: Pamela Hayden, Maggie Roswell

Premise: Flanders gets Homer a ticket for the Pigskin Classic football game between the Shelbyville Sharks and the Springfield Atoms. Homer's full of gratitude – and decides to become Flanders' friend.

Features: Kent Brockman, Bill and Marty at KBBL, the Flanderses, Lenny, Carl, Mr Burns, Milhouse, Mr and Mrs van Houten, Mayor Quimby, Moe, Dr Hibbert, Chief Wiggum, Rev. Lovejoy, Grampa, Helen Lovejoy.

Couch: The Simpsons rush in – to find two living rooms. They divide their bodies and sit down – twice.

Homage: Homer sings a corrupted version of Village People's 'Macho Man', and listens to Eddie Money's hit 'Two Tickets to Paradise'.

Moe's secrets: He reads sentimental novels (including *My Friend Flicka* and *Little Women*) to sick children in hospital.

Mmmmm: . . . sacrelicious.

Notes: This episode has some great existential musings from Lisa – the ending of the episode, in particular, is fantastic, with a glimpse of the 'next episode' – and contains some nice moments highlighting the differences between the Simpsons and the Flanderses.

98

1F15:

'Bart Gets an Elephant'

Written by John Swartzwelder
Directed by Jim Reardon
Also starring: Pamela Hayden, Maggie Roswell

Premise: 'KBBL is going to give me something stupid!' Bart wins a new pet – Stampy the elephant – from KBBL. Homer doesn't approve. Until he's approached by an ivory dealer.

Features: Moe, Bill and Marty at KBBL, Grampa, Chief Wiggum, Snake, Principal Skinner, Kent Brockman, Jasper, Helen Lovejoy, Milhouse, the van Houtens, the Flanderses, Nelson, Patty and Selma.

Couch: The Simpsons' eyes rush in – followed by their bodies.

Homage: 'Sixteen Tons' was a hit in 1955 for Tennessee Ernie Ford.

Mmmmm: . . . elephant friend.

Notes: Another favourite. It's hard to explain the special appeal of this episode. Perhaps it's because Homer is so exceptionally dumb. Or perhaps because it contains the 'D'oh!' 'A deer!' 'A female deer!' gag.

99

1F16:

'Burns' Heir'

Written by Jack Richdale   **Directed by** Mark Kirkland
Also starring: Pamela Hayden, Russi Taylor
Special guest voice: Phil Hartman (as Lionel Hutz)

Premise: Mr Burns nearly drowns in the bath. He realises he'll die without an heir. And rather than leave his wealth to the Egg Advisory Council he auditions for a suitable 'son'. Bart gets the job.

Features: Mr Burns, Smithers, Grampa, Hans Moleman, Martin, Ralph, Milhouse, Nelson, Krusty, Chief Wiggum, Lionel Hutz, Moe, Principal Skinner, Mayor Quimby, Lenny.

Couch: The spherical Simpsons bounce in.

Homage: The cinema commercial for groundbreaking sound refers to George Lucas' commercial for his THX sound process. The commercial that follows features Mr Burns alone in a field, just like Robin Williams in the trailer for *Toys* (Barry Levinson, 1992) and singing the archaic US cinema ad 'Let's All Go to the Lobby'. Mr Burns reviving from the dead in the bath is a nod to *Fatal Attraction* (Adrian Lyne, 1987) and Martin sings 'The Trolley Song' from *Meet Me in St Louis* (Vincente Minnelli, 1944). There are references to *A Christmas Carol* and *Nineteen Eighty-Four* in there as well.

Itchy and Scratchy in: 'The Buck Chops Here'.

Notes: Mr Burns shows the full range of his villainy, but this episode lacks the emotional punch of others in which members of the family are separated.

100
1F18:
'Sweet Seymour Skinner's Baadasssss Song'

Written by Bill Oakley and Josh Weinstein
Directed by Bob Anderson
Also starring: Doris Grau, Pamela Hayden,
Tress MacNeille, Maggie Roswell
Special guest voice: Marcia Wallace (as Ms Krabappel)

Premise: Skinner is fired by Superintendent Chalmers, and Flanders is installed as the new Principal. Skinner is alone and friendless – until Bart realises he needs an enemy in order to define his own personality . . .

Features: Grampa, Otto, Ralph, Martin, Nelson, Ms Krabappel, Milhouse, Groundskeeper Willie, Lunchlady Doris, Miss Hoover, Principal Skinner, Superintendent Chalmers, Ned Flanders, Kearney, Jimbo, Dolph, Apu, Mrs Skinner.

Couch: The Simpsons rush in – and Homer takes very unkindly to the FOX station logo in the corner of the screen.

Trivia: Ned Flanders' parents make their first appearance – they were to return in the episode 'Hurricane Neddie'.

Homage: The episode's title refers to the controversial blaxploitation movie *Sweet Sweetback's Baadasssss Song* (Melvin van Peebles, 1971). Skinner's use of a heat-seeking tracer to pin down the positions of Groundskeeper Willie and Santa's Little Helper within the school's ventilation system is a lift from *Alien* (Ridley Scott, 1979).

Notes for Brits: Joey Heatherton is an actress who appeared on numerous US celebrity panel games in the seventies.

Notes: Poor Skinner. The 100th episode – that explains the blackboard joke – is a fine one, with Principal Skinner's idea for a novel and the conduct of the staff at the Italian restaurant as highpoints.

101
1F19:
'The Boy Who Knew Too Much'

Written by John Swartzwelder   **Directed by** Jeffrey Lynch
Also starring: Pamela Hayden, Maggie Roswell, Russi Taylor
Special guest voices: Phil Hartman (as Lionel Hutz),
Marcia Wallace (as Mrs Krabappel)

Premise: Bart skips school – and slips into Freddy Quimby's 18th birthday party, where an altercation with a French waiter over the pronunciation of the word 'chowder' leads to a wrongful arrest. Only Bart can prove the accused's innocence – but in doing so he will give himself away to Principal Skinner. Worse still, Homer's on the jury – and when he discovers that an undecided jury stays for free in the Springfield Palace Hotel it looks like the wheels of justice will be turning a little slower than normal.

Features: Otto, Milhouse, Ms Krabappel, Martin, Principal Skinner, Groundskeeper Willie, Mayor Quimby, Wolfcastle, Chief Wiggum, Scott Christian, Kent Brockman, Attorney, Lionel Hutz, Moe, Dr Hibbert, Apu, Mrs Lovejoy, Jasper, Patty, Barney, Ned Flanders, Hans Moleman.

Couch: The Simpsons rush in – and find themselves the guests of David Letterman.

Trivia: Marge had a brother called Arnold who went on a killing spree.

Homage: Matt Groening appears in a cameo as a court artist. Bart fantasises of lazing with Huckleberry Finn from Mark Twain's classic children's novel of the same name. The series *McGonagall* is strongly reminiscent of Patty and Selma's beloved *McGyver*. And Homer gets to see a recut version of *Free Willie*. At the trial, his brain is singing the jingle to the early eighties ad campaign for Meow Mix catfood.

Note for Brits: 4H Clubs were designed to offer an alternative to bars for under 21s in the 1980s in a scoutish sort of environment.

Notes: This fine episode contains a memorable guest character in the French waiter Monsieur Lacosse, two great slapstick sequences involving the same, and displays Principal Skinner – pursuing Bart across the mountains like 'a non-giving-up school guy', and confessing that in some ways he's 'a small man; a petty, small man' – in particularly fine form.

102
1F21:
'Lady Bouvier's Lover'

Written by Bill Oakley and Josh Weinstein
Directed by Wes Archer
Also starring: Pamela Hayden
Special guest voice: Phil Hartman (as Troy McClure)

Premise: Grampa falls in love with Marge's mother Jackie. But she's fallen in love with Mr Burns. And Bart's sent off for an animation cel from Itchy and Scratchy using Homer's credit card.

Features: Krusty, Sideshow Mel, Jackie Bouvier, Patty and Selma, Grampa, Nelson, Apu, Android's Dungeon Guy, Mr Burns, Smithers, Jasper, Rev. Lovejoy.

Couch: The Simpsons rush in – and collide and shatter.

Trivia: Jackie Bouvier's friends – the actress Frances Farmer, the poet Sylvia Plath, and Zelda Fitzgerald (wife of the author F. Scott Fitzgerald) all had terribly unhappy and disastrous lives.

Homage: The aborted wedding, the scene of Grampa and Jackie on the bus and even the use of Simon and Garfunkel's 'The Sound of Silence' all come from *The Graduate*. Grampa performs Charlie Chaplin's potato dance from *The Gold Rush* (1925) to impress Jackie.

Hi, I'm Troy McClure, you may remember me from: such films as *The Boatjacking of Skyship '79* and *Hydro, The Man with the Hydraulic Arms*.

Songs: 'Play It Cool' sung to Grampa by Homer, and 'The Sound of Grampa' sung over the end credits.

Notes: Homer's nightmare vision of Bart, Lisa and Maggie as ordinary kids is a highlight of this especially crazy – surreal jokes, flashbacks and dream sequences whizz by at an alarming rate – instalment.

103
1F20:
'Secrets of a Successful Marriage'

Written by Greg Daniels   **Directed by** Carlos Baeza
Also starring: Pamela Hayden, Maggie Roswell
Special guest voices: Phil Hartman (as Lionel Hutz),
Marcia Wallace (as Ms Krabappel)

Premise: Homer gets a new job, lecturing at Springfield's adult education centre. The problem lies with his subject – his relationship with Marge. Soon the whole town has learnt their secrets and Marge throws Homer into the treehouse where he creates a replacement for her – a shrub.

Features: Moe, Lenny and Carl, Barney, Grampa, Groundskeeper Willie, Hans Moleman, Krusty, Sideshow Mel, Patty and Selma, Apu, Chief Wiggum, Ned Flanders, Principal Skinner, Otto, the Lovejoys, Smithers, Mr Burns, Lionel Hutz, Ms Krabappel, Milhouse.

Couch: The Simpsons rush in – and explode.

Homage: Homer sings the theme tune of US sitcom *Family Ties* at one point. His angry speech to Marge is a combination of lines from the movies *A Few Good Men* (Rob Reiner, 1992), *Patton* (Franklin Schaffner, 1970) and *Chinatown* (Roman Polanski, 1974). Smithers' flashback to his failed marriage recalls *Cat on a Hot Tin Roof* (Richard Brooks, 1958).

Notes: A confident finale to the fifth season, which had seen the series become progressively more surreal and self-aware.

Sixth Season

1994–1995
25 Episodes

104
1F22:
'Bart of Darkness'

Written by Dan McGrath   **Directed by** Jim Reardon
Also starring: Pamela Hayden, Maggie Roswell,
Russi Taylor

Premise: A heatwave hits Springfield, and the Simpsons' new 'Tinkler' pool makes Bart the most popular kid in town – until an accident leaves him bed-ridden and Lisa usurps his position. Idling at his bedroom window, Bart sees Ned Flanders digging a hole in his garden and crying 'I'm a murderer!'

Features: Hans Moleman, Spotty Boy, Principal Skinner, Otto, Martin Prince, Jimbo, Kearney, Dolph, Nelson, Sherri and Terri, Milhouse, Dr Hibbert, Krusty, Ned Flanders, Rod and Todd, Wiggum, Lou and Eddie, Ralph Wiggum, Wendell, Grampa, Maude Flanders.

Couch: The Simpsons are already in the living room, sat on mid-air: the sofa is missing. Then the parts of the sofa rush in and sit on them.

Trivia: Springfield's 911 police phoneline is touchtone automated – 'If you are being murdered or have committed a felony, please stay on the line.' Springfield has a wax museum featuring the Beatles and the original cast of *M*A*S*H*. Bart's temporary mental instability brings out his cockney obsession once more. Martin Prince's sexual preference is briefly called into doubt, and the episode ends touchingly with his rendition of Sinatra's 'The Summer Wind'.

Homage: The episode is, in part, a homage to the movie *Rear Window* (Alfred Hitchcock, 1954), adapted from a short story by Cornell Woolrich, in which the wheelchair-bound James Stewart spies a possible murder. Stewart's character pops up twice in lovingly re-created sequences. The Simpsons' first attempt to construct the pool is a lift from *Witness* (Peter Weir, 1985), and comes complete with Amish bystander. The pool dance display features Lisa in an Esther Williams-esque role. Bart's surreal play has touches of Chekhov. And the Itchy and Scratchy episode contains references to *Planet of the Apes* (Franklin J. Schnaffner, 1968), *Beneath the Planet of the Apes* (Ted Post, 1970) (the mind-bending mutants) and the *Star Trek* episode 'The Menagerie'.

Itchy and Scratchy in: 'Planet of the Aches'.

Look out for: Klassic Krusty, summertime reruns of Krusty's old shows, featuring (fictional) guest appearances from labour-leader George Meaney (in black and white, from 6 February, 1961) and sitar wizard Ravi Shankar. Also, Homer's instinctive response to anyone getting in the way of the TV screen.

Notes: This fine episode was made for the fifth season, but held over as the première for the sixth. For a moment you really believe Flanders has gone crazy. The eventual explanation for his murderous behaviour is hilarious.

105
1F17:
'Lisa's Rival'

Written by Mike Scully   **Directed by** Mark Kirkland

Also starring: Pamela Hayden, Maggie Roswell,
Russi Taylor
Special guest voice: Winona Ryder (as Allison Taylor)

Premise: Lisa's role as Springfield Elementary's gifted child is usurped by a saxophone-playing, well-read social liberal called Allison Taylor, who has skipped a year for being so bright. Lisa soon succumbs to Bart's suggestion to ridicule Allison in a school competition. Meanwhile, Homer's struck gold – or at least a pile of sugar.

Features: Principal Skinner, Ned Flanders, Todd Flanders, Rod Flanders, Janey, Ralph, Miss Hoover, Sherri and Terri, Grampa, Hans Moleman, Uter, Mr Largo, Jimbo Jones, Martin Prince, Mrs Skinner, Milhouse van Houten, Otto Mans, Nelson Muntz, Richard, Lewis, Wendell.

Couch: The merSimpsons swim towards the sofa.

Trivia: Allison is also a fan of Bleedin' Gums Murphy – his photo hangs on the wall of her trophy room. Bart is reading an edition of *Badboy's Life* while Marge opts for the bodice-ripper *Love in the Time of Scurvy*. Ralph's cat is called Mittens.

Homage: There's a line from *The Wizard of Oz,* an entire scene from *The Fugitive* (Andrew Davis, 1993), as Milhouse is tracked to a waterfall by the Feds, and another reference to Poe's short story 'The Tell-Tale Heart'. Best of all is Homer's sleepy, Cuban-accented soliloquy whilst guarding the sugar mountain: 'In America, first you get the sugar, then you get the power, then you get the women . . .' – which is lifted from *Scarface* (Brian De Palma, 1983).

Notes for Brits: Lisa's nightmare group of second bests, Born to Runner Up, includes herself, Art Garfunkel and John Oates (both familiar to non-Americans), and Jim Messina, who duetted on several occasions with Kenny Loggins, who isn't.

Notes: Despite being a Lisa show, it is poor Ralph Wiggum who steals the show with three great irrelevant replies, especially those concerning his cat's breath. One of a tiny handful of episodes in which we see Lisa as a schemer determined to win at all costs. This leads to great scenes between the Simpson siblings, especially Bart's idea to conquer Allison using a hose pipe.

106
2F33:
'Another Simpsons Clip Show'

Written by Penny Wise   **Directed by** David Silverman

Premise: Marge is concerned that she and Homer have set the kids a bad example in the field of romance. She invites the family to recount their romantic adventures. Cue the clips reel.

Couch: The Simpsons rush in – and get trodden on by a gigantic Monty Pythonesque foot.

Trivia: Marge is reading the novel *The Bridges of Madison County*. Lisa's still reading *Non-Threatening Boys* magazine, and is still in love with its cover star Corey Masterson.

Notes: There are large sections of romantic interludes from 'Jacques to Be Wild' ('Thank goodness I drove down that ironic street!' says Marge), 'The Last Temptation of Homer', 'I Love Lisa', 'Lady Bouvier's Lover' and 'The Way We Was'. There are also brilliant compositions of Bart's prank calls to Moe and 'Mmmmm's' from Homer. As good as a clips show can be.

107

2F01:

'Itchy & Scratchy Land'

Written by Jon Swartzwelder   **Directed by** Wes Archer
Also starring: Pamela Hayden, Maggie Roswell

Premise: The Simpsons take a vacation in Itchy & Scratchy Land – 'the violentest place on Earth'™ where nothing can possibly go wrong apart from the robot Itchys & Scratchys becoming rampaging killers.

Features: Krusty, Grampa, Dr Frink, Hans Moleman.

Couch: The Simpsons are beamed on to the sofa à la *Star Trek*.

Trivia: In the mid-eighties, the *Itchy & Scratchy* show included the characters Disgruntled Goat, Uncle Ant and Ku Klux Clam.

Homage: Where to start? Principally this episode quotes freely from *Jurassic Park* (Steven Spielberg, 1993) and *Westworld* (Michael Crichton, 1973), but there's also a shot-for-shot reconstruction of a sequence from *The Birds* (Alfred Hitchcock, 1963), and Homer's flashback to his holiday in Amish country re-creates a scene from *Witness* (Peter Weir, 1985).

Itchy and Scratchy in: 'The Last Traction Hero', 'Scratchtasia' and 'Pin-itchy-o'.

Notes: Theme park turns nightmare; an untypical episode, with an especially thin plot. But anyone that's been to Disneyland will get the point.

108

2F02:

'Sideshow Bob Roberts'

Written by Bill Oakley and Josh Weinstein
Directed by Wes Archer
Also starring: Henry Corden (as Fred Flintstone),
Pamela Hayden
Special guest voices: Kelsey Grammer (as Sideshow Bob),
Phil Hartman (as Lionel Hutz), Marcia Wallace (as
Ms Krabappel), Larry King (as himself), Dr Demento (as
himself)

Premise: The Republican Party needs a candidate to contest Springfield. Right-wing commentator Birch Barlow has a suggestion – Sideshow Bob!

Features: Grampa, Mayor Quimby, Sideshow Bob, Moe, Narney, Lenny and Carl, Principal Skinner, Ralph, Jasper, Mr Burns, Smithers, Dr Hibbert, Wolfcastle, Kent Brockman, Lionel Hutz.

Couch: The Simpsons eyes rush in – followed by their bodies.

Homage: Apart from *Bob Roberts* (Tim Robbins, 1992), in particular the scene where Bob enters Burns' meeting wrapped in the US flag, there are nods to *Citizen Kane* (Orson Welles, 1944) and, again, Jack Nicholson's angry speech from *A Few Good Men* (Rob Reiner, 1992). Lisa likes John Parr's 1985 hit 'St Elmo's Fire', for some reason.

Notes for Brits: Birch Barlow, author of *Only Turkeys Have Left Wings*, is a thinly veiled portrait of American right-wing commentator Rush Limbaugh. Stacey Koons was one of the police officers involved in the Rodney King affair.

Notes: A stunningly outspoken political satire that drew considerable disapproval from the Republican Party when it was aired in the run-up to the 1992 Presidential election.

109
2F03:
'Treehouse of Horror V'

Written by Greg Danula, Dan McGrath, David Cohen,
Bob Kushell   **Directed by** Jim Reardon
Additional cast: Doris Grau, Pamela Hayden, Russi Taylor
Special guest voice: Marcia Wallace (as Ms Krabappel)

Premise: Three more tawdry tales – 'The Shinning': the
Simpsons move into a house possessed by . . . something.
'Time And Punishment': Homer travels back in time and
accidentally creates a nightmare world for himself when he
returns – a world controlled by Flanders. And 'Nightmare
Cafeteria': in which Bart finds a new item on Lunchlady
Doris's menu – the kids.

Couch: The undead, disfigured Simpsons rush in.

Tombstones: Amusing Tombstones.

Homage: It's the turn of *The Outer Limits* to receive the
Treehouse of Horror treatment. There are also references
to *The Shining* (the entire first segment is an affectionate
parody), *Terminator 2*, and *Jurassic Park*. The reference to
Brazilian time-travellers is bizarre – we draw a blank.

Mmmmm: . . . fuzzy.

Song: 'One', sung by the Undead.

Notes: Another fine entry to the Treehouse canon.

110
2F04:
'Bart's Girlfriend'

Written by Jonathan Collier   **Directed by** Susie Dietter

Also starring: Pamela Hayden, Maggie Roswell
Special guest voice: Meryl Streep (as Jessica)

Premise: Jessica Lovejoy is the sweet, angelic daughter of the local vicar. But Bart sees another side of her, a malevolent and mischievous girl out for attention. Exactly the qualities that will make him fall in love with her.

Features: Sherri (or is it Terri?), Milhouse, Lewis, Ralph, Richard, Nelson, Mr and Mrs van Houten, Rev. Lovejoy, Miss Hoover, Captain McCallister, Helen Lovejoy, Martin Prince, Miss Allbright, Dr Hibbert, Groundskeeper Willie, Principal Skinner, Ms Krabappel, Ned Flanders, Maude Flanders, Todd Flanders, Rod Flanders, Grampa, Moe, Jasper, Lenny, Carl, Hans Moleman, Otto Mans, Apu, Chief Wiggum.

Couch: The family's eyes get to the sofa first, joined by their bodies.

Homage: Bart and Jessica's romance is, appropriately, accompanied by 'Misrilou', the theme of *Pulp Fiction* (Quentin Tarantino, 1994).

Notes for Brits: Janet Reno is the United States Attorney General.

Notes: Poor Bart gets picked on very cruelly by Jessica in a cleverly drawn study of pre-pubescent love. We're very fond of the scene in which Bart leaps out of the window at the church, and Homer cries, 'He's jumped out of the window!'

111
2F05:
'Lisa on Ice'

Written by Mike Scully   **Directed by** Bob Anderson
Also starring: Pamela Hayden, Tress MacNeille,
Russi Taylor

Special guest voice: Marcia Wallace (as Ms Krabappel)

Premise: Competition between Lisa and Bart takes on extraordinary proportions when Apu discovers that Lisa makes an excellent ice hockey goalie. Trouble is, Bart plays for the other team . . .

Features: Kent Brockman, Milhouse, Martin Prince, Sherri and Terri, Lewis, Richard, Jimbo Jones, Kearney, Nelson Muntz, Edna Krabappel, Dolph, Ralph Wiggum, Chief Wiggum, Apu, Uter, Snake, Grampa, Moe, Groundskeeper Willie, Miss Hoover, Krusty, Dr John Frink, Hans Moleman, Jasper.

Couch: The family are bounced into the ceiling by the sofa.

Trivia: The elementary school kids named their assembly room 'The Butthead Hall'.

Homage: *Rollerball* (Norman Jewison, 1975) provides some inspiration here.

Look out for: The volleyball deflated by Lisa's hair; Edna's alphabetical homework call, with which she traps Bart at 'B'.

Notes: A fabulous episode for Lisa and Bart, although with a special mention for a few seconds of tremendous Edna Krabappel wickedness.

112
2F06:
'Homer: Bad Man'

Written by Greg Daniels   **Directed by** Jeff Lynch
Also starring: Pamela Hayden, Maggie Roswell,
Tress MacNeille
Special guest voice: Dennis Franz (as 'Homer Simpson')

Premise: Homer and Marge visit a candy trade fair where Homer steals the unique Gummi di Milo. This becomes attached to the butt of the kids' baby-sitter, and when Homer pulls it off, she accuses him of sexual molestation and Homer becomes public enemy number one.

Features: Apu, Dr John Frink, Smithers, Kent Brockman, Moe, Barney, Lenny, Dr Hibbert, Bumblebee Man, Grampa, Groundskeeper Willie.

Couch: The sofa and room zoom into the distance, pursued by the Simpsons.

Trivia: Other Gummi treats include Gummi Cows' Heads and Gummi Jaw Breakers. Ashley bribes Bart with the video game cartridge 'Disembowler IV'. The other apologies on the Rock Bottom Correction List are: People's Choice Award is America's Greatest Honor; Styrofoam is not made from kittens; The UFO was a paper plate; The nerds on the internet are not geeks; The word 'cheese' is not funny in and of itself; The older Flanders boy is Todd not Rod; Lyndon Johnson didn't provide the voice of Yosemite Sam; If you are reading this, you have no life; Roy Rogers was not buried inside his horse; The other UFO was an upside-down salad spinner; Our universities are not hotbeds of anything; Mr Dershowitz did not literally have four eyes; Our viewers are not pathetic sexless food tubes; Audrey Hepburn never weighed 400 pounds; The 'Cheers' gang is not a real gang; Salt water does not 'chase the thirsties away'; Licking an electrical outlet will not turn you into a Mighty Morphin Power Ranger; Cats do not eventually turn into dogs; Bullets do not bounce off fat guys; Recycling does not deplete the ozone; The authors of this book were paid – a little – to transcribe all this; Everything is 10% fruit juice; Janet Reno is evil; V8 juice is not one-eighth gasoline; Ted Koppel is a robot; Women aren't from Venus and men aren't from Mars; Fleiss does not floss; Quayle is familiar with common bathroom procedures; Bart is bad to the bone; Godfry Jones' wife is cheating on him; The Beatles haven't reunited to enter kick-boxing competitions; The 'bug' on your TV screen can see into your home; Everyone on TV is better than you; The people who are writing this have no life.

Homage: Homer deals with the guards at the Candy Convention in an explosive fashion reminiscent of *Die Hard* (John McTiernan, 1988). Gentle Ben comes from the US sixties kids' show of the same name. Kent Brockman's reference to 'the Simpson estate' is reminiscent of the news coverage of O.J. Simpson's flight from the police after the death of his wife Nicole and Ronald Goldman.

Song: 'Under the Sea' sung by the Simpsons.

Notes: Thankfully we, unlike his own family, know Homer is wholly innocent, but nevertheless, he does ask for it. And Rock Bottom is such a good parody of those oh-so-well-meaning exposé programmes. Surprisingly, it's not one of Kent Brockman's – he's relegated to helicopter duty this show. Dennis Franz is great as bad Homer.

113
2F07:
'Grampa vs. Sexual Inadequacy'

Written by Bill Oakley and Josh Weinstein
Directed by Wes Archer
Also starring: Pamela Hayden, Maggie Roswell
Special guest voice: Phil Hartman (as Troy McClure)

Premise: Homer needs something to make him more sexually potent, and Grampa has the answer – an elixir. It's not long before they fall out. Homer has to come to terms with a few home truths Grampa has told him.

Features: Troy McClure, Mayor Quimby, Grampa, Ned Flanders, Maude Flanders, Dr John Frink, Mr and Mrs van Houten, Dr Hibbert, Milhouse, Nelson, Ralph, Barney.

Couch: The family dance, on tiptoes, across a recurring living room set.

Homage: On discovering someone has bought his book, Al Gore plays 'Celebration', a 1980 hit for Kool and the Gang.

Hi, I'm Troy McClure, you may remember me from: *Good Time Slim, Uncle Doobey and the Great 'Frisco Freak Out.*

Notes: An amazing episode, in which Homer actually has an argument with someone, rather than backing down. As he and his father drift further apart, so the family are at a loss at what to do. You can't help but feel sorry for Grampa as a piece of Simpson family history goes up in flames.

114

2F08:

'Fear of Flying'

Written by David Sacks   **Directed by** Mark Kirkland
Also starring: Pamela Hayden
Special guest voices: Anne Bancroft (as Dr Zweig), Ted Danson, Woody Harrelson, Rhea Perlman, John Ratzenberger, George Wendt (as the cast of *Cheers*)

Premise: After impersonating a pilot and endangering lives, Homer wins the family a free holiday flight. But Marge is terrified of flying. Why? Is it anything to do with her father – who was an airline pilot?

Features: Moe, Barney, Carl, Lenny, Smithers, Grampa, Bill from KBBL, Principal Skinner, Patty and Selma, Mrs Bouvier, Mr Bouvier.

Couch: The Simpsons rush in – and take centre place in a high-kicking, unicycling, elephant-acrobaticking showbiz extravaganza.

Trivia: Homer's favourite record of all time is 'It's Raining Men' by The Weather Girls, and he has a terrible fear of sock puppets.

Homage: The title refers to Erica Jong's novel *Fear of Flying*, a bold and humorous exploration of female sexuality. There are references to *Swarm* (Irwin Allen, 1980), *Home Alone* (Chris Columbus, 1990), *It's A Wonderful Life* (Frank Capra, 1946) (Homer's speech to Marge about getting out of Springfield), *North by Northwest* (Alfred Hitchcock, 1959) (Marge and her mother at the cornfield), *Alive!* (Frank Marshall, 1992), and *Prince of Tides* (Marge remembering her psychologist's name as Loewenstein). Homer enters the bar from *Cheers,* prompting a detail-packed re-creation of a typical episode featuring the voices of the cast, while Marge fantasises about sixties sci-fi series *Lost in Space* (with Marge as Mrs Robinson, Homer as Dr Smith and Lisa as the Robot ('Danger! Danger! My hooks are flailing wildly!').

Notes: Marge's father looks suspiciously like Moe. A good Marge-centric episode with plenty of clever set pieces – the tributes to *Cheers* and *Lost in Space* are fantastic.

115

2F09:

'Homer the Great'

Written by John Swartzwelder
Directed by Jim Reardon
Also starring: Pamela Hayden, Maggie Roswell
Special guest voice: Patrick Stewart (as Number One)

Premise: Homer becomes the leader of the legendary Stonecutters – and promptly brings them into disrepute.

Features: Arnie Pie, Lenny, Carl, Moe, Principal Skinner, Chief Wiggum, Grampa, Sideshow Mel, Krusty, Mr and Mrs van Houten, Miss Hoover, Jasper, Barney, Mr Burns, Smithers, Herman, Dr Hibbert, Kent Brockman, Groundskeeper Willie, Mayor Quimby.

Couch: The Simpsons rush in – to an Escher engraving.

Trivia: Americans may think that 911 is their Emergency Services phone number, but the Stonecutters know it is really 912. Homer's Revenge List includes: The Bill of Rights; Grandpa; Fat-Free Lard; Gravity; Emmys; Darwin; H2-Whoa!; Billy Crystal; God; Soloflex; The Boy; Stern Lecture Plumbing and Econo-Save. Grampa Simpson is a member of The Elks; The Masons; The Communists; The Gay and Lesbian Alliance (of which he is President) and, of course, The Stonecutters.

Homage: Homer emerges in his finery exactly like *The Last Emperor* (Bernardo Bertolucci, 1987).

Song: 'We Do' sung by The Stonecutters.

Notes: A brilliant crack at freemasonry, with all the secret signs, one-upmanship, rituals and unusual membership rules. Add to this Patrick Stewart's amazing voice and you have one of the better episodes of the series. The homage to *The Last Emperor* is especially good.

116

2F10:

'And Maggie Makes Three'

Written by Jennifer Crittenden
Directed by Swinton O. Scott III
Also starring: Pamela Hayden, Maggie Roswell

Premise: Inspired by an especially dull night's TV viewing, Homer has a flashback to the distant days of 1993 and the birth of Maggie.

Features: Patty and Selma, Carl and Lenny, Chief Wiggum, Apu, Moe, Barney, Mr Burns, Smithers, Dr Hibbert, Captain McCallister, Maude Flanders, Helen Lovejoy, Jackie Bouvier, Ruth Powers, Mrs van Houten.

Couch: Homer enters as James Bond, viewed down the barrel of a gun.

Homage: The Simpsons are watching *Knight Boat* at the start of the episode, a reference to the eighties kids' adventure series *Knight Rider* ('Oh, there's a canal every week,' moans Bart).

Notes: A surprisingly traditional episode. The flashback to 1993 seems a bit odd, but this is a good example of a story that doesn't overly rely on set pieces and confounded expectations for its success.

117
2F11:
'Bart's Comet'

Written by John Swartzwelder
Directed by Bob Anderson
Also starring: Pamela Hayden, Maggie Roswell

Premise: As a punishment, Bart is forced to join Seymour Skinner at 4.30 a.m. to do a spot of astronomy. Bart spots a new comet which is, unfortunately, on a collision course for Springfield. And who has the only shelter? The Flanderses, of course.

Features: Principal Skinner, Groundskeeper Willie, Richard, Martin Prince, Milhouse, Nelson, Lewis, Jimbo Jones, Sherri and Terri, Wendell, Mayor Quimby, Moe, Dr John Frink, Rev.

Lovejoy, Arnie Pie, Kent Brockman, the Flanderses, Barney, Apu, Krusty, Dr Hibbert, Chief Wiggum, Otto, Capt McCallister, Dolph, Jimbo Jones, Kearney, Carl, Dr Nick Riviera, Helen Lovejoy, Patty and Selma, Mrs Hibbert, Sideshow Mel, Lenny, Mr Largo, Mr and Mrs van Houten.

Couch: In black and white, the Simpsons are animated Max Fleischer-style.

Trivia: Bart's nickname given to him by the SuperFriends is Cosmos. Oh, and for those interested in such things, Kent Brockman's list of gay people is made up of *Simpsons* production staff including Matt Groening, David Silverman, Bill Oakley and David Mirkin.

Homage: The plot mirrors that of *Meteor* (Ronald Neame, 1979). There are also some nods to *Back to the Future*. The nerdy gang the Super Friends are named after a seventies Hanna Barbera cartoon series.

Notes: An excellent episode, in which just about everyone in Springfield becomes friends – and a great moment when the ever-pious Maude Flanders happily sacrifices her Neddy. Homer's clever plan to escape Springfield – by driving away – is also worthy of mention.

118
2F12:
'Homie the Clown'

Written by John Swartzwelder   **Directed by** Mark Kirkland
Also starring: Pamela Hayden
Special guest voices: Dick Cavett (as himself), Johnny Unitas (as himself), Joe Mantegna (as Don Tony)

Premise: Krusty's luck has run out – the Mafia are after him. Homer's luck has run out, too – he's enrolled at clown school and pretending to be Krusty.

Features: Krusty, Carl and Lenny, Ralph, Chief Wiggum, Apu, Ned Flanders, Milhouse.

Couch: The sofa runs in – and sits on the Simpsons.

Trivia: Krusty's products include Krusty Monopoly, the Krusty Krowd Kontrol Barrier, and the Lady Krusty range of feminine toiletries.

Homage: The episode's title refers to a character called Homie the Clown featured in US comedy series *In Living Color*. Homer's compulsion to make a clown sculpture reflects Richard Dreyfus' similar problem in *Close Encounters of the Third Kind* (Steven Spielberg, 1979), and at one point he hears a song from *The Godfather* (Francis Ford Coppola, 1972). Krusty lights a cigarette with a copy of *Action Comics #1*, the rarest and most valuable comic of all time.

Notes: 'Clowns are funny.' Notable for its scenes of Homer on trying to emulate Krusty's mini-trike loop the loops.

119

2F13:

'Bart vs. Australia'

Written by Bill Oakley and Josh Weinstein
Directed by Wes Archer
Also starring: Pamela Hayden
Special guest voice: Phil Hartman

Premise: Bart tries to discover if water does go clockwise in the southern hemisphere and in doing so destroys good relations between the US and Australia. The Australians demand that he flies down under to apologise – and face the revenge of a boot up the butt.

Features: Milhouse.

Couch: The merSimpsons swim underwater to the sofa.

Trivia: The South O' the Equator Gift Shoppe has a sign that reads PEDRO SEZ 'GETS HIGH KOALA-T!' and a baseball cap which claims POBODY'S NERFECT IN AUSTRALIA. The Parliament building which is actually the PARLIA-MENT-HAUS DER AUSTRIA, with an extra AL scribbled in.

Homage: *Crocodile Dundee* – the 'now this is a knife' sequence is used again. Yahoo Serious was the Australian star and director of *Young Einstein* (1991).

Look out for: The slide show given by Conover to show that America lost interest in everything Australian after *Crocodile Dundee*'s run had finished.

Notes: Best if watched with Australians who will be, per-haps understandably, aggrieved at their portrayal. After the attack on the French, this is a vicious, unkind, offensive and wonderfully amusing slaughter of Australian culture by the makers of *The Simpsons*.

120

2F14:

'Homer vs. Patty & Selma'

Written by Brent Forrester   **Directed by** Mark Kirkland
Special guest voices: Mel Brooks (as himself),
Susan Sarandon (as Ballet Mistress)

Premise: Homer is desperately short of cash and ends up taking out a loan from his sisters-in-law, who then belittle him at every opportunity, knowing he cannot fight back. Meanwhile, Bart discovers a new gift – he is an excellent ballet dancer.

Features: Patty, Selma, Chief Wiggum, Ms Krabappel, Principal Skinner, Milhouse, Jimbo Jones, Nelson, Dolph, Kearney, Sherri and Terri, Ralph Lewis, Richard, Groundskeeper Willie, Barney, Moe, Carl, Lenny, Hans Moleman.

Couch: The family 'beam' on to the sofa *Star Trek*-style.

Trivia: It is physical education sign-up day at Springfield Elementary, and among the sports on offer are: Ballet, Football, Hockey, Baseball, Kickball, Lap Running, Badminton, various Martial Arts and Gender Issues in Sport. Among the reasons Homer cannot get a good credit rating is because once, back in 3rd Grade, he grabbed a dog by its hind legs and pushed it around like a vacuum cleaner.

Look out for: Homer literally throwing Patty and Selma out of the house, and accidentally chucking Marge out as well.

Notes: Quite a fun one this, although Bart's ballet career comes to an unsurprising conclusion. Skinner's delight at Bart's choice is a joy to behold, by the way. Patty and Selma have rarely been more evil than here – they are fabulously cruel.

121

2F31:

'A Star is Burns'

Written by Ken Keeler   **Directed by** Susie Dietter
Also starring: Pamela Hayden, Doris Grau
Special guest voices: Maurice la Marche (as George C. Scott),
Jon Lovitz (as Jay Sherman),
Phil Hartman (as Charlton Heston)

Premise: Springfield decides to have a film festival and Marge invites Jay Sherman to help judge it. Mr Burns decides to make a movie, and ensure it will win by bribing everyone involved.

Features: Kent Brockman, Barney, Principal Skinner, Grampa, Lenny, Carl, Apu, Otto, Mr Largo, Moe, Ms Krabappel, Krusty, Mayor Quimby, Patty, Selma, Milhouse, Miss Hoover, Chief Wiggum, Eddie, Lou, Herman, the Flanderses, Rainier Wolfcastle, Mr Burns, Smithers, Bumblebee Man, Dr Hibbert, Snake, Hans Moleman, Rev. Lovejoy, Nelson.

Couch: The relative size of the family is reversed, so that Homer is a tiny child and Maggie a giant.

Trivia: The new McBain film is called *Let's Get Silly*. Among the films are *A Burns For All Seasons* (made by Monty Burns), *Pukeahontas* (Barney Gumble), *Bright Lights, Beef Jerky* (Apu), *Moe Better Blues* (Moe Szyslak) and *Man Getting Hit by Football* (Hans Moleman).

Homage: Jay Sherman is the central character of the animated series *The Critic*, which shares many production personnel with *The Simpsons*.

Itchy and Scratchy in: 'Four Funerals and a Wedding'.

Mmmmm: . . . beer nuts.

Song: The Rapping Rabbis cover MC Hammer's 1990 hit 'U Can't Touch This'.

Notes: Barney's film is magnificent, but it's easy to see why Homer wants Hans Moleman to be the winner. Jay Sherman perhaps proves here, even more so than in *The Critic*, just why that show failed. He's too flawed to be likeable.

122

2F15:

'Lisa's Wedding'

Written by Greg Daniels   **Directed by** Jim Reardon
Also starring: Doris Grau, Pamela Hayden, Maggie Roswell
Special guest voice: Mandy Patinkin (as Hugh Parkfield)

Premise: Lisa visits a fortune teller who spins her a story set in the strange world of 2010, when she is destined to fall in love with a young English aristocrat.

Features: Mr Burns, Smithers, Patty, Selma, Principal Skinner, Ms Krabappel, Miss Hoover, Lunchlady Doris, Milhouse, Martin Prince, Moe, Chief Wiggum, Kent Brockman, Ned Flanders, Rev. Lovejoy, Dr Hibbert, Krusty, Mayor Quimby, Troy McClure, Lenny, Carl, Nelson, Dr John Frink.

Couch: The springs in the sofa bounce the Simpsons into the ceiling.

Trivia: The Fortune Teller shows Lisa two cards – Death, indicating change, and – horror of horrors – The Happy Squirrel! In 2010, Lisa and Hugh are studying at the Dr and Mrs Dre Hall at Eastern Uni. Springfield's water supply contains three-eyed fish and a fish with the head of a cow. Lisa and Hugh are Jim Carrey fans, visiting a film fair where they show forty of his films including *The Mask* and *Ace Ventura VI*. The Rolling Stones have recently toured with their Steel Wheelchair Tour 2010, and Lisa Bart now works for the Down With Buildings Demolition Co and has been married twice. Kent Brockman offers a list of arrested celebrities. These are: The Baldwin Brothers Gang; Dr Brad Pitt; John John John Kennedy; George Burns; Infamous Amos' Grandson and Sam; The Artist Formerly Known as (symbol); Tim Allen Jnr; Senator and Mrs Dracula; The Artist Formerly Known as Buddy Hackett; Madonnabots Series K; Sideshow Ralph Wiggum; Martha Hitler and

Johnny Neutrino. Heather Locklear remains at large. Kent's show is on CNNBCBS, a division of ABC. The wedding invitation to Lisa's wedding reads: *Mr and Mrs Homer J. Simpson request the pleasure of your company at the marriage of their daughter Lisa Marie to Hugh St. John Alastair Parkfield at the Springfield Meadow. Sunday One PM August 1, 2010.*

Homage: *Four Weddings and a Funeral* (Mike Newell, 1994) provides Hugh's name. The romance in *Love Story* (Arthur Hiller, 1970) begins, as here, with a dispute over a book in a college library. There are also lots of incidental references – sound-effects and the like – to *Star Trek.*

Notes: The whole scenario of this episode places it well within the top five all-time greats as we see not only the world of tomorrow but how the Simpsons cope with it. Presumably both Grampa Simpson and Jackie Bouvier are no longer with us, but just about everyone else makes it to the wedding.

123

2F18:

'Two Dozen and One Greyhounds'

Written by Mike Scully   **Directed by** Bob Anderson
Also starring: Tress MacNeille, Frank Welker

Premise: Santa's Little Helper is restless, but when he meets a female greyhound, She's The Fastest, he falls in love. Before long, the Simpsons have twenty-five puppies to contend with – until Mr Burns sees a good opportunity to increase his winter wardrobe.

Features: Mr Burns, Smithers, Ned Flanders, Principal Skinner, Kent Brockman, Chief Wiggum, Eddie, the van Houtens, Grampa, Jasper, Rev. Lovejoy.

Couch: The sofa and living room vanish into the distance, chased by the family.

Trivia: Brockman presents a cookery show called *Kent's Kitchen*. The puppies whose names we see are Rover, Rover II, Fido, Fido II, Rex, Rex II, Spot, Cleo, Dave, Dave II, Jay, Jay II, Paul, Paul II, Branford, Branford II, Sleepy, Dopey, Grumpy, Grumpy II, Donner, Blitzen, King, Queenie, Prince and the Puppy Formerly Known as Prince. Mr Burns calls one of the puppies Monty.

Homage: *One Hundred and One Dalmations* provides the title and some of the iconography ('He wants to be one of the Models Inc!' says Bart as the pups watch TV). *Star Trek* (the pet shop clerk's Vulcan mind-meld with Santa's Little Helper). The two dogs get free food from Luigi's restaurant, and their spaghetti-sucking antics are a lift from Disney's *Lady and the Tramp* (1955).

Song: Mr Burns puts on a rollicking musical number celebrating his capture of the puppies.

Notes: A great one for animal lovers, with Santa's Little Helper getting some good moments – as does Snowball II when he gets jealous about the puppies. We would have loved to see a *Simpsons* character as Cruella De Ville, though.

124

2F19:

'The PTA Disbands'

Written by Jennifer Crittenden
Directed by Swinton O Scott III
Also starring: Doris Grau, Pamela Hayden, Maggie Roswell, Russi Taylor
Special guest voice: Marcia Wallace (as Ms Krabappel)

Premise: Cash flow has become a serious problem for Springfield Elementary and, helped in no small way by Bart, the teachers rebel against Skinner. All-out anarchy ensues. Can Ms Krabappel and Principal Skinner sit down and remedy the situation without killing each other?

Features: Sherri and Terri, Nelson, Ms Krabappel, Principal Skinner, Ralph, Otto, Richard, Lewis, Uter, Lunchlady Doris, Miss Hoover, Mr and Mrs van Houten, Groundskeeper Willie, Mr Largo, Jimbo Jones, Mrs Jones, Dolph, Kearney, Moe, Chief Wiggum, Ned Flanders, Jasper, John Frink, Chalmers, Grampa, Snake.

Couch: The living room has become an Escher engraving.

Trivia: Books banned by other schools (and therefore still at Springfield Elementary) include *Theory of Evolution*, *Sexus*, *40 Years of Playboy*, *Steal This Book*, *Hop on Pop*, *The Satanic Verses – Junior Illustrated Version*, and *Tek War*. (The latter's a forbidden text in the real world only in that it's written by William Shatner.)

Notes: 'Grade me!' A jolly little romp where Bart's deviousness actually gets the better of him and he realises he has to repair the damage. Possibly the best of the school episodes. And we love Lisa's School Strike Preparedness Survival Kit.

125

2F32:

'Round Springfield'

Written by Joshua Sternin and Jeffrey Ventimilin
Story by Mike Reiss and Al Jean
Directed by Steven Dean Moore
Also starring: Pamela Hayden, Doris Grau
Special guest voices: Marcia Wallace (as Ms Krabappel), Phil Hartman (as Lionel Hutz), Steve Allen (as himself), Ron Taylor (as Bleedin' Gums)

Premise: Life loses its meaning for Lisa when, as Bart recovers in hospital, she finds Bleedin' Gums Murphy close to death in the next room. She tries to make sense of her grief and loneliness.

Features: Krusty, Sideshow Mel, Ms Krabappel, Principal Skinner, Chalmers, Android's Dungeon Guy, Dr Hibbert, Milhouse, Martin Prince, Richard, Lunchlady Doris, Groundskeeper Willie, Dr Nick Riviera, Kent Brockman, Scott Christian, Moe, Barney, Ralph, Chief Wiggum, Grampa, Lou, Eddie, Rev. Lovejoy, Lionel Hutz, Hans Moleman.

Couch: The relative size of the family is reversed, so that Homer is a tiny child and Maggie a giant.

Trivia: The Springfield Elementary School Charter explains that 'teachers cannot be held accountable if Bart Simpson dies or if Milhouse van Houten is eaten by the school snake.' We see a flashback to 'Moaning Lisa', Bleedin' Gums Murphy's first appearance. There is a suggestion that Julius Hibbert and Bleedin' Gums Murphy are long-lost brothers – perhaps they are both related to the orphanage director who brought up Herb Powell (see 'Oh Brother, Where Art Thou?'). Bleedin' Gums Murphy released only one LP, 'Sax on the Beach', and his hobby was collecting Fabergé eggs.

Notes for the Uneducated: The title refers to jazz legend Thelonious Monk's ''Round Midnight'.

Look out for: Homer explaining about the 'Do Not Feed the Bears' sign. And one of the show's absolute classics – Grampa seeing the Grim Reaper everywhere – 'Ahhh! Death!'

Notes: A real tear-jerker as a semi-regular character dies and the impact on Lisa is gut-wrenching. A nice study of the various reactions to death and a moment of true delight as Bart buys Lisa 'Sax on the Beach' for no other reason than it'll make her happier than him.

126

2F21:

'The Springfield Connection'

Written by Jonathan Collier   **Directed by** Mark Kirkland
Additional cast: Marcia Wallace, Pamela Hayden,
Tress MacNeille, Maggie Roswell
Special guest voice: Phil Hartman (Lionel Hutz)

Premise: A chance encounter with Springfield's criminal lowlife launches Marge on a new career as a cop. How will her lawless family cope?

Features: Dr Hibbert, Snake, Chief Wiggum, Lou and Eddie, Lionel Hutz, Apu, Mr Burns, Principal Skinner, Mrs Skinner, Jimbo, Kearney, Dolph, Maude Flanders, Ms Krabappel, Helen Lovejoy, Moe, Ned Flanders, Barney, Lenny, Hans Moleman, Carl, Herman, Rev. Lovejoy, Milhouse and Grampa.

Couch: Homer enters as James Bond.

Homage: *Hill Street Blues* is the main influence, with a briefing scene at the police station and a hint of its theme tune in the incidental music. There's also a skit on crime camcorder documentaries such as *Cops*. *Police Academy* (Hugh Wilson, 1984) supplies the overeager trainee at police college, and Marge's freeway jump recalls *Speed* (Jan de Bont, 1994). And the title and Herman's illegal activities refer to *The French Connection* (William Friedkin, 1971).

Note for Brits: The US police use 'McGruff, the crime dog' in public relations.

Mmmmm: . . . incapacitating.

Notes: Homer's attempt to run after Marge as she chases Snake is very impressive. But the highlight of this episode has to be Marge's training, especially her sharpshooting on the firing range.

127

2F22:

'Lemon of Troy'

Written by Brent Forrester   **Directed by** Jim Reardon
Also starring: Pamela Hayden, Tress MacNeille, Russi Taylor
Special guest voice: Marcia Wallace (as Ms Krabappel)

Premise: The people of Springfield and the people of neighbouring Shelbyville have despised each other for centuries. Now the battle's coming to a head – over a lemon tree.

Features: Grampa, Nelson, Martin, Todd, Ned Flanders, Dr Frink, Milhouse, the van Houtens, Ms Krabappel, Jebediah.

Couch: The primitively animated Simpsons rush in – and judder.

Homage: Milhouse quotes the chorus of Prince's 1984 hit 'When Doves Cry'. We also hear Louis Armstrong's 1968 hit 'What a Wonderful World'.

Song: Martin sings a grateful folk song in honour of Nelson.

Notes: There are some nice ideas in this episode – Bart and his chums all have near-doubles in Shelbyville – but this is a strangely pedestrian outing, and seems hidden away – wisely – at this point in the season.

128

2F16:

'Who Shot Mr Burns?' Part One

Written by Bill Oakley and Josh Weinstein
Directed by Jeffrey Lynch
Also starring: Doris Grau, Pamela Hayden, Maggie Roswell
Special guest voice: Tito Puente (as himself)

Premise: Springfield Elementary strikes it rich. But when Mr Burns steals the school's wealth to create a revolutionary new device – a screen to block out the sun's rays – he encourages the wrath of a number of Springfield's citizens. A very large number.

Features: Principal Skinner, Groundskeeper Willie, Ms Krabappel, Nelson, Milhouse, Ralph Wiggum, Miss Hoover, Mr Burns, Smithers, Superintendent Chalmers, Lenny, Carl, Lunchlady Doris, Otto, Mr Largo, Ned Flanders, Moe, Barney, the two Barflies, Grampa, Quimby, Dr Hibbert, Captain MacAllister, Sideshow Mel, Krusty, Apu, Snake, Jimbo, Selma, Chief Wiggum.

Couch: The Simpsons rush about the living room on tiptoes – with sinister fixed grins. They didn't do it.

Homage: The principal influence is 'Who Shot J.R.?', the cliffhanger episode of the 1980 season of *Dallas*. Just before he's shot, Mr Burns is paraphrasing Simon and Garfunkel's '59th Bridge Street Song'.

Notes: A superb end to the season – and what's more, it's a genuine whodunnit. There's no cheating – all the clues are there.

Seventh Season

1995–1996
24 Episodes

129

2F20:

'Who Shot Mr Burns?' Part Two

Written by Bill Oakley and Josh Weinstein
Directed by Wes Archer
Special guest voice: Tito Puente (as himself)

Premise: Mr Burns is still alive – and now it's up to Chief Wiggum to apprehend the murderer. Prime suspect Smithers is in the clear – and Simpson DNA is found on Mr Burns' suit.

Features: Smithers, Mr Burns, Kent Brockman, Lou and Eddie, Ned Flanders, Chief Wiggum, Grampa, Moe, Barney, Carl, the two barflies, Snake, Bumblebee Man, Groundskeeper Willie, Otto, Krusty, Principal Skinner, Lenny, Dr Colossus, Sideshow Mel, Jasper, Superintendent Chalmers, Spotty Boy, Dr Nick Riviera, Apu.

Couch: The Simpsons rush in – and find themselves lined up for a mug shot.

Trivia: Sideshow Mel gives his full name as Melvin van Horne. The DNA test displays many family names of Springfield characters and members of the production team.

Homage: The opening of the episode recalls the infamous first episode of *Dallas*'s 1986 season, in which Pam Ewing found her dead husband Bobby alive and well and showering, which led to the revelation that the entirety of the previous season had been a dream. Smithers' dream about himself and Mr Burns in *Speedway Squad* mirrors the sixties American series *Mod Squad*. Groundskeeper Willie's interrogation pays homage to Sharon Stone's interrogation in *Basic Instinct* (Paul Verhoeven, 1992). Chief Wiggum's surreal dream is a tribute to the similar dream experienced by Kyle McLachlan investigating the murder of Laura Palmer in *Twin Peaks*. Homer's escape recalls the crashing prison train from *The Fugitive*.

Notes for Brits: Smithers' confession 'I'm not a Catholic – but, well, I tried to march in the St Patrick's Day Parade' is a reference to the furore surrounding the banning of gay organisations from New York's parade in 1995.

Song: 'Señor Burns', the vengeful mambo performed by Tito Puente and his Latin Jazz Ensemble.

Notes: A superb conclusion. And the solution isn't disappointing at all.

130

2F17:

'Radioactive Man'

Written by John Swartzwelder   **Directed by** Susie Dietter
Also starring: Pamela Hayden, Doris Grau, Maggie Roswell
Special guest voices: Phil Hartman (as Lionel Hutz),
Mickey Rooney (as himself)

Premise: A Hollywood film crew decide to film a new *Radioactive Man* movie in Springfield. All they have to face is a greedy mayor, a reluctant child star and a once-only special effects shot involving flesh-stripping acid.

Features: Milhouse, Android's Dungeon Guy, Mayor Quimby, Chief Wiggum, Principal Skinner, Ms Krabappel, Miss Hoover, Hans Moleman, Nelson, Sherri and Terri, Martin Prince, Moe, Barney, Kent Brockman, Mr and Mrs van Houten, Lunchlady Doris, Grampa, Lionel Hutz, Krusty, Rainer Wolfcastle, Lenny, Carl, Apu, Mr Largo, Herman, Otto, Ralph, Snake.

Couch: A colour photocopy of the family slides on to the sofa.

Trivia: Among the newsgroups that the Android's Dungeon Guy subscribes to are rec.arts.corewar, rec.org.mensa, alt. comics.radioactiveman, rec.arts.startrek.fandom, alt. binaries. pictures.erotica and alt.nerd.obsessive. On sale in the comic store are copies of *Bat Boy*, *Birdguy*, *Dogkid*, *Cat Girl*, *Snake Kid*, *Bat Chick*, *Treeman*, *Power Person*, *Man-Boy*, *Mr Hop*, *The Human Bee*, *Lava Lady*, *Nick*, *Star Dog*, *Iguana Girl*, *Radiation Dude* and *Mister Amazing*.

Homage: The closing scenes of Hollywood are set to 'Lean on Me', a 1972 hit for Bill Withers. Radioactive Man seems closer to Batman than any other superhero, with several of the sixties *Batman* series gimmicks being used in this episode. The Scoutmaster closely resembles Paul Lynde, the voice of animated characters such as the Hooded Claw – nemesis of Penelope Pitstop. Radioactive Man and Fallout Boy are trapped at one point in Aquaworld, which looks very similar to *Waterworld*.

Moe's secrets: He played Smelly in the original *L'il Rascals* shorts.

Notes: A wonderful pastiche on the Tim Burton *Batman* movies, with Milhouse an obvious candidate for Fallout Boy. Our favourite heroes: Mr Hop and Iguana Girl.

131

3F01:

'Home Sweet Home-Diddily-Dum-Doodily'

Written by Jon Vitti   **Directed by** Susie Dietter
Also starring: Pamela Hayden, Tress MacNeille,
Maggie Roswell, Frank Welker
Special guest voice: Marcia Wallace (as Ms Krabappel)

Premise: While Homer and Marge are away on a three-hour trip to the Mingled Waters Health Spa, the Child Welfare Board swoop. Bart, Lisa and Maggie are taken to a foster family – the Flanderses. Bart and Lisa are appalled by the religious regime – but Maggie looks like succumbing . . .

Features: Grampa, Ms Krabappel, Nelson, Milhouse, Groundskeeper Willie, Principal Skinner, Ned, Maude, Rod and Todd Flanders, Female Judge, Mrs Skinner, Cletus, Rev. and Mrs Lovejoy.

Couch: The Simpsons are occupying the squares normally reserved for the Brady Bunch.

Trivia: There's an equestrian statue of 'Swartzwelder' outside the town hall. Titles on the Flanderses' bookshelf include *Today's Family Gnostic Bible*, *Aramaic Sentencing* and *Who Begat Whom*.

Notes for Brits: *My Three Sons* was a very long-running, and rather anodyne, US sitcom. Poco were a folk-rock group of the seventies.

Itchy and Scratchy in: 'Foster Pussycat! Kill! Kill!'

Song: 'We Got You, Babe' sung by Ned and Maude Flanders to Maggie.

Notes: *My Three Sons* was a very long-running, and rather anodyne, US sitcom. Possibly one of the most disturbing episodes, as Bart and Lisa are dragged into the Flanderses' sinister lifestyle. The ending, as Ned tried to baptise the kids, is nail-biting stuff – and Maggie's second first-word is a truly shocking moment. It's astonishing that anything this radical made it on to prime time TV. The final moments are perhaps the most moving in the entire series, a wonderful affirmation of everything the series, and the Simpson family, are about.

132

3F02:

'Bart Sells His Soul'

Written by Greg Daniels   **Directed by** Wesley Archer
Also starring: Pamela Hayden, Tress MacNeille, Maggie
Roswell, Russi Taylor

Premise: Bart scoffs at the very concept of soul – and sells his to Milhouse for $5. Soon he finds that automatic doors won't open to him, that the pets hiss at the sight of him, and that he doesn't find Itchy and Scratchy funny any more. Meanwhile, Moe's had a brainwave. To boost trade he's converting his tavern into 'Uncle Moe's Family Feedbag'.

Features: Rev. Lovejoy, Ralph, Milhouse, Dr Hibbert, Barney, Moe, the two barflies, Carl, Rod and Todd Flanders, Jimbo, Dolph, Kearney, Apu, Mrs van Houten, Sherri and Terri, Martin, Nelson, Ned Flanders, Maud Flanders, Chief Wiggum, Snake, Krusty, Android's Dungeon Guy.

Couch: The Simpsons rush in – in motorised clown carts.

Trivia: Moe reads YOUR GIMMICKY RESTAURANT by Bennigan and Fuddrucker.

Homage: 'In A Gadda Da Vida' a seven-minute-long prog-rock smash for Iron Butterfly.

Itchy and Scratchy in: 'Skinless in Seattle'.

Notes: Undoubtedly the most disturbing episode of the series, with Bart's nightmare of losing his soul – illustrated by a macabre playground where all the souls of his playmates are visible, and his is tagging along with Milhouse – more frightening than funny. The scene of the desperate, soulless Bart attempting to steal the soul of Ralph Wiggum is also memorable for its weirdness. An illustration of just how far the series could go by this point.

133

3F03:

'Lisa the Vegetarian'

Written by David S. Cohen   **Directed by** Mark Kirkland
Also starring: Doris Grau, Pamela Hayden,
Tress MacNeille, Maggie Roswell, Russi Taylor
Special guest voices: Phil Hartman (as Troy McClure),
Linda McCartney (as herself), Paul McCartney (as himself)

Premise: Homer's planning a barbecue. Which is a big problem – because Lisa, inspired by a visit to the Storeytown Kids' Park, has decided to forsake all meat.

Features: Grampa, Ned Flanders, Miss Hoover, Ralph, Lunchlady Doris, Principal Skinner, Groundskeeper Willie, Janey, Barney, Dr Hibbert, Chief Wiggum, Mr Burns, Smithers, Sherri and Terri, Kent Brockman, Apu.

Couch: The Simpsons rush in as outlines – and get filled in by robotic paint guns.

Homage: Linda McCartney quotes, appropriately, a line from the Beatles' song 'Octopus's Garden'. The reference to hidden messages in reversed Beatles songs refers to the (mistaken) belief that 'Paul Is Dead' was spoken backwards on the 'Sergeant Pepper' album. The end credits play out with

McCartney's 'Maybe I'm Amazed', with a recipe for lentil soup read by Paul played backwards over it.

Hi, I'm Troy McClure, you may remember me from: 'Meat and You: Partners in Freedom' (Number 3F03 in the *Resistance is Useless* series of educational films). And other educational films such as $2-3 = Negative Fun$, and *Firecrackers: The Silent Killers*.

Itchy and Scratchy in: 'Esophagus Now'. An especially disgusting entry to the canon.

Notes: 'You don't win friends with salad!' Lisa's finest hour – you'll cheer as she saves the life of an earthworm, triggers the school's Independent Thought alarm system and makes a pig fly. A very simple, very memorable episode with superb guest cameos from the McCartneys.

134

3F04:

'Treehouse of Horror VI'

Written by John Swartzwelder, Steve Tombkins,
David S. Cohen
Directed by Bob Anderson
Also starring: Russi Taylor
Special guest voices: Marcia Wallace (as Ms Krabappel),
Paul Anka (as himself)

Premise: 'Attack of the 50 Ft Eyesores': in which Springfield is menaced by advertising hoardings brought to life by celestial energy. 'Nightmare On Evergreen Terrace'; in which Groundskeeper Willie haunts the dreams of the kids of Springfield Elementary. And 'Homer ^3': in which Homer becomes lost in the mysterious third dimension.

Couch: The hanged Simpsons dangle down over the sofa.

Homage: The three segments are direct pastiches of *Attack of the 50 Ft Woman* (Nathan Hertz, 1958), the *Nightmare On Elm Street* movies, and the *Twilight Zone* episode 'Little Girl Lost' respectively. There are also references to *Mork and Mindy*, *Terminator 2*, *The Pagemaster* (Martin Prince's dream), *Tron*, and *The Black Hole* (the appearance of the third dimension). When Homer emerges into our world at the episode's climax, the library from the computer game 'Myst' can be seen matted on to the horizon.

Mmmmm: . . . sprinkles . . . . erotic cakes.

Song: 'Just Don't Look' sung by Paul Anka and Lisa.

Notes: Complex, very assured and very clever, this feels like The Simpsons moving into a whole new era. The computer graphics are outstanding, and the final scene – as Homer enters our dimension – is one of the highlights of the entire series.

135

3F05:

'King-Size Homer'

Written by Dan Greaney   **Directed by** Jim Reardon
Also starring: Pamela Hayden
Special guest voice: Joan Kenley

Premise: 'All my life I've been an obese man trapped inside a fat man's body.' Homer needs to gain 61 lbs in order to be classified as disabled and thus be allowed to work at home.

Features: Smithers, Mr Burns, Carl, Lenny, Dr Hibbert, Dr Nick, Arnie Pie, Ned Flanders, Milhouse, Nelson, Jimbo Jones, Spotty Boy, Ralph.

Couch: The Simpsons rush in – as sparking clockwork toys.

Trivia: Products seized on by Homer include Ham Ahoy!, Much Ado About Stuffing, Tubbb!, Cheezs And Rice, and Uncle Jim's Country Fillin'. He visits THE VAST WAISTBAND clothing store. Homer goes to see the movie HONK IF YOU'RE HORNY starring Pauly Shore and Faye Dunaway.

Homage: The scene where Bart, Milhouse and friends crowd outside the window of the Simpsons' house to spy on the obese Homer is a lifted scene from *What's Eating Gilbert Grape?* (Lasse Hallstrom, 1993).

Mmmmm: . . . I can feel three kinds of softness.

That's Homer Simpson, sir: 'one of your chair moisteners from Sector 7G.'

Notes: Homer's antics with the computer ('Press any key? There is no any key!') and Mr Burns running exercise classes ('push out the jive, bring in the love!') are plus points, but this isn't one of the best episodes. Homer's at his most irritating and childish here – you really want Marge to beat him up.

136

3F06:

'Mother Simpson'

Written by Richard Appel
Directed by David Silverman
Also starring: Pamela Hayden, Maggie Roswell
Special guest voices: Glenn Close (as Grandma Simpson), Harry Morgan (as Bill)

Premise: Homer fakes his own death to avoid work. At his graveside he meets a woman who claims to be his mother – a woman who's been hiding from Mr Burns since she attempted to destroy his experimental germ warfare plant in the sixties.

Features: Mr Burns, Smithers, Carl, Lenny, Flanders, Rev. Lovejoy, Maud Flanders, Helen Lovejoy, Patty and Selma, Hans Moleman, Grampa, Chief Wiggum, Kent Brockman, Spotty Boy.

Couch: The Simpsons rush in – and get cleared by a skittle-clearing thing.

Homage: Harry Morgan reprises his role from the crime TV show *Dragnet*. Maggie dances to the theme of *Rowan & Martin's Laugh-In*, and we hear 'Sunshine Of Your Love' by Cream and 'All Along the Watchtower' by Jimi Hendrix in reference to Grandma Simpson's sixties rebellion.

Notes for the Uneducated: 'Steal This Book' was written by sixties activist Abbie Hoffman.

Notes: In which we discover where Lisa got her brains and determination to fight social and political injustices, how Homer developed an inferiority complex, and that Smithers is a big fan of Swedish popsters Abba. Gag-packed, and very touching.

137

3F08:

'Sideshow Bob's Last Gleaming'

Written by Spike Ferestein
Directed by Dominic Polcino
Also starring: Pamela Hayden, Tress MacNeille,
Russi Taylor
Special guest voices: Kelsey Grammer (as Sideshow Bob),
R. Lee Ermey (as Colonel Habaplap)

Premise: On a day trip from Springwood Minimum Security Prison to an air base, Sideshow Bob conceives a fiendish plot to be rid of his second greatest enemy – television. And his first greatest enemy – Bart. And also his sister Lisa – to whom he's fairly indifferent.

Features: Krusty, Sideshow Mel, Sideshow Bob, Chief Wiggum, Spotty Boy, Lou, Milhouse, Grampa, Martin, Moe, Dr Hibbert, Mayor Quimby, Dr Frink, Bumblebee Man.

Couch: The merSimpsons swim into their underwater living room.

Trivia: The 'esteemed representatives of television' are Kent Brockman, Bumblebee Man, Doctor Who (the Tom Baker model familiar to US viewers through endless reruns on public broadcast 'pledge' TV stations), and Krusty.

Homage: The nuclear explosion sequence, the bunker refuge of the US Army, and the trigger-happy General all come from *Dr Strangelove* (Stanley Kubrick, 1963). R. Lee Ermery's role as Colonel Habaplap is a close cousin to his role in *Full Metal Jacket* (Stanley Kubrick, 1987). Sideshow Bob is seen at one point of the episode debating with Australian media tycoon Rupert Murdoch.

Notes: Probably the least satisfying of Sideshow Bob's gleamings – but there's enough slapstick and satire (on surprising targets, including box kites) to keep things ticking along nicely.

138

3F31:
'138th Episode Spectacular'

Written by Penny Wise   **Directed by** 'Pound Foolish'
Special guest voice: Phil Hartman (as Troy McClure)

Premise: Troy McClure presents yet another clip show devoted to America's favourite non-prehistoric cartoon family – 23 per cent original footage. But this time there's unreleased material from previous episodes in the gag bag.

Features: Troy McClure.

Couch: The Simpsons rush in – lots of times and in lots of different ways.

Trivia: We get to see excised sections from the episodes 'Krusty Gets Kancelled', '$pringfield', 'Mother Simpson', 'Treehouse of Horror IV', 'Homer and Apu' and 'Burns' Heir', plus an alternative solution to 'Who Shot Mr Burns?'

Homage: The unseen material from 'Homer and Apu' takes a swipe at the hundreds of movies produced by the Bombay film industry, while James Bond turns up in '$pringfield'.

Hi, I'm Troy McClure, you may remember me from: such Fox Network specials as 'Alien Nose-Job' and '5 Fabulous Weeks of "The Chevy Chase Show".'

Notes: The out-takes are up to standard, and there are a number of great self-referential moments. It was nice of them to own up that Bleedin' Gums Murphy was never popular.

139

3F07:

'Marge Be Not Proud'

Written by Mike Scully **Directed by** Steven Dean Moore
Also starring: Pamela Hayden, Tress MacNeille,
Maggie Roswell
Special guest voices: Phil Hartman (as Troy McClure),
Lawrence Tierney (as Brodka)

Premise: Marge won't buy Bart the video game 'Bonestorm' for Christmas. So Bart applies 'the four-fingered discount' – and ends up estranged from his own mother.

Features: Krusty, Grampa, Nelson, Android's Dungeon Guy, Troy McClure, Milhouse, Mrs van Houten, Jimbo, Dolph, Kearney.

Couch: The Simpsons rush in – and Homer pulls a giant plug from the floor, sucking them all down.

Hi, I'm Troy McClure, you may remember me from: such public service videos as *Designated Drivers: The Lifesaving Nerds* and *Phony Tornado Alarms Reduce Readiness*.

Notes: A Christmas special in all but name, and a touching look at the relationship between Marge and her growing Bart.

140

3F09:

'Two Bad Neighbors'

Written by Ken Keeler   **Directed by** Wes Archer
Also starring: Pamela Hayden, Tress MacNeille,
Maggie Roswell

Premise: The Simpsons have new neighbours – ex-President George Bush and his wife Barbara. But George and Bart don't get on.

Features: Grampa, the Flanderses, Apu, Lenny and Carl, Chief Wiggum, Dr Hibbert, Milhouse, Principal Skinner.

Cameos: Everyone's at the rummage sale.

Couch: A big game hunter has bagged the Simpsons.

Notes for Brits: In 1990 George Bush had expressed his wish for the American family to be 'more like the Waltons than the

Simpsons . . .' Six years passed before the Simpsons took their revenge.

Homage: The relationship between Bart and George Bush is a homage to the US sitcom *Dennis the Menace*, in which a young scamp terrorised an older neighbour. Grampa refers to Grover Cleveland, the only President to have served two non-consecutive terms in office.

Notes: Very strange, this episode takes *The Simpsons* into a whole new dimension of political satire. The lampooning of a single public figure is a startling move. Works much better for Americans, we're told.

141

3F10:

'Team Homer'

Written by Mark Scully   **Directed by** Mark Kirkland
Also starring: Doris Grau, Pamela Hayden, Russi Taylor

Premise: Homer puts together a bowling team. All's going well – until feeble, unsporting Mr Burns demands to come on side. Principal Skinner's got plans, too – he's going to introduce school uniforms.

Features: Quimby, Krusty, Bumblee Man, Groundskeeper Willie, Patty and Selma, Nelson, the Flanderses, Moe, Barney, Apu, Otto, Wiggum, Mr Burns, Smithers, Ms Krabappel, Martin, Jimbo.

Couch: The Simpsons rush in – as do a family of mice.

Homage: Homer's stolen Oscar was awarded to Dr Haing S. Nor as best supporting actor in *The Killing Fields* (Roland Joffe, 1984). He sings a snatch of Styx's 1985 hit 'Mr Roboto'.

Notes: One of our least favourite episodes. The sub-plot, involving new school uniforms, is a lot more satisfying than the bowling story, with the fashion parade a particular high-light.

142

3F11:

'Scenes from the Class Struggle in Springfield'

Written by Jennifer Crittenden   **Directed by** Susie Dietter
Also starring: Pamela Hayden, Tress MacNeille,
Maggie Roswell
Special guest voice: Tom Kite (as himself)

Premise: Marge buys a Chanel suit – knocked down to $90 from $2800 – and gets an invite to join the career women of the Springfield Glen Country Club – Proud Home of the Tippling Gadabout. And where Homer can practise his golf.

Features: Bumblebee Man, Grampa, Cletus, Apu, Mr Burns, Krusty, Kent Brockman, Lenny, Carl, Mr Burns, Smithers, Patty and Selma, Spotty Boy.

Couch: The Simpsons rush in, into eerie darkness.

Homage: The title refers to *Scenes from the Class Struggle in Beverly Hills* (Paul Bartel, 1989).

Mmmmm: . . . open-based club sandwich.

That's Homer Simpson, sir: 'one of your fork and spoon operators from Sector 7G.'

Notes: Marge looks great in her Chanel, the golf scenes between Homer and Mr Burns are brilliant, and there are many true, touching moments as Marge struggles valiantly to improve herself. Yet again, it's tempting for the viewer to urge Marge on and get the hell away from the family.

143

3F12:
'Bart the Fink'

Story by Bob Kushell   **Teleplay by** John Swartzwelder
Directed by Jim Reardon
Also starring: Pamela Hayden, Tress MacNeille
Special guest voice: Bob Newhart (as himself),
Phil Hartman (as Troy McClure)

Premise: Bart unwittingly lands Krusty in deep, deep trouble with the tax authorities, who rename his show *Herschel Krustofsky's Clown-Related Entertainment Show*. But how far will Krusty go to avoid the IRS? Auctioning his pornography? Suicide in his private plane the *I'm-On-A-Rolla-Gay*? Or faking his own death and starting a new life as a yachtsman?

Features: Android's Dungeon Guy, Milhouse, Jimbo, Krusty, Kent Brockman, Spotty Boy, Moleman, Patty and Selma, Jasper, Principal Skinner, Mrs Skinner, Superintendent Chalmers, Chief Wiggum, Troy McClure, Sideshow Mel, Dr Hibbert, Captain MacAllister.

Couch: A colour photocopy of the Simpons slips on to the sofa.

Trivia: All Krusty's Sideshows but Bob turn up to his funeral (including Sideshow Luke Perry).

Hi, I'm Troy McClure, you may remember me from: such showbiz funerals as *Andre the Giant, We Hardly Knew Ye* and *Shemp Howard, Today We Mourn a Stooge*.

Notes for Brits: The sign on the side of the bus reading 'ARE YOU MISSING "MAD ABOUT YOU" RIGHT NOW? NBC TV Sundays at 8' is a direct reference to the sitcom slotted opposite *The Simpsons* during this season.

Notes: 'What good is respect without the moolah to back it up?' Very fast and very good, with plenty of gags and effective set pieces. Bob Newhart's eulogy to Krusty is especially memorable.

144

3F13:

'Lisa the Iconoclast'

Written by Jonathan Collier
Directed by Mike B. Anderson
Additional cast: Pamela Hayden, Tress MacNeille,
Maggie Roswell
Special guest voices: Phil Hartman (as Troy McClure),
Donald Sutherland (as Hollis Hurlbutt),
Marcia Wallace (as Ms Krabappel)

Premise: 'A noble spirit embiggens the smallest man' – the inspirational words of town founder Jebediah Springfield. As bicentennial celebrations loom, and Homer gets a job as Town Crier, Lisa makes a dread discovery. Was Jebediah in truth the ruthless pirate Hans Sprungfeld?

Features: Troy McClure, Milhouse, Ms Krabappel, Miss Hoover, Principal Skinner, Kearney, Ralph Wiggum, Quimby, Ned Flanders, Dr Hibbert, Rev. Lovejoy, Chief Wiggum, Android's Dungeon Guy, Apu, Moe, Barney, the two barflies (who get told to shut up by Moe), Groundskeeper Willie, Grampa, Helen Lovejoy, Mr Burns, Smithers, Mrs Hibbert, Mother Skinner, Jasper, Sherri and Terri, Janey, Lewis, Lou and Eddie, Mrs Winfield.

Couch: The Simpsons are inside the boxes normally reserved for the Brady Bunch.

Hi, I'm Troy McClure, you may remember me from: the movie *Young Jebediah Springfield* (a Rental Films presentation of a Watch & Learn feature).

Notes for the Uneducated: William Dawes and Samuel Oatus, mentioned by Hurlbutt, are such minor revolutionaries that we can't find any trace of them. The Howard Hughes will and the Hitler diaries were genuine forgeries, but there's never been a retraction of the emancipation proclamation. Adlai Stevenson II (1900–1965) was a presidential candidate in the 1950s. In Homer's dream of 1781, the additions to the flag wanted by George Washington are the shapes of the breakfast cereal Lucky Charms. There appear to be eighteenth-century cameos of Marge and Homer on the wall of the museum.

Song: 'Camptown Races' sung by the skull of Jedediah Springfield ventriloquised by Chief Wiggum. The episode plays out with an ode to Jebediah.

Notes: Homer's fantasy of the fight between Sprungfeld and George Washington, replete with action movie clichés, is fantastic. A clever, Lisa-centric episode. In fact, Bart and Maggie barely appear.

145
3F14:
'Homer the Smithers'

Written by John Swartzwelder
Directed by Steven Dean Moore
Additional cast: Tress MacNeille

Premise: Smithers blames himself for neglecting Mr Burns, and is sent on vacation. A temporary replacement is needed – and, not wanting to be outshone, Smithers chooses Homer.

Features: Smithers, Mr Burns, Lenny and his wife, Carl and his wife, Moe, Chief Wiggum, Dr Hibbert, Barney.

Couch: The Simpsons are zizzing about the living room in circus mini-motors dressed in fezzes. They stop and toot their horns.

Homage: There's yet another reference to *A Clockwork Orange* (Stanley Kubrick, 1971) in the sequence of Smithers feeding Mr Burns peanuts at his bedside.

Notes for Brits: Mr Burns recalls the days of Postum, a hot drink, designed to rival tea and coffee, that floundered in the early days of the century. His use of 'ahoy, hoy!' to answer the phone was also common telephone etiquette in the very first days of the telephone. *Little Rascals*, Hal Roach's cutesy 1930s cinema shorts about a gang of street kids, are on the US's syndication roundabout. President Taft was in office from 1909 to 1913.

That's Homer Simpson, sir: 'one of your organ banks from sector 7G.' ('All of the recent events of your life have revolved around him in some way.')

Look out for: Smithers' vacation, complete with volleyball, disco dancing and all-male speedboat-triangle displays. Homer is on top form, forgetting the first word of Mr Burns' dictation and making a very unusual breakfast.

Notes: Mrs Burns makes her only contemporaneous appearance (to date), although she does appear briefly in flashback in 'Rosebud'. A very good episode, and an unusually straightforward one for this surreal season.

146

3F15:

'A Fish Called Selma'

Written by Jack Barth   **Directed by** Mark Kirkland
Additional cast: Phil Hartman (as Troy McClure),
Pamela Hayden
Special guest voice: Jeff Goldblum (as McArthur Parker)

Premise: Troy McClure's career is looking up at last. All he has to do to satisfy Hollywood's casting agents is quash the speculation about his personal life. And that means marriage. And marriage means Selma.

Features: Troy McClure, Chief Wiggum, Patty and Selma, Grampa, Dr Hibbert, Lenny, Carl, Spotty Boy, Moe, Krusty, Kent Brockman, Mrs Bouvier, Rev. Lovejoy, Mayor Quimby, Apu.

Couch: The Simpsons have become sparking clockwork toys. But they manage to reach the sofa – except Homer.

Trivia: One of Troy's movies is playing on TV in the 'Movie For A Rained-Out Ball Game' slot. At the Pimento Grove restaurant, we see celebrity photographs of Krusty and Rainier Wolfcastle (from the Springfield universe) and previous special guest voice artists including Liz Taylor, Bette Midler, Leonard Nimoy, Barry White, Sting, James Woods and Phil Collins (among others). Next to its feature on Troy, the *Springfield Shopper* carries an article about Wolfcastle titled 'Look Who's Drunk'.

Homage: The Muppets are very well satirised in a sequence featuring Miss Piggy and Kermit. Selma's romantic cigarette play with Troy recalls *Now, Voyager* (Irving Rapper, 1942), and the musical version of *Planet of the Apes* (Franklin J. Schaffner, 1968) contains a parody of Falco's 1984 hit 'Rock Me Amadeus'. The episode's title refers to *A Fish Called Wanda* (Charles Crichton, 1988), in connection with the rumours about Troy McClure's bizarre sex life that have dogged his career.

Hi, I'm Troy McClure, you may remember me from: such films as: *The Muppets Go Medieval* (1977) co-starring Dyan Cannon, *The Greatest Story Ever Hulaed*, *They Came to Burgle Carnegie Hall*, *Meet Joe Blow*, *Give My Remains to Broadway*, *The Verdict Was Mail Fraud*, *Leper in the Back Field*, *Astronaut Gemini 3*, *Incident at Noon*, *My Darling Beefeater*, *Locker Room Towel Fight: The Blinding of Harry Driscoll*, *The Electric Gigolo*, and *The Contrabulous*

Fabtraption of Professor Hufnagel. And he stars in the play *Stop the Planet of the Apes I Want to Get Off* and is up for a part in *McBain IV: Fatal Discharge*.

Song: 'Dr Zaius, Dr Zaius' sung by Troy and the cast of *Stop the Planet of the Apes*.

Notes: Troy McClure gets a starring role at last. We finally discover – nearly – the reason for his stalled career, get to see his revolving dome home, and learn of his emotional inadequacies (at least where human females are concerned). This episode fits into the Selma-marriage sub-genre, and her previous unhappy alliances are referred to at the wedding.

147

3F16:

'The Day the Violence Died'

Written by John Swartzwelder
Directed by Wesley Archer
Also starring: Pamela Hayden, Tress MacNeille
Special guest voices: Kirk Douglas (as Chester J. Lampwick), Phil Hartman (as Lionel Hutz), Alex Rocco (as Roger Myers), Jack Sheldon (as Amendment 2B), Suzanne Somers (as herself)

Premise: It's the 75th anniversary of Itchy and Scratchy, but one person not celebrating is bum Chester J. Lampwick. He tells Bart he created Itchy in 1919 – so there's the small matter of $800,000,000 in outstanding royalties to be settled.

Features: Kent Brockman, Android's Dungeon Guy, Otto, Milhouse, Grampa, Lionel Hutz, Krusty, Apu.

Couch: The Simpsons rush in – but they're blanked-out silhouettes. Robotic spray-painting restores their colour.

Trivia: The other members of the Itchy and Scratchy family are Brown-Nose Bear, Disgruntled Goat, Flatulent Fox, Rich Uncle Skeleton and Dinner Dog.

Homage: The cryogenic fate of Roger Myers Snr refers to the myth that Walt Disney's body was similarly frozen after death. The cartoon replacement for Itchy and Scratchy is a parody of the early seventies educational cartoon series *Schoolhouse Rock*.

Notes for Brits: Amendment 2B was designed by right-wingers to amend the American Constitution to forbid the burning of the US flag, and was regarded by its opponents as the thin end of a political wedge. The surprise witnesses at the trial include the McCrary twins, famed in the States as the fattest twins on Earth.

Itchy and Scratchy in: The Itchy and Scratchy 48-hour diamond anniversary marathon – 'celebrating 75 years of ribtickling brutality and hilarious atrocities', including 'Remembrance of Things Slashed'. We also see 'Itchy & Scratchy meet Fritz the Cat', a seventies blaxploitation-style outing. Lampwick provides Itchy's solo premier 'Manhattan Madness' (1919) as proof of his claim, which is refuted by another screening of 'Steamboat Itchy' (as seen in 'Itchy & Scratchy The Movie'). And there's an unnamed cartoon featuring Itchy in a team-up with God (yes, God).

Song: 'I'm Amendment 2B' sung by Amendment 2B.

Notes: A great episode, with some clever observations on ideas and copyright, and a superb – and sinister – twist ending featuring the return of both Bart and Lisa from their days on *The Tracey Ullman Show*.

148

3F17:

'Bart on the Road'

Written by Richard Appel

Directed by Swinton O. Scott III
Also starring: Pamela Hayden, Jim Lau, Tress MacNeille,
Russi Taylor

Premise: A fake ID gives Bart the chance to take to the road.
Accompanied by Milhouse, Nelson and Martin – and using
the alibi of the National Grammar Rodeo – he sets off for
Knoxville, Tennessee, home of the fantastic Sun Sphere.

Features: Principal Skinner, Patty and Selma, Milhouse, Mr
van Houten, Martin Prince, Nelson, Moe, Barney, the two
barflies, Smithers.

Couch: The Simpsons are deposited on to the sofa like
bowling pins.

Trivia: Springfield Elementary's address is 19 Plympton
Street. Principal Skinner's holiday is booked with Sky-
AmeriWestica. Mr and Mrs Prince are seen for the first time
since the first season. According to his fake driver's licence,
Bart is 4′ 9, with black eyes, and weighs 85 lbs. It gives the
Simpsons' address as 742 Evergreen Terrace.

Homage: *Naked Lunch* (David Cronenberg, 1992) is the
movie adaptation of William Burroughs' novel dealing with
heroin addiction, homosexuality and hallucinogens.

Hello, can I speak to: Ura Snotball.

Notes: This contains some superb and touching character
scenes between Homer and Lisa, a fascinating glimpse of
Marge's insecurities, and some nice touches – Nelson's love
of Andy Williams, Martin's toy dog – that take it above the
series' very high average.

149

3F18:

'22 Short Films About Springfield'

Written by Richard Appel, David S. Cohen,
Jonathan Collier, Jennifer Crittenden, Greg Daniels, Brent
Forrester, Rachel Pulido, Steve Tompkins, Josh Weinstein,
and Matt Groening
With writing supervised by Greg Daniels
Directed by Jim Reardon
Also starring: Pamela Hayden, Tress MacNeille,
Maggie Roswell, Russi Taylor
Special guest voice: Phil Hartman (as Lionel Hutz)

Premise: Er, 22 short films about Springfield. Including a
dastardly plot by Herman to set off a nuke, Homer trapping
Maggie in a newspaper vending machine, and Lisa getting
gum caught in her hair. And lots of oranges falling on the
Bumblebee Man.

Features: Grampa, Dr Nick, Jasper, Moe, Barney, Snake,
Principal Skinner, Superintendent Chalmers, Mother Skinner,
Chief Wiggum, Lou and Eddie, Bumblebee Man, Herman,
Rev. Lovejoy, Ned Flanders, Groundskeeper Willie, Captain
McCallister, Otto, Dr Hibbert, Sideshow Mel, Lionel Hutz,
Uter, Android's Dungeon Guy, Milhouse, Mr van Houten,
Nelson, Dr Frink.

Couch: The sea monkey Simpsons swim in and sit in front of
a barnacled treasure chest.

Homage: The title comes from *32 Short Films About Glenn
Gould* (François Girard, 1993). The sequence involving Wiggum and his men – 'Now this is a burger' – is lifted straight
from *Pulp Fiction* (Quentin Tarantino, 1994). There are also
echoes of Tarantino's *Reservoir Dogs* in Herman threatening
to torture Milhouse when he's tied to a chair.

Moe's secrets: He provided NASA with the Voyager spacecraft.

Songs: Theme to 'Skinner and the Superintendent'. Theme to 'Cletus, The Slack-Jawed Yokel'. Theme to 'Professor Frink'.

Notes: An untypical episode, and a very good one. We get to see little character pieces that wouldn't sustain a full episode but work brilliantly as cameos, and for once the Simpsons take a back seat, allowing us to see many of the other characters in unfamiliar situations of their own. Our favourite of the 22: 'Skinner and the Superintendent', as poor Seymour attempts to palm Chalmers off with a lunch of Krustyburgers disguised as 'steamed hams'.

150

3F19:

'Raging Abe Simpson and his Grumbling Grandson in "Return of the Flying Hellfish" '

Written by Jonathan Collier   **Directed by** Jeffrey Lynch
Also starring: Pamela Hayden, Tress MacNeille, Maggie Roswell, Russi Taylor
Special guest voice: Marcia Wallace (as Ms Krabappel)

Premise: In World War II, Grampa was commander of the Hellfish – a crack commando unit whose loot of Nazi treasure has lain undisturbed for fifty years. But now all the Hellfish have died. Apart from Grampa and Mr Burns. And it's time to grab the treasure.

Features: Principal Skinner, Ms Krabappel, Milhouse, Nelson, Martin, Rev. Lovejoy, Mr Burns, Smithers, Jasper, Ned Flanders.

Couch: There's a giant plug in the living room. Homer pulls it out – and the family are sucked in.

Trivia: The seven dead Hellfish were Sheldon Skinner, Ernie Gumble, Asa Phelps, Iggy Wiggum, Milton 'Ox' Haas, Ethell Westgrin and Griff McDonald.

Homage: The Flying Hellfish organisation's activities in wartime Germany recall *The Dirty Dozen* (Robert Aldrich, 1967). Grampa repeats part of Dorothy's closing speech from *The Wizard of Oz*.

Notes for Brits: Grampa's reference to a 'liberty sausage' refers to the patriotic renaming of German products such as frankfurters and sauerkraut during the world wars.

Notes: Notable for Mr Burns' impersonation of Marge, some spectacular action sequences, and some good underwater scenes – but not especially brilliant.

151
3F20:
'Much Apu About Nothing'

Written by David S. Cohen   **Directed by** Susie Dietter
Also starring: Pamela Hayden, Tress MacNeille,
Maggie Roswell, Russi Taylor
Special guest voice: Joe Mantegna (as Don Tony)

Premise: 'We're Here, We're Queer, We Don't Want Any More Bears!' is the rallying cry of Homer's new anti-bear vigilante group. But when the bear is sorted out, the city needs another scapegoat. Illegal immigrants fit the bill – and their number includes Apu.

Features: Ned Flanders, Rod and Todd, Maude Flanders, Kent Brockman, Chief Wiggum, Lou and Eddie, Barney, Moe, Lenny, Mayor Quimby, Principal Skinner, Helen

Lovejoy, Uter, Nelson, Groundskeeper Willie, Grampa, Apu, Professor John Frink, Kearney, Don Tony, Selma.

Cameos: everybody's in the Vigilante Group. Also Bumblebee Man, Dr Nick Riviera, Mr Burns, Hans Moleman.

Couch: A hunter rushes in – having shot and bagged the Simpsons.

Trivia: Lunchlady Doris has become Postlady Doris. Homer's paycheck gives him $362.19 pay after deductions. If Grampa's memoir is to be relied on, the Simpsons emigrated to the US from Ireland when he was a child. According to his fake ID, Apu was born on 9 January 1962. Magazines at the Kwik-E-Mart include Golf Novice, Low Rider and UFO.

Notes for Brits: Proposition 24 is very similar to California's Proposition 187, which proposed the rescinding of employment rights and benefits from immigrants.

Moe's secrets: He has to sit the written citizenship test.

Notes: 'When are people going to learn – democracy doesn't work!' One of the most outspoken, and certainly angriest of episodes succeeds as a savage satire on the scapegoating of immigrants. Homer has never been so frighteningly dumb, although he does come through with a rousing liberal speech.

152

3F22:

'Summer of 4 ft 2'

Written by Dan Greaney   **Directed by** Mark Kirkland
Also starring: Pamela Hayden, Tress MacNeille,
Maggie Roswell, Russi Taylor
Special guest voices: Christina Ricci (as Erin), Marcia
Wallace (as Ms Krabappel)

Premise: Flanders offers the Simpsons the use of his beach house in Little Pwagmattasquarmsettport – the perfect setting for Lisa's attempt to shake off her dorky feathers and become a fully dysfunctioning slacker-kid with her new friends Erin, Rick, Dean and Ben.

Features: Milhouse, Ms Krabappel, Eddie, Martin, Nelson, Miss Hoover, Ralph Wiggum, Ned Flanders.

Couch: The Simpsons are colour-photocopied on to the sofa.

Trivia: *Newsweek* has dubbed Springfield 'America's Crudbucket'.

Homage: Lisa has a vision of Alice and the Mad Hatter from Lewis Carroll's *Alice's Adventures in Wonderland* (they are re-created very faithfully from the John Tenniel illustrations of the original publication), Pippi Longstocking from the books by Astrid Lindgren, and the urbane Eustace B. Tilley from the *New Yorker* magazine. Milhouse refers to the US sitcom *Blossom*.

Notes: 'Like, you know, whatever.' This episode will strike a chord with anyone that's ever tried to fit in with the crowd, and is a neat critique of East Coast port towns, Generation X, and 4th July fireworks. Lisa gets to show the many facets of her character, and there's a superb slapstick sequence as Homer tries to dispose of a firework.

153

3F21:

'Homerpalooza'

Written by Brent Forrester   **Directed by** Wesley Archer
Also starring: Pamela Hayden, Tress MacNeille
Special guest voices: Cypress Hill (as themselves),
Peter Frampton (as himself), The Smashing Pumpkins (as themselves), Sonic Youth (as themselves)

Premise: 'Why do we need new bands? Everyone knows rock attained perfection in 1974!' Homer's feeling out of touch with the youth of today – so he takes Bart and Lisa to Hullabalooza, the biggest alternative music festival. And ends up as star attraction in its pageant of the trans-mundane – or, more accurately speaking, its freakshow.

Features: Otto, Milhouse, Jasper, Nelson, Janey, Barney, Grampa, Jimbo Jones, Mr Burns, Smithers.

Couch: The Simpsons rush in – into darkness.

Homage: We hear the songs 'Winners And Losers' by Grand Funk Railroad, 'Mississippi Queen', and 'Frankenstein' by the Edgar Winters Group. 'You Make Me Feel Like Dancing' by Leo Sayer is Homer's favoured disco record. 'Appetite for Destruction' and 'Don't Fear the Reaper' were hits for Guns 'N' Roses and Blue Oyster Cult respectively.

Notes: One of the most memorable episodes, if not one of the greatest – the satire on youth counterculture is well handled, and Homer's flashback to his youth is fabulous. But the best bits are the guest slots from Cypress Hill, Sonic Youth and the Smashing Pumpkins. It's a statement of the credibility of *The Simpsons* that they allow themselves to be sent up so mercilessly.

Eighth Season

1996–1997
25 Episodes

154
4F02:
'Treehouse of Horror VII'

Written by Ken Keeler, Dan Greaney, David S. Cohen
Directed by Mike B. Anderson
Special guest voice: Phil Hartman (as Bill Clinton)

Premise: 'The Thing & I': in which Bart discovers his evil twin, Hugo Simpson; 'The Genesis Tub' in which Lisa creates a city of tiny people; and 'Citizen Kang', in which the two Rigellians run for the presidency – by assuming the forms of Clinton and Dole.

Couch: The Simpsons rush in – to find the Grim Reaper waiting.

Homage: *Independence Day* (the alien takeover on 'Inauguration Day'), *Basket Case* (the evil twin). Lisa's city looks like one you might create using the computer game 'Sim City'. Homer sings 'Fish Heads', a novelty semi-hit for Barnes & Barnes in 1981.

Look out for: The contents of the Simpsons' attic – ephemera from many, many previous episodes.

Notes: A cracking start to the eighth season. *The Simpsons*, it seems, just gets better and better.

155

3F23:

'You Only Move Twice'

Written by John Swartzwelder
Directed by Mike Anderson
Also starring: Albert Brooks (as Hank Scorpio),
Pamela Hayden, Tress MacNeille

Premise: Offered a job by Globex, the Simpsons move to Cyprus Creek. But the nuclear plant Homer is now working for hides a deadly secret – its boss is none other than East Coast super villain Hank Scorpio – not that Homer notices.

Features: Smithers, Otto, Apu, Ned Flanders, Rev. Lovejoy, Moe, Barney, Bumblebee Man, Kent Brockman, Krusty, Sideshow Mel, Captain McAllister, Android's Dungeon Guy, Mayor Quimby, Mr Burns, Dr Nick Riviera, Dr Hibbert, Snake, Chief Wiggum, Principal Skinner, Mrs Skinner, Chalmers, Groundskeeper Willie, Milhouse, Richard, Lewis, Martin Prince, Nelson.

Couch: The family parachute on to the sofa.

Homage: Loads of James Bond movies, but most obviously *You Only Live Twice*, *A View to a Kill* and a whole sequence from *Goldfinger* – in which Homer's stupidity actually kills Sean Connery's Bond.

Good gags: Without a doubt, one of the all-time best sight gags is Lisa's Disney-esque skipping through the forest, saying hello to Mr Chipmunk and Mrs Owl, only to have the owl kill the chipmunk as soon as her back is turned. And look out for Apu's heartfelt goodbye.

Song: the episode plays out with the superb pseudo-Bond theme 'Scorpio'.

Notes: A tremendous episode, with some really good moments, most of them involving Bart, Lisa and Marge's loathing for Cyprus Creek. The remedial kids are fab (especially Warren) and Lisa's second chipmunk encounter is inspired. Scorpio is a good character, especially his Christopher Walken-esque killing spree.

156

4F03:

'The Homer They Fall'

Written by Jonathan Collier
Directed by Mark Kirkland
Also starring: Paul Winfield (as Lucious Sweet),
Michael Buffer (as himself),
Phil Hartman (as Lionel Hutz)

Premise: When Dr Hibbert discovers that Homer has an abnormally thick skull, Moe decides that Homer should become a boxer. Then Dreaderick Tatum gets out of jail and Homer becomes his World Heavyweight opponent – much to Marge's alarm.

Features: Android's Dungeon Guy, Milhouse, Lewis, Martin Prince, Wendell, Richard, Dolph, Kearney, Jimbo Jones, Janey, Moe, Grampa, Dr Hibbert, Barney, Lenny, Snake, Carl, Jasper, Rainer Wolfcastle, Kent Brockman, Krusty, Dr Nick, Patty, Selma, Dr John Frink, Mr Burns, Smithers.

Couch: The Western Simpsons rush in – and the sofa takes off like a wild bucking bronco.

Trivia: On the wall in Moe's secret HQ – the ladies' washroom – are posters of his past fights including a couple of *Simpsons* production team in-jokes – Oakley, Kirkland and Silverman.

Homage: The *Rocky* movies provide much of the episode's imagery. The closing song, 'People Who Need People', was originally sung by Barbra Streisand in 1968. The layout of the comics store resembles the interior control panel of the Tardis from British SF series *Doctor Who*.

Moe's secrets: He was a boxing manager before he became a bartender.

Notes: A pastiche on Mike Tyson's return to the boxing circuit after his time in jail, and his conversion to Christianity. Sadly, this makes for the dullest, one-joke episode of the entire series.

157
4F05:
'Burns, Baby, Burns'

Written by Ian Maxtone-Graham
Directed by Jim Reardon
Also starring: Tress MacNeille
Special guest voice: Rodney Dangerfield (as Larry)

Premise: Larry, Mr Burns' long-lost illegitimate son, turns up to learn about his roots, only to incur his father's wrath. In an attempt to get sympathy, Larry joins forces with Homer and fakes his own kidnapping.

Features: The Flanderses, Mr Burns, Smithers, Moe, Barney, Chief Wiggum, Lou, Eddie, Kent Brockman, Hans Moleman, Groundskeeper Willie, Principal Skinner, Lenny, Carl, Otto, the van Houtens, Dr Hibbert, Dr Nick, Miss Hoover, Apu, Jimbo Jones.

Couch: Bubble versions of the family settle on the sofa – and then pop.

Trivia: Lily and Monty Burns watch *Gone With the Wind* at the Springfield Cinema, while Larry, Homer and Hans Moleman have to make do with *Too Many Grandmas!* starring Bo Derek and Olympia Dukakis.

Look out for: Homer's brain going off on its own to escape Ned Flanders.

Notes: A fun episode, with Rodney Dangerfield putting a lot of pathos into Larry – and Homer's impassioned speech atop the cinema at the climax is one of his funniest moments.

158

4F06:

'Bart After Dark'

Written by Richard Appel   **Directed by** Dominic Polcino
Also starring: Tress MacNeille, Pamela Hayden, Maggie Roswell
Special guest voice: Phil Hartman (as Lionel Hutz)

Premise: While Lisa and Marge join a host of celebrities to clean up animals caught in an oil slick, Homer sends Bart to work in a burlesque house, Maison Derriere, run by the seductive Belle. Marge returns – and vows to have the joint closed down.

Features: Kent Brockman, Captain McCallister, Rainier Wolfcastle, Milhouse, Nelson, Martin Prince, Ralph, Mr Burns, Smithers, Lionel Hutz, Grampa, Herman, Dr Nick Riviera, Principal Skinner, Ned Flanders, Maude Flanders, Helen Lovejoy, Rev. Lovejoy, Mayor Quimby, Lenny, Carl, Ruth Powers, Kirk van Houten, Luanne van Houten, Moe, Groundskeeper Willie, Miss Hoover, Hans Moleman, Sideshow Mel, Ms Krabappel, Sanjay, Apu, Chief Wiggum, Otto, Dr Hibbert, Mrs Wiggum, Mrs Skinner, Chalmers, Patty, Selma, Cletus, Barney, Jasper, Lou and Eddie, Mr

Largo, Mr Lovejoy, Bumblebee Man, Krusty, Jimbo Jones, Kearney, Dolph, Android's Dungeon Guy.

Couch: The sofa is replaced by a pastiche of the cover collage from The Beatles' 1967 album 'Sgt Pepper's Lonely Hearts Club Band'. It features: Hans Moleman, Patty, Selma, Apu, Barney, Radioactive Man, Rev. Lovejoy, Skinner, Sideshow Bob, Otto, Smithers, Mr Burns, Marvin Munroe, Herb Powell, Ned, Jimbo, Kearney, Dolph, Eddie, Lou, Nelson (holding a Krusty doll), Bleedin' Gums Murphy, Chief Wiggum, Sherri and Terri, Kent Brockman, Ms Krabappel, Grampa, Miss Hoover, Dr Hibbert, Quimby, Cletus, his wife Brandine, Android's Dungeon Guy, Moe, Troy McClure, Lionel Hutz, Krusty, Princess Kashmir, Martin, Milhouse, and Itchy and Scratchy. The Simpsons occupy the place of the 'Sergeant Pepper' era Beatles, while the sixties Beatles are represented by the Simpsons as they appeared in the Tracey Ullman shorts. At the front, 'The Simpsons' is spelled out in pink sugar-coated doughnuts, with Santa's Little Helper and Snowball II, Blinky the fish in a bowl, a baby Homer and Jebediah Springfield's head amongst the memorabilia.

Trivia: Marge is 37 and is a third-generation Springfield resident. Former US president Eisenhower has been a punter at Belle's Maison Derriere.

Homage: *The Best Little Whorehouse in Texas* (Colin Higgins, 1982) provides the character of Belle, much of Maison Derriere's design, and Marge's campaign to clean up Springfield. The *O-pe-Ra* show going out of control incident recalls the 1995 edition of *The Jenny Jones Show* after which one of the guests shot another dead.

Itchy and Scratchy in: 'Good Cats, Bad Choices'.

Look out for: Lisa and her peach tree. Bart's exploration of Maison Derriere: 'I have been grossly misinformed about witches.'

Song: 'The Spring in Springfield' sung by Belle.

Notes: The cynical attack on celebrities jumping on the bandwagon to save cute, fluffy seals caught in oil slicks is spot on and Tress MacNeille's Belle is a wonderful character.

159
4F04:
'A Milhouse Divided'

Written by Steve Tompkins
Directed by Steven Dean Moore
Also starring: Pamela Hayden, Tress MacNeille,
Maggie Roswell

Premise: After a disastrous dinner party at the Simpsons, the van Houtens decide to divorce. This makes Homer consider the state of his own marriage and whether he treats Marge with the respect she deserves.

Features: Otto, Rev. Lovejoy, Helen Lovejoy, Dr Hibbert, Kirk van Houten, Luanne van Houten, Milhouse, the Flanderses, Nelson, Kearney, Patty and Selma, Grampa, Jackie Bouvier.

Couch: Bart is flickering like a badly tuned portable TV.

Trivia: Ned Flanders likes Woody Allen movies (but can't stand Woody Allen himself) while Homer reads *Hot Lotto Picks Weekly*. Homer describes the Love Is . . . newspaper cartoon as 'a comic strip about two naked eight-year-olds who aren't married'. Homer has taken to wearing half-moon spectacles to read.

Homage: The van Houtens' bitter destruction of each other's possessions recalls *War of the Roses* (Danny DeVito, 1989).

Look out for: Otto leaving The Pot Palace – 'This is flagrant false advertising.' The meatball on the carpet (why is Lisa eating meatballs if she's a vegetarian?) and Homer's attempts at soothing sea sounds to send Marge to sleep.

Notes: More drama than comedy, and very honest in its dealings with the van Houtens' divorce and its effects on Milhouse. Subsequent episodes do not suggest that the van Houtens have reconciled.

160
4F01:
'Lisa's Date With Density'

Written by Mike Scully   **Directed by** Susie Dietter
Also starring: Pamela Hayden, Tress MacNeille,
Maggie Roswell, Russi Taylor

Premise: To her own horror, Lisa develops a crush on Nelson Muntz. She sets out to uncover the charming, sophisticated, good-natured young man she believes exists beneath the veneer of sadistic bully and general bad-doer. Back home, Homer's causing problems with his new automatic telephone-dialling system.

Features: Principal Skinner, Chalmers, Kearney, Apu, Ned Flanders, Chief Wiggum, Eddie, Lou, Janey, Wendell, Sherri and Terri, Richard, Jimbo Jones, Kearney, Dolph, Nelson, Groundskeeper Willie, Milhouse, Ralph Wiggum, Ms Krabappel, Captain McCallister, Miss Hoover, Lewis, Mr Burns, Mr Largo, Todd Flanders, Uter, Martin Prince, Grampa, Jasper, Dr Frink, Mrs Skinner.

Couch: The sofa and the family are suspended upside down.

Trivia: Chalmers owns a 1979 Honda Accord while Kearney has a Hyundai. Homer tries to add things to his doughnut that are not sprinkles – including a Mars Bar, a Twizzler and a Jolly Rancher.

Homage: Lisa's doomed romance with 'just misunderstood' Nelson, and his flight from the cops, pay homage to *Rebel Without a Cause* (Nicholas Ray, 1955) – even parts of Lisa's costume are similar to Natalie Wood's from the movie.

Notes for the Uneducated: Lisa's description of Nelson – 'a riddle wrapped in a mystery inside an enigma' – was Winston Churchill's opinion of Russia at the outbreak of World War II.

Notes: Nelson takes centre stage for the first time. Also impressive for the desperate stunts of the lovesick Milhouse, who, even after Nelson has beaten him up for apparently making a pass, will still do anything for uncaring Lisa.

161

4F07:

'Hurricane Neddy'

Written by Steve Young   **Directed by** Bob Anderson
Also starring: Pamela Hayden, Maggie Roswell,
Tress MacNeille
Special guest voice: Jon Lovitz (as Jay Sherman)

Premise: The terrible Hurricane Barbara destroys the Flanderses' home and the Leftorium. Ned's neighbours try to help him out by building him a new one. When he sees what they've done, he finally flips – and after an astonishing outburst, admits himself into the Calmwood Mental Hospital. What dark secrets might therapy reveal?

Features: Kent Brockman, Apu, Android's Dungeon Guy, Rev. Lovejoy, Groundskeeper Willie, Jasper, Helen Lovejoy, Patty, Selma, Ms Krabappel, Maude Flanders, Kirk van Houten, Dr Nick Riviera, Chalmers, Principal Skinner, Jimbo Jones, Krusty, Moe, Cletus, Lionel Hutz, Kearney, Troy McClure, Lenny, Luanne van Houten, Dr Frink, Snake, Miss

Hoover, Mayor Quimby, Ralph, Grampa, the Flanderses, Dr Hibbert, Barney, Captain McCallister, Lou, Eddie, Otto, Carl, Hans Moleman, Milhouse, Richard.

Couch: There is no sofa – just a big sign pointing to a couch vending machine.

Trivia: The original Hall of Records in Springfield was mysteriously blown away in 1978. Lisa is reading *The How, Why and Huh? Book of the Weather*.

Homage: *Twister* and *The Wizard of Oz* provide much of the hurricane imagery.

Look out for: The arrival of Hurricane Barbara in a clever version of the series' titles.

Notes: An explanation for why Ned Flanders speaks like he does, and some amusing set pieces involving Homer and the psychotherapist assigned to Ned Flanders' case.

162
3F24:
'El Viaje Misterioso del Nuestro Homer'(The Mysterious Voyage of Homer)

Written by Ken Keeler   **Directed by** Jim Reardon
Also starring: Maggie Roswell
Special guest voice: Johnny Cash (as the coyote)

Premise: Homer gorges down a superhot pepper at the Springfield Chili Cook-Out and commences a bizarre psychic journey under the guidance of his coyote spirit guide. His advice – he must discover his true soul mate and bond with him.

Features: Bumblebee Man, Lenny, Rev. Lovejoy, Helen Lovejoy, Dr Nick, Nelson, Mr Burns, Otto, Ms Krabappel,

Carl, Lunchlady Doris; Herman, Dr Frink, Ned Flanders, Todd Flanders, Rod Flanders, Smithers, Moe, Chief Wiggum, Eddie, Lou, Miss Hoover, Jimbo Jones, Jasper, Ralph, Dr Hibbert, Mayor Quimby, Krusty, Barney, Kent Brockman, Captain McCallister.

Couch: The family parachute on to the sofa – except Homer, who drops like a stone.

Trivia: Amongst the various chili stands are Muntz Family Chili (it takes weeks to make Muntz); Old Eliku's Yale-Style Saltpeter Chili, Professor Frink's Virtual Chili, Moe's Chili Bar and Firehouse Ned's Five-Alarm Chili. Homer's record collection includes albums by Jim Nabors, Flint Campbell and The Doodletown Pipers.

Homage: *Dances With Wolves* (Kevin Costner, 1990) provides a lot of the Native American imagery.

Look out for: The smug tortoise.

Notes: Homer's chili-induced trip is brilliant, complete with the surreal tortoise and Indian spirit guide.

163
3G01:
'The Springfield Files'

Written by Reid Harrison   **Directed by** Steven Dean Moore
Also starring: Tress MacNeille, Pamela Hayden
Special guest voices: Leonard Nimoy (as himself),
Gillian Anderson (as Scully), David Duchovny (as Mulder)

Premise: Homer sees a little green alien floating through the forest. His wild claims of contact with 'greys' bring him to the attention of two FBI agents and a cigarette smoking man. However, not even they will believe him . . .

Features: Carl, Lenny, Mr Burns, Smithers, Jasper, Dr Hibbert, Hans Moleman, Barney, Moe, Grampa, Chief Wiggum, Milhouse, Kent Brockman, Otto, Apu, Ned Flanders, Rev. Lovejoy, Mr Largo, Martin Prince, Ralph Wiggum, Richard, Lewis, Jimbo Jones, Helen Lovejoy, Krusty, Groundskeeper Willie, Ms Krabappel, Lunchlady Doris, Dr Nick.

Couch: The Simpsons arrive at the sofa via rocket backpacks.

Trivia: Marge reads *Better Homes Than Yours* magazine, while Lisa spends her time with *Junior Skeptic*. Moe has a breathalyser which starts with Tipsy, then Soused, Stinkin' and finally Boris Yeltsin.

Homage: *The X-Files* aside, the alien line-up which the FBI agents show Homer includes Gort from *The Day the Earth Stood Still* (Robert Wise, 1951), Marvin the Martian from Warner Bros *Looney Tunes*, Chewbacca from *Star Wars*, ALF from the TV series of the same name, and one of the Rigellians from the 'Hallowe'en' specials.

Look out for: Mulder's ID badge photograph.

Notes: Despite the *X-Files* duo only cropping up for about ten minutes in the middle (and for the singalong at the end) a very clever episode, with the line-up one of the best visual gags in ages. Having Duchovny and Anderson is a definite plus, but Leonard Nimoy's part feels too brief after his previous cameo in 'Marge vs. the Monorail'.

164

4F08:

'The Twisted World of Marge Simpson'

Written by Jennifer Crittenden   **Directed by** Chuck Sheetz
Also starring: Tress MacNeille, Maggie Roswell

Special guest voices: Marcia Wallace (as Ms Krabappel), Joe Mantegna (as Don Tony), Jack Lemmon (as Frank)

Premise: Kicked out of the Ladies' Investorettes' Franchise Circle, Marge sets up a pretzel business, but Ms Krabappel and the others fight back. In a desperate bid to help, Homer goes to Fat Tony D'Amico – and starts a Mafia war between the factions.

Features: Helen Lovejoy, Mrs Skinner, Luanne van Houten, Ms Krabappel, Maude Flanders, Ned Flanders, Wiggum, Lenny, Mr Burns, Cletus, Bumblebee Man, Principal Skinner, Smithers, Mr Largo, Dr Hibbert, Hans Moleman, Eddie, Lou, Grampa.

Couch: The Simpsons pop up through holes in the sofa and floor, to be hit by a large hammer.

Trivia: The Investorettes, against Marge's wishes, invested in a Mexican wrestler called El Bombastico. At the ball game, Mr Burns wins the 1997 Pontiac AstroWagon.

Notes: A clever, and rather unusual, idea for an episode that shows a frightening bitchiness beneath the middle-class veneer of smalltown businesswomen.

165

4F10:

'Mountain of Madness'

Written by John Swartzwelder   **Directed by** Mark Kirkland

Premise: Mr Burns decides that his workers need to understand the true meaning of teamwork. He takes them all to snowy Mount Useful for a survivalist exercise. Homer is teamed up with his boss, and things start to go wrong before you can say 'avalanche'.

Features: Mr Burns, Smithers, Carl, Lenny.

Couch: Grampa is asleep on the sofa, folded out as a bed. The others fold it back up, him still inside, and sit upon it.

Trivia: Burns decides to test his workers with a fire drill – the other options on his control panel include Meltdown Alert, Mad Dog Drill and Blimp Attack.

Look out for: Homer's advice on how to bring a bowl of dip towards yourself without standing up.

Notes: Mr Burns and Homer are thrown together, and begin to lose their minds. An inventive episode, with several memorable moments – the Simpsons' skidding car, the avalanche scene, Smithers' bitterness at Mr Burns picking Homer as his partner . . .

166
3G03:
'Simpsoncallafragilisticexpiala-D'oh!-cious'

Written by Al Jean and Mike Reiss
Directed by Chuck Sheetz

Also starring: Pamela Hayden, Maggie Roswell

Premise: Marge is starting to have a nervous breakdown. Just as it looks like she'll blow, help arrives in the shape of magical nanny Shary Bobbins ('Gawd bless 'er').

Features: Krusty, Grampa, Milhouse, Jasper, Mr and Mrs van Houten, the Flanderses, Principal Skinner, Mrs Skinner, Chalmers, Chief Wiggum, Ralph, Carl, Dr John Frink, Captain McCallister, Moe, Dr Hibbert, Barney, Apu, Kearney, Hans Moleman, Snake, Nelson, Groundskeeper Willie, Jimbo Jones, Mr Burns, Smithers, Rainier Wolfcastle.

Couch: The sofa is empty and the Simpsons aren't rushing in – they've locked themselves out.

Trivia: Krusty is trying out the Krusty Komedy Klassics – and then realises that KKK is not a very sensible abbreviation. Charles Bronson and Rainier Wolfcastle both feature on the *Before They Were Famous* show.

Homage: *Mary Poppins* (Robert Stevenson, 1964) provides the basis for the entire episode – and *Mrs Doubtfire* (Chris Columbus, 1993) turns up on the doorstep as well.

Itchy and Scratchy in: 'Reservoir Cats'.

Song: There's a hilarious parody of 'A Spoonful of Sugar' sung by Shary and the Simpsons.

Notes: This reworking of *Mary Poppins* is treated with so much love it stands out as one of the series all-time best episodes – although for those not familiar with the source material, a lot of the jokes may pass them by. A tremendously clever idea, wonderful song pastiches and Maggie Roswell's Shary Bobbins is a terrific creation.

167
4F12:
'The Itchy & Scratchy & Poochie Show'

Written by David S. Cohen
Directed by Steven Dean Moore
Also starring: Pamela Hayden, Tress MacNeille
Special guest voices: Phil Hartman (as Troy McClure and Lionel Hutz), Alex Rocco (as Roger Myers)

Premise: Itchy and Scratchy need a new co-star – and a super-cool dog is created, for which Homer provides the voice. Trouble is, nobody likes Poochie.

Features: Krusty, Sideshow Mel, Ralph, Nelson Muntz, Milhouse, Hans Moleman, Miss Hoover, Otto, Jimbo Jones, Kearney, Troy McClure, Lionel Hutz, Android's Dungeon Guy, Grampa, Patty and Selma, Moe, Jasper, Ned Flanders, Barney, Lenny, Carl, Kent Brockman.

Couch: The sofa is replaced by a pastiche of the cover collage from the Beatles' 1967 album 'Sgt Pepper's Lonely Hearts Club Band'.

Hi, I'm Troy McClure, you may remember me from: such cartoons as 'Christmas Ape' and 'Christmas Ape Goes to Summer Camp'.

Itchy and Scratchy in: 'Why Do Fools Fall in Lava?'

Itchy and Scratchy and Poochie in: 'The Beagle has Landed'.

Look out for: June's story about voicing Roadrunner. 'Cheap bastards!'

Notes: The inclusion of Roy is a clever dig at the whole concept of adding hip characters to a line-up for no reason other than ratings, and then dropping them, mirroring the entire Itchy and Scratchy plot. A very neat episode which, like 'The Front', is a good parody of the cartooning business. Poochie might not have worked (his ultimate fate is inspired) but let's hope we see June Bellamy again.

168
4F11:
'Homer's Phobia'

Written by Ron Hauge   **Directed by** Mike B. Anderson
Also starring: Pamela Hayden
Special guest voice: John Waters (as John)

Premise: When Homer realises that Bart's new friend, camp antiques dealer John, is gay, he begins to fear for Bart's sexual orientation and sets out to ensure his son is a 'real' man.

Features: Milhouse van Houten, Lewis, Richard, Ralph, Rod Flanders, Principal Skinner, Smithers, Barney, Moe.

Couch: The sequence is being uploaded from a computer, but fails to load quickly enough and so is cancelled.

Trivia: John works at Cockamamie's, a store for the kitsch and camp. Among the badges there which Skinner looks at are campaign ones such as I Fell For Dole. Click With Dick. I Like Ike. I Still Like Ike and Quayle Can't Fail. There is a poster for the movie *Clank Clank You're Dead*, and Homer's record collection includes records by the New Christy Minstrels, Loony Laura, The Wedding of Lynda Bird Johnson and Ballads of the Green Berets by S/Sgt Barry Sadler.

Homage: Homer and John dance to 'I Love the Nightlife (Disco Round)' by Alicia Bridges, a 1978 hit, while the Steel Mill guys bop along to 'Gonna Make You Sweat (Everybody Dance Now)', a 1990 hit for C & C Music Factory featuring Freedom Williams. This track is also played out over the closing titles. Bart meanwhile dons a Cher wig and sings along to her 'Shoop Shoop Song (It's in His Kiss)', a number one hit in 1991.

Look out for: Smithers' and John's tête-à-tête in the diner. 'So, this is your sick mother.'

Notes: After many years of almost hitting the mark with gay storylines (OK, so we had Waylon confirmed doing the conga on holiday and Karl a possibility in 'Simpson & Delilah'), here comes the most wonderfully camp one, with Homer's spot-on reactions, some delightful stereotypes at the Steel Mill and Bart's blissful innocence of the whole thing. Only *The Simpsons* could do this so tongue-in-cheek that nobody could get in a tizzy about it. Very good indeed.

169

4F14:

'Brother from Another Series'

Written by Ken Keeler   **Directed by** Pete Michels
Also starring: Pamela Hayden
Special guest voices: Marcia Wallace (as Ms Krabappel),
Kelsey Grammer (as Sideshow Bob), David Hyde Pierce
(as Cecil)

Premise: Sideshow Bob is out of jail, a reformed man, working alongside his brother on a massive dam project. Only Bart holds any distrust for the man who has sworn to kill him.

Features: Krusty, Snake, Sideshow Bob, Mayor Quimby, Carl, Smithers, Miss Hoover, Lenny, Ned Flanders, Moe, Barney, Principal Skinner, Groundskeeper Willie, Mr van Houten, Dr Hibbert, Sideshow Mel, Chief Wiggum, Eddie, Lou, Dr Nick, Charlie, Jasper, Milhouse, Ms Krabappel, Cletus, Ralph.

Couch: The sofa and the family are suspended upside down from the ceiling, until they drop to the floor.

Homage: The US hit comedy series *Frasier*, which stars Kelsey Grammer in the title role.

Notes: To get the full benefit of this excellent episode, you need to a) know Sideshow Bob's entire background and b) watch *Frasier*, in which David Hyde Pierce plays Kelsey Grammer's younger brother. The repartee between the two brothers is magnificent – this could almost be an episode of

Frasier, it is so witty and sharp. And yet it still has a good *Simpsons* story with a twist in the tail.

170

4F13:

'My Sister, My Sitter'

Written by Dan Greaney   **Directed by** Jim Reardon
Also starring: Pamela Hayden, Tress MacNeille,
Maggie Roswell

Premise: Lisa is earning herself a good reputation as a reliable babysitter, until she has to look after a vengeful Bart when Marge and Homer visit the new, late-night shopping mall built at the old harbour.

Features: Kent Brockman, Miss Hoover, Rev. Lovejoy, Helen Lovejoy, Jasper, Principal Skinner, Lunchlady Doris, the Flanderses, Chief Wiggum, Ralph, Dr Hibbert, Mayor Quimby, Snake, Herman, Nelson Muntz, Martin Prince, Rainier Wolfcastle, Hans Moleman, Moe, Barney, Smithers, Dr John Frink, Android's Dungeon Guy, Dr Nick, Apu, Ms Krabappel, Lenny, Otto, Sideshow Mel.

Couch: The Simpsons are swept away by a crashing wave and only the television set survives.

Trivia: Lisa reads The Babysitter's Club book #14 – *The Formula Formula*, while Janey is on book #20 – *The President's Baby Is Missing*. Among the shops at Squidport are Turban Outfitters, Just Rainsticks, It's A Wonderful Knife, My 1st Tattoo, Much Ado About Muffins (to eat or not to eat), Crypto Barn, Itchy and Scratchy Store (Poochie Close-Out), Malaria Zone, Bloaters and Planet Hype, a restaurant owned by Rainier Wolfcastle. Dr Hibbert's surgery number is

555-3642, while Dr Nick Riviera, based at 44 Bow Street, is on 555-NICK (We Stitch and Don't Snitch).

Look out for: Homer trapped by the fountain. Maggie high on too much caffeine.

Notes: A clever episode, if a little disjointed – the two stories don't gel as well as normal.

171

4F15:

'Homer vs. the Eighteenth Amendment'

Written by John Swartzwelder   **Directed by** Bob Anderson
Also starring: Pamela Hayden, Tress MacNeille,
Maggie Roswell
Special guest voices: Joe Mantegna (as Don Tony),
Dave Thomas (as Rex Banner)

Premise: After a riotous St Patrick's Day parade in which Bart gets drunk, the town discover that prohibition was never repealed in Springfield. Rex Banner is brought in to replace the ineffectual Chief Wiggum, creating a new wave of speakeasies, masterminded by Homer and Moe.

Features: Carl, Lenny, Moe, Barney, barflies, Grampa, Kent Brockman, Chief Wiggum, Mrs Wiggum, Lou, Eddie, Skinner, Ms Krabappel, Miss Hoover, Groundskeeper Willie, Milhouse, Martin, Nelson, Jimbo, Dolph, Kearney, Sherri and Terri, Lewis, Richard, Ralph, Janey, Rev. Lovejoy, Helen Lovejoy, Ned Flanders, Maude Flanders, Mr van Houten, Mrs van Houten, Dr Hibbert, Sylvia, Quimby, Android's Dungeon Guy, Krusty, Apu, Herman, Cletus, Dr Nick Riviera.

Couch: The Western Simpsons rush in – and the sofa takes off like a wild bucking bronco.

Trivia: Dr Hibbert calls his wife Bernice rather than Sylvia.

Homage: *The Untouchables* (Brian de Palma, 1987) and just about every other prohibition/gangster flick you care to mention.

Notes for Brits: Prohibition was the forbidding of the manufacture of alcohol in America in 1920, brought in under the Eighteenth Amendment to the Constitution. It was repealed in 1933 under the Twenty-first Amendment.

Look out for: Lisa's actions mimicking Marge's when they discover Homer's beer factory in the cellar. The NO ENTRY sign on the cellar door is written in English, Spanish, French, German and Japanese. Everything goes green for the Irish Festival (itself another great *Simpsons* moment of unparalleled xenophobia) including Marge's hair and Lisa's dress.

Notes: A nice episode in which Homer actually devises a clever plan to keep the beer flowing, one which even Marge approves of. We like the catapult, including the rather dark moment as a cat tests it out.

172
4F09:
'Grade School Confidential'

Written by Rachel Pulido   **Directed by** Susie Dietter
Also starring: Pamela Hayden, Tress MacNeille,
Maggie Roswell, Russi Taylor
Special guest voice: Marcia Wallace (as Ms Krabappel)

Premise: After a disastrous party at the Princes', Edna Krabappel and Seymour Skinner find true love at last: with each other. But when Bart finds out, he becomes embroiled in their attempts to keep their clandestine affair secret.

Features: Mr Burns, Smithers, Carl, Lenny, Moe, Barney, Patty, Selma, Grampa, Jasper, Kent Brockman, Chief

Wiggum, Mrs Wiggum, Agnes Skinner, Skinner, Miss Hoover, Groundskeeper Willie, Mr Largo, Otto, Lunchlady Doris, Superintendent Chalmers, Milhouse, Martin, Nelson, Jimbo, Dolph, Kearney, Sherri and Terri, Lewis, Richard, Wendell, Ralph, Janey, Allison, Rev. Lovejoy, Helen Lovejoy, Ned Flanders, Maude Flanders, Mrs van Houten, the Princes, Dr Hibbert, Ruth Powers, Krusty, Sideshow Mel, Bumblebee Man, Sanjay, Herman, Dr Nick Riviera.

Couch: Bubble versions of the family settle on the sofa and then pop.

Trivia: Seymour Skinner is a 44-year-old virgin and Agnes collects pictures of cakes cut out from magazines. She's been doing this since 1941. Edna is used to dining alone: soup for one, salad for one, wine for three!

Look out for: The outrageous closing joke with the champagne cork popping and Edna's response. Possibly the show's most risqué moment ever.

Notes: A delightful episode that finally brings to fruition one of the series' longest running gags: Edna and Seymour's mutual attraction. What is doubly refreshing is that it remains a constant in the subsequent episodes. Awww, bless 'em.

173

4F16:

'The Canine Mutiny'

Written by Ron Hauge   **Directed by** Dominic Polcino
Also starring: Pamela Hayden, Tress MacNeille,
Frank Welker

Premise: When Bart applies for and receives a Money Bank credit card, he goes on a spending spree which includes buying a new, highly well-bred dog, Laddie the Collie. But what of poor Santa's Little Helper? He is given away, until Bart's conscience pricks him.

Features: Mr Burns, Smithers, Moe, Patty, Selma, Kent Brockman, Chief Wiggum, Lou, Eddie, Agnes Skinner, Groundskeeper Willie, Otto, Milhouse, Sherri and Terri, Rev. Lovejoy, Quimby, Android's Dungeon Guy, Don Tony.

Couch: Grampa is asleep on the sofa, which is folded out as a bed. The others fold it back up – him still inside – and sit upon it.

Trivia: At the party in Mr Mitchell's house, the cops get stoned to 'Jammin' ', a 1977 hit for Bob Marley and the Wailers. Marge meanwhile boogies down to the sounds of The Kinks' 'You Really Got Me', coming out of her frying-pan radio some years after its original 1964 release. Amongst the mail to arrive at 742 Evergreen Terrace are the following helpful pamphlets: Gas Your Termites; Freeze Your Termites; Zap Your Termites; Save the Termites. On the form he returns, Bart uses Homer's Social Security number (123–456789 – Homer's birthday is 13 July by the way) and claims he is a Butt Doctor by profession. Using Santa's Little Helper's name, the credit card comes addressed to Santos L. Halper. Once he's rich, Bart's spending spree at the Android's Dungeon includes issues of *Zebra Girl*, *Zillionaire* and *Zoid-zilla*. He's also after *The Radioactive Man Collection* trade paperback. Mr Mitchell lives at 57 Mt. Auburn Street.

Homage: *Lassie Come Home* (Fred M. Wilcox, 1943) and every other tedious family *Lassie* movie and TV spin-off ever since.

Look out for: Santa's Little Helper's attempts to get the mail, Lisa on her pills, and Bart's dream of Santa's Little Helper's fate on the high seas. We also like the visit to Springfield Park, where dogs meet to sniff each other and bark. Laddie the dog, by the way, can herd sheep, use a flushing lavatory, water the flowers, and do CPR. He can also sniff out pot.

Notes: A sweet episode, although similar in nature to 'Dog of Death' (8F17) in tone, as Bart tries to get his old dog back from its new life. The jokes at the blind man's expense are, of course, thoroughly offensive and simply wonderful.

174

4F17:

'The Old Man and the Lisa'

Written by John Swartzwelder   **Directed by** Mark Kirkland
Also starring: Tress MacNeille
Special guest voice: Bret Hart (as himself)

Premise: After Mr Burns loses everything due to bad financial management, he goes to live in the Springfield Retirement Castle and enlists Lisa's help in turning him into an ecology-friendly businessman, so he can rise up once again. Lisa forgets, however, that leopards never really change their spots.

Features: Mr Burns, Smithers, Lenny, Moe, Barney, Grampa, Jasper, Kent Brockman, Skinner, Ms Krabappel, Milhouse, Nelson, Martin, Ralph, Mrs van Houten, Dr Hibbert, Ruth Powers, Krusty, Spotty Boy.

Couch: The Simpsons pop up through holes in the sofa and floor, to be hit by a large hammer, à la a Whack-A-Mole game.

Trivia: Burns' motto for good business is to bypass such weaknesses as family, religion and friendship. Smithers was born in 1954. Burns' biography, started in 'Blood Feud' (7F22), *Will There Ever Be A Rainbow?*, has now been published and Lisa owns a copy. The residents of the Retirement Castle are watching a TV movie called *Colonel Dracula Joins the Navy*, and they later do their aerobics to the rather appropriate sounds of Billy Ray Cyrus' 1992 hit 'Achy,

Breaky Heart'. Oh, and at the Castle, according to Grampa, the residents are not allowed to use the library, read newspapers, nor use either the games room or the activity room. They may, however, stare out of the Staring Window.

Notes for Brits: Bret Hart is one of those flamboyant American wrestler-types who goes by the name The Hitman. Ooh, scary!

Look out for: We love the idea of Smithers, briefly, getting his heart's desire, as Burns moves into his apartment. And keep an eye out for Maggie recognising Burns and holding her fingers up like a gun at him. L'il' Lisa's Animal Slurry has many uses, including a protein-based animal feed, insulation for low-income housing, a high explosive, and a topnotch engine coolant.

Notes: An odd episode with a not-too-unexpected outcome. The best bits are undoubtedly Burns learning his way around a supermarket and Lisa's realisation of what Burns has been up to. 'Oh dear God', she breathes. And who can truly blame her?

175

4F18:

'In Marge We Trust'

Written by Donick Carey **Directed by** Steven Dean Moore
Also starring: Pamela Hayden, Tress MacNeille, Maggie Roswell, Frank Welker, Karen Maruyama (as dancer), Gede Watanable (as factoryman), Denice Kumagai (as dancer)
Special guest voice: Sab Shimono (as Mr Sparkle)

Premise: While Homer is horrified to find his face being used to advertise a Japanese cleaning powder ('a magnet for food stuffs who will banish dirt to the land of wind and ghosts'), Marge calls Rev. Lovejoy's bluff and volunteers to take on his workload at the church, successfully becoming The Listen Lady. Lovejoy, as a result, has a crisis of career.

Features: Lenny, Moe, Barney, Kent Brockman, Chief Wiggum, Mrs Wiggum, Agnes Skinner, Skinner, Ms Krabappel, Miss Hoover, Milhouse, Jimbo, Dolph, Kearney, Rev. Lovejoy, Helen Lovejoy, Ned Flanders, Maude Flanders, Mr van Houten, Mrs van Houten, Captain McCallister, Dr Hibbert, Sylvia, Ruth Powers, Hans Moleman, Sideshow Mel, Dr Nick Riviera.

Couch: A vending machine drops a couch from the ceiling on to Homer.

Trivia: Amongst the attractions at the zoo are Aardvark Paark; Baboon County, USA; Habitat for Huge Manatees; Elephant-Cage and The Emu Experience. Tim seeks guidance from St Lucius, St Eleutherius, St Bartholomew and St Donikus. When Timothy Lovejoy arrived to work in Springfield, Ned Flanders was already there and The Bump was a popular dance craze, so it was around 1974 then. He has a number of noises to awaken his congregation, including a bird, an ambulance siren, and a disco whistle, and his next sermon will be entitled 'The Miracle of Shame'. In fact, he actually gives one called 'Conquest of the County of the Apes'. The Springfield Library does indeed keep phone directories for Hokkaido in Japan, and to call there uses 19 number presses. Springfield Dump has a sign saying NO LITTERING.

Itchy and Scratchy in: 'Deaf Comedy Blam!'

Look out for: Marge listens to a number of local problems. Ned, of course, has to deal with the boys terrorising him in the Leftorium, while Helen worries about Timothy. Less important perhaps are Captain McCallister's lost Nintendo Gameboy, Sideshow Mel's dreams of falling, Skinner and his mother fighting over the television, Moe losing his will to live (his cat also has a problem, but we never find out what), and Lenny having lied to Carl about his marriage. Keep an eye out as well for Snowball II trapped under the floorboards, the Mr Sparkle advertisement with its two-headed cow, and the in-joke of the family believing someone is watching them.

Notes: A rare case of both storylines being worthy of full episodes in their own right, this is a cracking episode which highlights the unduly neglected Rev. Lovejoy and makes you realise Homer isn't the only one ready to kill Ned Flanders! Great stuff.

176
4F19:
'Homer's Enemy'

Written by John Swartzwelder   **Directed by** Jim Reardon
Also starring: Pamela Hayden, Russi Taylor, Frank Welker

Premise: A new worker, Frank Grimes, arrives at the Plant, and despite Homer being . . . well, Homer, the two fall out. Slowly but surely, Frank goes mad as he tries to convince everyone else that Homer is a menace to society. Bart, meanwhile, buys a run-down factory for a dollar and decides he and Milhouse will run it.

Features: Mr Burns, Smithers, Carl, Lenny, Moe, Barney, Kent Brockman, Chief Wiggum, Mrs Wiggum, Mr Largo, Milhouse, Martin, Ralph, Rev. Lovejoy.

Couch: Bart is flickering like a badly tuned portable TV.

Trivia: Carl and Lenny, as well as Frank Grimes, have Masters Degrees in Nuclear Physics. Homer doesn't. Bart's factory is at 35, Industry Way: dead opposite Moe's bar. Lisa has an IQ of 156 and Homer has photos of himself in space, with the Smashing Pumpkins, and with Gerald Ford. Since he became the Plant's safety inspector, accidents have doubled, meltdowns trebled and, according to Lenny, Homer should have died 316 times.

Look out for: Bart's method of jet propulsion with the fire extinguisher and Ralph building his model of the powerplant from a Malibu Stacy Dream House. Lovely.

Notes: A terrific episode that both highlights why Homer is a walking disaster and yet underscores just why we love him so. Frank is right: how can such a walking disaster area have gone into space or dined with Gerald Ford? Poor Frank! This is one of the series' darkest episodes and ends on a real downer but is nevertheless also one of the wittiest and cleverest in ages.

177
4F20:
'The Simpsons Spin-Off Showcase'

Written by David S. Cohen, Dan Greaney, Steve Tompkins
Directed by Neil Affleck
Also starring: Pamela Hayden, Tress MacNeille
Special guest voices: Phil Hartman (as Troy McClure),
Tim Conway (as himself), Gailard Sartain (as Big Daddy)

Premise: Troy McClure explains that every so often, TV network executives need to take elements from popular shows and spin them off into their own series. Three times this has happened with *The Simpsons*, although none of them has been picked up and gone to a series. As a special treat, here they are.

Features: Smithers, Lenny, Moe, Barney, Selma, Grampa, Jasper, Kent Brockman, Chief Wiggum, Skinner, Groundskeeper Willie, Jimbo, Dolph, Kearney, Ralph, Dr Hibbert, Captain McCallister, Hans Moleman, Judge Snyder.

Trivia: The only shows on Fox's current evening line-up are *The Simpsons*, *The X Files* and *Melrose Place*. Amongst the shows Troy uses to demonstrate the power of spin-offs are *The Ropers* (out of *Man About the House*), *Laverene and Shirley* (one of three spin-offs from *Happy Days*) and *Rhoda* (out of two from *The Mary Tyler Moore Show*). On their variety show, the Simpsons sing a variety of confectionery-themed songs: 'I Want Candy', a 1965 hit for the Tremeloes; 'Peppermint Twist', originally by Joey Dee and the Starliters in 1962. Jasper handles 'Lollipop', the 1958 song by the Chordettes, and Smithers, rather kinkily, goes for Devos' 1980 song 'Whip It', complete with cracking whip!

Homage: *Magnum PI* obviously, as well as sitcoms along the lines of *Mister Ed*, *I Dream of Jeannie* and *Bewitched*. And in their own show, the Simpsons come over very much like the *Partridge Family*. And Grampa singing 'Daisy Bell' comes straight from *2001:A Space Odyssey* (Stanley Kubrick, 1968).

Hi, I'm Troy McClure, you may remember me from: such spin-offs as *Sons of Sanford & Son* and *After Mannix*.

Look out for: There are three spin-offs. *Chief Wiggum PI* sees Springfield's finest moving to bust crime in New Orleans, alongside Skinner, or Skinny Boy, as he's known. The Simpsons guest star. *The Love-Matic Grampa* sees Abe's spirit inhabiting a Love Machine in Moe's bar and thus he helps Moe find true love. Homer guest stars. And *The Simpson Family Smiley-Time Variety Hour*, a big variety show in which Lisa refused to take part and is replaced by a late-teens blonde beauty. Tim Conway guest stars. It also features the Waylon Smithers dancers and the Springfield Baggy Pants Players.

Notes: A very clever spin on the alternates offered by the Treehouse of Horrors run. Each of the spin-offs is very clever in its own way. The canned, and always inappropriate, laughter on *The Love-Matic Grampa* is inspired, the *Partridge Family* spin on The Simpsons family is great and although *Chief Wiggum PI* is the weakest, it still has a few good moments. Also a rarity: there's no couch sequence!

178

4F21:

'The Secret War of Lisa Simpson'

Written by Richard Appel   **Directed by** Mike B. Anderson
Also starring: Pamela Hayden, Tress MacNeille,
Maggie Roswell
Special guest voices: Marcia Wallace (as Ms Krabappel),
Willem Dafoe (as Commandant)

Premise: To try and put an end to Bart's wayward lifestyle, Homer and Marge opt to enrol him in a military school. Delighted to see that the discipline and curriculum at the school are far better than at Springfield Elementary, Lisa signs up as well. However, the other, all-male, students accept Bart but despise Lisa, and the two siblings find themselves on opposite sides of the popularity fence once more.

Features: Grampa, Jasper, Chief Wiggum, Lou, Eddie, Skinner, Miss Hoover, Milhouse, Martin, Nelson, Sherri and Terri, Lewis, Richard, Wendell, Ralph, Janey, Dr Frink.

Couch: The sofa and family are suspended upside down from the ceiling, until they drop to the floor.

Trivia: Rommelwood, the military school, has never had a female student in all 185 years of its existence. Marge ends the audio-cassette letters to Lisa, and on one she sings 'You Are My Sunshine'.

Look out for: The bizarre motto for the camp is 'I'll Die Before I Surrender, Tim'. And we like Maggie putting extra pacifiers in her ears!

Notes: A very dull episode indeed, a waste of Willem Dafoe, and a hackneyed Bart versus Lisa plot that outlives its welcome very early on. The three boys Bart befriends might just as well be Jimbo, Dolph and Kearney, and Rommelwood might just as well be Springfield Elementary. All this proves is that when the chips are down, the younger Simpsons stick together and overcome adversity. But they nearly always do.

Ninth Season

1997–1998
26 Episodes

179
4F22:
'The City of New York vs. Homer Simpson'

Written by Ian Maxtone-Graham
Directed by Jim Reardon
Also starring: Tress MacNeille, Joan Kenley, Michael Dees

Premise: Six months after Barney lost Homer's car in a drunken stupor, it turns up in New York and Homer must fetch it back. However, Homer's previous visit to the Big Apple was hardly inspiring and he's fearful of going back. Marge and the kids, however, see it as a great excuse for a day out shopping and sightseeing.

Features: Carl, Lenny, Moe, Barney, barflies.

Couch: The Family are dressed like the Harlem Globetrotters.

Trivia: The Duffmobile that comes to Moe's arrives to the song 'Oh Yeah', a 1985 single by Swiss popstars Yello. Once drunk, Homer and the others attempt a chorus of 'Macarena', the 1996 hit for Spanish duo Los Del Rio. When Homer was last in New York, the movie houses were showing *The Godfather Part II* and he was hearing Scott Joplin's 'The Entertainer'. Over the credits, a version of 'New York, New York', made popular by Frank Sinatra, is played. The Simpsons go to New York via Atlanta, and Homer appears not to know what a wheelclamp is. Back home, 91 per cent of road traffic accidents in Springfield are caused by Homer, Barney, Lenny, Carl and the two barflies.

Homage: Homer versus the Carriage driver in Central Park has more than a passing resemblance to the chariot race in *Ben-Hur* (William Wyler, 1959).

Look out for: Woody Allen dumping his trash on Homer's head, and Bart's visit to the MAD offices where he sees such luminaries as Alfred E. Neumann, Spy versus Spy, and cartoonist Dave Berg. Amongst the shows on Broadway are Tommy Tune in *Gotta Mince*, *Ernest Goes to Broadway*, Neil Simon's *More About Brooklyn*, and magician David Copperfield's *Astonishing Girlfriend*. They all go to see *Kickin It*, a musical journey through the Betty Ford Center. It stars Liza Minnelli and has a central character very similar to comedian Lenny Bruce. Oh, and Bart mistaking the three old Jewish men for ZZ Top: politically incorrect of course, but this is *The Simpsons*.

Notes: An odd episode because it's set almost entirely away from familiar *Simpsons* territory. It highlights the fears many small towners have about big cities, particularly New York, which has radically changed since Homer's first visit in the seventies and so, while Homer's side of the story shows the inhospitable side of the city, Marge and the kids have a fun day out, proving that New York is actually one of the most pleasant cities in America.

180
4F23:
'The Principal and the Pauper'

Written by Ken Keeler   **Directed by** Steve Moore
Also starring: Tress MacNeille, Maggie Roswell
Special guest voices: Marcia Wallace (as Ms Krabappel),
Martin Sheen (as Seymour Skinner)

Premise: On the day of the town's celebrating Principal Skinner's 20 years at the school, Springfield is rocked by a scandal. Seymour Skinner isn't Seymour Skinner at all: his real name is Armin Tamzarian. He was an orphan street punk from Capitol City who took the real Skinner's identity during Vietnam. As the town begins to adjust to the real Skinner taking over as Principal, the disgraced Tamzarian returns to his old life away from Edna, Agnes and his beloved pupils.

Features: Carl, Lenny, Barney, barflies, Grampa, Jasper, Kent Brockman, Chief Wiggum, Agnes Skinner, Skinner, Miss Hoover, Groundskeeper Willie, Otto, Mr Largo, Superintendent Chalmers, Milhouse, Martin, Nelson, Jimbo, Sherri and Terri, Lewis, Richard, Wendell, Ralph, Janey, Allison, Rev. Lovejoy, Helen Lovejoy, the Flanderses, Mr van Houten, Mrs van Houten, The Hibberts, Ruth Powers, Quimby, Hans Moleman, Apu, Sanjay, Judge Snyder, Rainier Wolfcastle.

Couch: The family are wearing spacesuits, and the couch blasts off.

Trivia: Groundskeeper Willie has also served Springfield Elementary for 20 years. Every Friday night, Agnes and Seymour make cut-out silhouettes. The real Sergeant Skinner was believed killed on a mission and, upon meeting Agnes, when he took Skinner's effects home, Tamzarian decided to take Skinner's place. Agnes has known all along. The real Skinner was in fact a hostage in a shoe factory and only released last week.

Homage: Sort of Mark Twain's book *The Prince and the Pauper*, which lends its title to this. And the war sequences owe everything to just about any movie you can think of which focuses on relationships in war zones, from *Saving Private Ryan* to *Full Metal Jacket* and so on.

Look out for: Bart's version of the 'Pledge of Allegiance' sung to the tune of Toni Basil's sadly unforgettable 1982 hit 'Mickey'.

Notes: One of the series' all-time best episodes, mainly because it shows us a human side, not just of Principal Skinner, but of his hectorish Mom as well. The revelation that she was as much a party to the deception as Tamzarian is delightful, as is Judge Snyder's brief cameo as he legally changes the Principal's name to Seymour Skinner. Martin Sheen steals the show though in a brief but important slice of *Simpsons* history.

181

3G02:

'Lisa's Sax'

Written by Al Jean   **Directed by** Dominic Polcino
Also starring: Pamela Hayden, Maggie Roswell, Doris Grau
Special guest voice: Fyvush Finkel (as Krusty the Klown)

Premise: After an argument between Bart and Lisa destroys the girl's beloved saxophone, Marge and Homer settle down to explain to her how it came about that she has one. Of course, there's a great deal of extraneous information to impart alongside this.

Features: Moe, Barney, Patty, Selma, Grampa, Skinner, Groundskeeper Willie, Lunchlady Doris, Milhouse, Nelson, Jimbo, Sherri and Terri, Lewis, Richard, Wendell, Ned Flanders, Todd, Rod, Dr Hibbert, Hans Moleman, Apu.

Couch: The family pop out from Homer like Russian dolls.

Trivia: In the TV movie *The Krusty the Klown Story*, he is married to Mia Farrow – shades of unsubtle digs at Woody Allen, one suspects. Lisa plays Gerry Rafferty's 1978 hit 'Baker Street' on her sax, which is bought from King Toots. In the flashbacks to 1990, Homer is watching *Twin Peaks*, David Lynch's surreal TV show – although no such scene involving the Giant dancing with the White Horse ever actually occurred. Bart's first day at school moves along to the sounds of Bobby McFerrin's inexplicably popular 1988 novelty hit 'Don't Worry, Be Happy'. Dr Hibbert is dressed like Mr T from the successful TV series *The A Team*. Lisa is almost sent to Miss Tillingham's School for Snotty Girls and Mamas' Boys. When younger, Milhouse drank soya milk as he had an allergy to the pasteurised stuff. He will also grow up, according to the school psychologist, to be gay.

Notes for Brits: '*The Simpsons* is recorded in front of a live studio audience': a common phrase that preceded many US sitcoms of the seventies and eighties. It was an attempt to move away from the canned laughter track previously used. Here it is, of course, used ironically. There is no laughter track at all. Which might have been quite fun for once.

Look out for: Willie's sign: ACH! KEEP OFF THE GRASS at school. Bart being read *Curious George and the Ebola Virus*, a pastiche of the popular books by H. A. Rey. Homer dreaming firstly of Lisa winning a Nobel prize for kickboxing and later of playing foozball with Michelangelo's *David* and Munch's *Scream*. Homer also dreams of Patty and Selma melting, which he rather enjoys. Best gag of all has to be the comment about good parenting, followed by Maggie wandering around with a power drill.

Notes: A terrific episode, full of amusing self-referential wit (in 1990, Tracey Ullman was singing, entertaining and using crudely drawn filler-material on her TV show apparently) and it is especially nice to finally discover what it was that caused Bart to go down the path to the darkside.

182
5F02:
'Treehouse of Horror VIII'

Written by Mike Scully, David S. Cohen, Ned Goldreger
Directed by Mark Kirkland

Also starring: Pamela Hayden, Tress MacNeille, Maggie Roswell
Special guest voice: Marcia Wallace (as Ms Krabappel)

Premise: *The Homega Man* in which Homer thinks he's the last man left alive after a nuclear explosion, until he meets the Brotherhood. *Fly Versus Fly* sees Bart and a fly swap body parts. *Easy Bake Coven* is set during the Salem Witch Trials, and sees the Bouvier family terrorising the neighbourhood.

Features: Kang, Kodos, Mr Burns, Carl, Lenny, Moe, Patty, Selma, Kent Brockman, Chief Wiggum, Mrs Wiggum, Lou, Eddie, Agnes Skinner, Skinner, Miss Hoover, Groundskeeper Willie, Otto, Superintendent Chalmers, Ralph, Nelson, Rev. Lovejoy, Helen Lovejoy, Ned Flanders, Maude Flanders, Mr van Houten, Mrs van Houten, Dr Hibbert, Quimby, Captain McCallister, Dr Frink, Android's Dungeon Guy, Sideshow Mel, Herman.

Couch: The family are electrocuted à la Death Row.

Trivia: After the nuclear war, Homer dances outside the church (he's put HOMER ROCKS on the sign) to Edwin Starr's 1970 hit, 'War'.

Homage: *The Omega Man* (Boris Sagal, 1970) is the basis for the first story. The second is obviously *The Fly* (Kurt Neumann, 1958) and the third is Arthur Miller's play *The Crucible* and its various filmic incarnations and variations on that theme.

Look out for: Homer not getting any of Gary Larson's *Far Side* cartoons, his planning to pee in one transmat booth, having positioned the other by the loo and, best of all, the opening scene. In this, a Fox Network censor tries to explain why *The Simpsons* needs a 'G' rating but is then repeatedly stabbed until we get a '21' rating.

Notes: After a couple of iffy 'Treehouses' recently, this season's offering is the best in a long while, with all three

233

stories of top-drawer quality, and even a cameo by everyone's favourite Rigellians!

183

5F01:

'The Cartridge Family'

Written by John Swartzwelder   **Directed by** Pete Michels
Also starring: Pamela Hayden, Tress MacNeille

Premise: After post-soccer violence sets the streets of Springfield ablaze, Homer joins the NRA and arms himself. Marge, on the other hand, hates the idea of a gun in the family and eventually takes the kids and leaves until Homer can make himself part with his pistol.

Features: Mr Burns, Smithers, Carl, Lenny, Moe, Barney, barflies, Selma, Patty, Kent Brockman, Chief Wiggum, Lou, Eddie, Agnes Skinner, Skinner, Groundskeeper Willie, Otto, Superintendent Chalmers, Milhouse, Nelson, Jimbo, Dolph, Kearney, Snake, Rev. Lovejoy, Helen Lovejoy, Ned Flanders, Ruth Powers, Mr van Houten, Dr Hibbert, Quimby, Don Tony, Bumblebee Man, Krusty, Sideshow Mel, Apu, Sanjay, Spotty Boy, Herman, Cletus, Rainier Wolfcastle, Dr Nick Riviera.

Couch: The family run in, bums on fire, and douse themselves on the waterlogged couch.

Trivia: Patty and Selma still live at 1599 Spinster City Apartments. At the Springfield Stadium, on the night of the soccer (Mexico versus Portugal, by the way, with a welcome from football legend Pele), is advance notice that tomorrow it is the 'Monsters of Poetry' night. Ex-Con Security's logo is FROM THE BIG HOUSE TO YOUR HOUSE. At the NRA meeting is a notice to COME IN AND SHOOT YOUR MOUTH OFF. Homer believes NRA stands for Nachos, Rifles and Alcohol.

Homage: The title, but nothing else, is swiped from the seventies TV series *The Partridge Family*.

Notes for Brits: The National Rifle Authority is a very powerful lobby in America, determined to uphold the constitutional right for citizens to bear arms. Having no such law in Britain, many of us may well sympathise with Lisa's comment that the ideology is about 200 years out of date. Despite the tragedies of recent years, no US administration seems likely to take the risk of repealing such a law. Yet.

Look out for: Willie and his Scottish pals knowing how to start a good fight, Homer's temptation to shoot everything from a Target stores truck, Patty and Selma, and even Ned Flanders. Marge, when holding the pistol, suddenly understands the attraction, to the strains of Laurie Johnson's magnificent theme to the sixties TV show *The Avengers*.

Notes: One of the most politically unambiguous episodes ever: it's very clear which side of the argument the creators of *The Simpsons* come down on in the gun debate. Sadly the episode itself is very dull and the plot isn't sustainable, but it does offer up the gem of Lisa reminding Homer that Maggie shot Mr Burns. Homer thought Smithers did it, which, Lisa acknowledges, makes more sense.

184
5F03:
'Bart Star'

Written by Donick Carey **Directed by** Dominic Polcino
Also starring: Pamela Hayden, Tress MacNeille,
Maggie Roswell, Russi Taylor
Special guest voices: Roy Firestone (as himself), Joe
Namath (as himself), Mike Judge (as Hank Hill)

Premise: After Ned Flanders coaches the local kids' football team to victory after victory, a jealous Homer takes over, putting Bart as the star player. Not only is this something Bart doesn't want, but also, by replacing Nelson Muntz with Bart, the team hasn't a hope.

Features: Mr Burns, Smithers, Carl, Lenny, Patty, Selma, Grampa, Jasper, Kent Brockman, Chief Wiggum, Mrs Wiggum, Miss Hoover, Groundskeeper Willie, Otto, Milhouse, Martin, Nelson, Sherri and Terri, Lewis, Richard, Wendell, Uter, Janey, Allison, Helen Lovejoy, the Flanderses, Mr van Houten, Mrs van Houten, Ruth Powers, Dr Hibbert, Quimby, Bumblebee Man, Troy McClure, Rainier Wolfcastle, Krusty, Sideshow Mel, Apu, Sanjay, Dr Nick Riviera.

Couch: The Simpsons are caught in a car-crusher.

Trivia: The Free Health Fair welcomes cheapskates and Dr Nick has a booth helping you identify what sex you are. Homer meanwhile has made up Skittle-Brau, a lager with candy in it.

Notes for Brits: This one is about American Football. Apparently it has some rules, but what exactly they are is anyone's guess.

Look out for: Bart quoting the Thing from the Marvel Comics series, *The Fantastic Four*: 'It's Clobberin' Time', while Lisa has a sudden loss of interest in joining the team when they welcome her rather than stop her, as a great twist. There's a nice cameo from the *King of the Hill* cartoon series cast, and we particularly like the idea that Homer was once a classy gymnast until Grampa ruined his confidence. Homer, during the credits, kicking everyone off the team, including the Gracie Film's 'Shush' lady.

Notes: A fun episode, where you root for Bart – and, unusually, Nelson – all the way through. Homer is just too stupid for words, but that's excusable because we finally see Ned Flanders lose it, big time!

185
5F04:
'The Two Mrs Nahasapeemapetilons'

Written by Richard Appel
Directed by Steven Dean Moore
Also starring: Tress MacNeille, Maggie Roswell
Special guest voices: Marcia Wallace (as Ms Krabappel),
Andrea Martin (as Apu's Mom), Jan Hooks (as Manjula)

Premise: Apu realises that his arranged marriage is about to take place, but he's not met the bride-to-be in years and decides (prompted by Homer) that the only way to avoid this is to tell his mother in India that he's already married. Trouble is, Mom comes over to meet her daughter-in-law who we know better as Marge Simpson.

Features: Mr Burns, Smithers, Carl, Lenny, Moe, Barney, barflies, Patty, Selma, Grampa, Jasper, Kent Brockman, Chief Wiggum, Mrs Wiggum, Skinner, Miss Hoover, Otto, Milhouse, Rev. Lovejoy, Helen Lovejoy, Ned Flanders, Maude Flanders, Mr van Houten, Mrs van Houten, Ruth Powers, Dr Frink, Hans Moleman, Krusty, Sideshow Mel, Captain McCallister, Apu, Sanjay.

Couch: Bart uses a spraycan to graffiti the family on to the couch.

Trivia: No bids for Barney or the other men at the charity auction, but Apu is bought for $926. Kirk van Houten hopes Luanne van Houten has enough money left to pay her alimony! Manjula was betrothed to Apu in exchange for ten goats, an electric fan and a textile factory. While enjoying his bachelorhood, Apu sings 'Hot Blooded', a 1978 hit for Foreigner, while at the wedding, an Indian version of the Carpenters' 1970 song '(They Long to Be) Close to You' can be heard.

Notes for Brits: Gunter and Ernst (minus their trademark white tiger here) are two American equivalents of the Gladiators.

Notes: A good fun episode, introducing Manjula and giving a delightful guest turn to Andrea Martin as Apus' tetchy mother. How amusing to note that it's Kirk who needs money from Luanne after their divorce!

186

5F05:

'Lisa the Skeptic'

Written by David S. Cohen   **Directed by** Neil Affleck
Also starring: Pamela Hayden, Tress MacNeille,
Maggie Roswell, Russi Taylor
Special guest voices: Marcia Wallace (as Ms Krabappel),
Phil Hartman (as Lionel Hutz), Stephen Jay Gould
(as himself)

Premise: During a school archaeological dig, Lisa finds the skeleton of an angel on the site where a new shopping mall is to be erected. Homer takes it home and, while the experts argue its validity, and the clerics its divinity, charges people to come and see it. Which is fine, until one day the angel flies away.

Features: Mr Burns, Smithers, Carl, Lenny, Moe, Barney, Patty, Selma, Grampa, Jasper, Kent Brockman, Chief Wiggum, Mrs Wiggum, Lou, Eddie, Agnes Skinner, Skinner, Miss Hoover, Groundskeeper Willie, Otto, Superintendent Chalmers, Milhouse, Martin, Nelson, Jimbo, Dolph, Kearney, Sherri and Terri, Lewis, Richard, Wendell, Ralph, Uter, Snake, Rev. Lovejoy, Helen Lovejoy, the Flanderses, Mr van Houten, Mrs van Houten, Dr Hibbert, Sylvia, Quimby, Bumblebee Guy, Dr Frink, Android's Dungeon Guy, Krusty, Sideshow Mel, Apu, Manjula, Sanjay, Herman, Cletus, Judge Snyder.

Couch: The family can't get near the couch because it's now part of an occupied male sauna.

Trivia: Homer sings a pastiche of 'Up, Up and Away', the 1966 hit for the Johnny Mann Singers, substituting balloon with motorboat. He watches *Springfield's Dumbest Criminals* on TV.

Look out for: Smithers, believing the world is to end, finally letting go and giving Mr Burns a snog. Much good may it do him.

Notes: A brilliant spin on crowd hysteria and its manipulation by big businesses, or as it is here, the building contractors. Lisa's firm belief that angels don't exist and the whole thing is a scam is borne out, but nevertheless, there is a lovely moment where even she begins to question her own convictions. A good episode for both her and her relationship with Marge.

187

5F06:

'Reality Bites'

Written by Dan Greaney　　**Directed by** Swinton Scott
Also starring: Pamela Hayden, Tress MacNeille,
Maggie Roswell
Special guest voice: Phil Hartman (as Lionel Hutz)

Premise: Marge takes a job with Lionel Hutz's Red Blazer Reality, an estate agency, but finds her morals on shaky ground when she has to sell properties to friends that aren't up to scratch. Despite that, she still manages to convince the Flanderses to move to the quaintly named Murder House.

Features: Carl, Lenny, Moe, Barney, Jasper, Kent Brockman, Chief Wiggum, Skinner, Ms Krabappel, Kearney, Jimbo, Snake, the Flanderses, Helen Lovejoy, Mrs van Houten,

Dr Hibbert, Sylvia, Captain McCallister, Hans Moleman, Sideshow Mel, Apu.

Couch: A human hand spins the picture, leaving everything a blur of colour.

And introducing: Gil.

Trivia: Lenny likes azaleas, and we learn for the first time that Sideshow Mel's wife is called Barbara. Ned moves from number 744 Evergreen Terrace in a van rented from U-Break-It, while Lionel Hutz's motto is 'You'll Never Go Nuts with Lionel's Huts'. Best sign is outside the Real Estate Test room: $75 OR BEST OFFER. Skinner's childhood sweetheart was Debbie-Sue, who died in a car crash. According to Wiggum, a 318 is the offence of waking a police officer.

Homage: Rod Flanders talks via his finger in the Murder House, in the same way as Jack Nicholson's red rum growling son does in *The Shining* (Stanley Kubrick, 1980).

Look out for: A brief cameo from George Bush. Snake setting a trap with Acme Piano Wire (a nod to the Warner Brothers' Roadrunner cartoons) and Kirk van Houten loses his arm in the trap, although it has been surgically replaced later. Ned Flanders screams like a girl (still, what can you expect?) and keep an eye out for the dove on his cheque.

Notes: A simple but enjoyable romp, with the final few minutes in the Murder House particularly funny. Best thing though is the introduction of the hapless Gil, destined to always be a ray of light in any episode!

188

5F07:

'Miracle on Evergreen Terrace'

Written by Ron Hauge   **Directed by** Bob Anderson

Also starring: Pamela Hayden, Tress MacNeille, Maggie Roswell
Special guest voice: Alex Trebek (as himself)

Premise: After Bart burns the Christmas tree and all their presents down, the rest of the family believe his story that it was all stolen. Kent Brockman interviews them, leading to the whole community rallying around and, ultimately, the Simpsons become rich. Trouble is, when the truth is revealed, their neighbours want their money back.

Features: Mr Burns, Smithers, Carl, Lenny, Moe, Barney, Grampa, Jasper, Kent Brockman, Chief Wiggum, Lou, Eddie, Agnes Skinner, Skinner, Ms Krabappel, Miss Hoover, Groundskeeper Willie, Otto, Superintendent Chalmers, Milhouse, Jimbo, Sherri and Terri, Ralph, Rev. Lovejoy, Helen Lovejoy, the Flanderses, Mr van Houten, Dr Hibbert, Sylvia, Quimby, Hans Moleman, Android's Dungeon Guy, Krusty, Sideshow Mel, Apu, Captain McCallister.

Couch: The couch is inside a snowglobe that then gets shaken.

Trivia: Selma gives Bart cash for Christmas, while he gets an Inferno Buster 3000 from his parents, which is what starts the fire. Lisa is unsurprised to be getting a yellow sweater.

Homage: The title owes much to *Miracle on 34th Street* (George Seaton, 1947) but not the plot. The two orphans could have walked straight out of *Annie* (John Houston, 1982).

Notes for Brits: Alex Trebek hosts the gameshow *Jeopardy*.

Look out for: Homer's attempts to justify parking in the disabled parking space, Lisa strangling Bart with a cry of 'Why you little . . .' and Marge somehow managing to lose $5200 on *Jeopardy*. Oh, and after all these years, Homer thinks his neighbour is called Ted! Bless him.

Notes: A deliberately mawkish Christmas episode that is low on good jokes (although the Simpsons watching their own fire on TV is a good start) and a retread of any number of episodes where Bart does wrong, feels guilty and eventually has to fess up. The only real ray of sunshine is the closing moments when the neighbours get their revenge but the Simpsons find the family spirit after all.

189

5F24:

'All Singing, All Dancing'

Written by Steve O'Donnell   **Directed by** Mark Ervin

Premise: Told entirely in verse, this is yet another clips show, linked by Snake's attempts to rob the Simpsons, but put off by their singing. Needless to say, all the clips feature songs.

Features: Snake.

Couch: The floor is a conveyor belt and Homer trips and falls under the couch, repeatedly trying to get up but sucked under.

Trivia: The family ask Homer to hire either *Waiting to Exhale* (Deborah Schindler, 1995) or *Emma* (Douglas MacGrath, 1996) but he rents *Paint Your Wagon* (Joshua Logan, 1969), assuming it's a traditional Clint Eastwood Western. Of course, it isn't, but it does make Lisa realise that she finds Lee Marvin singing 'dreamy'.

Look out for: A good selection of clips, actually, from 'Homer's Barbershop Quartet', 'Bart After Dark', 'Boy Scoutz 'n the Hood', 'Homer and Apu', 'Krusty Gets Cancelled', 'Two Dozen and One Greyhounds', 'Marge versus the Monorail', 'Bart Sells his Soul' and 'Homer the Great'.

Song: Not a song as such, but the last word goes to the family singing 'There is something worse, and it really does blow, when a long-running series, does another clip show.' Indeed.

Notes: For a clips show (the fourth, as they point out via a strategically placed banner in the living room), it's not bad, and it's always a pleasure to hear Mr Burns sing his song from 'Two Dozen and One Greyhounds'. The only one missing really is Dr Zaius from 'A Fish Called Selma'. We like Snake's attempts to stop the theme tune over the closing credits, too.

190
5F08:
'Bart Carny'

Written by John Swartzwelder **Directed by** Mark Kirkland
Also starring: Pamela Hayden, Tress MacNeille
Special guest voice: Jim Varney (as Cooder)

Premise: After trying their hand at the carny lifestyle, Homer and Bart lose their new friend Cooder's business. To make amends, they allow Cooder and his son, Spud, to stay for a while, but then find them very hard to get rid of.

Features: Moe, Chief Wiggum, Lou, Eddie, Agnes Skinner, Skinner, Nelson, Snake, Ned Flanders, the Princes, Android's Dungeon Guy, Krusty.

Couch: As the family sit, Nelson Muntz pulls the couch away from beneath them. Ha-Ha!

Look out for: Some of Colonel Tex's attractions at the fairground, particularly Humphrey the Talking Camel and the Tooth Chipper, a creaky rollercoaster. Spud is double-jointed throughout his body, which is really rather gross!

Notes: One of the most dismally unfunny episodes ever, lifted only by the brief appearance of a talking camel and Homer's clever way of getting Cooder and Spud out of his home. Whereas most of the series's politically incorrect moments are funny and well-observed, this episode seems to be saying that fairground folk and travellers really are deeply unpleasant criminals who are both irredeemable and unworthy of help. Nasty-taste-in-the-mouth time.

191

5F23:

'The Joy of Sect'

Written by Steve O'Donnell
Directed by Steven Dean Moore
Also starring: Pamela Hayden, Tress MacNeille
Special guest voice: Marcia Wallace (as Ms Krabappel)

Premise: A new cult has established itself in Springfield, the Movementarians, whose unseen master promises them all a better life on the distant planet Blisstonia. One by one, Springfield's residents join in, until only one woman can expose them.

Features: Mr Burns, Smithers, Carl, Lenny, Moe, Barney, Jasper, Kent Brockman, Agnes Skinner, Skinner, Miss Hoover, Groundskeeper Willie, Otto, Jimbo, Dolph, Kearney, Rev. Lovejoy, Helen Lovejoy, the Flanderses, Mr van Houten, Mrs van Houten, Ruth Powers, Hans Moleman, Android's Dungeon Guy, Krusty, Sideshow Mel, Apu, Manjula, Spotty Boy, Dr Frink, Cletus, Gerald the Baby, Dr Nick Riviera.

Couch: The Simpsons are tiny and clamber on to the couch, but Santa's Little Helper eats Homer.

Trivia: Homer goes fishing and sings about the sport to Nelson Riddle's theme to the sixties *Batman* TV show. Mr Burns only pays $3 tax per year. When Marge makes her bid for freedom, she is pursued by a Rover from the cult sixties TV series *The Prisoner*; they use Ron Grainer's excellent theme as well.

Look out for: Mr Burns' attempts to make himself popular, particularly his Michael Jacksonesque statues, and his intention to use the trademarks from both Kellogg's Special K breakfast cereal and also Disneyland's Mickey Mouse ears. We also like the robotic Barney the Dinosaur and the idea that Timothy Lovejoy would torch his church for the insurance money. But the best joke of the episode is that while Bart owns a L'il Bastard General Mischief Kit which he plans to use to effect an escape from the Movementarians, they in turn get him with their L'il Bastard Brainwashing Kit. Great!

Notes: An odd one this, with lots of good moments. It's a nice twist to see Burns determined to be loved, but another one where the central joke isn't strong enough to last the whole episode.

192
5F11:
'Das Bus'

Written by David S. Cohen   **Directed by** Pete Michel
Also starring: Pamela Hayden, Tress MacNeille, Russi Taylor
Special guest voices: Phil Hartman (as Troy McClure),
Jack Ong (as Fisherman), James Earl Jones (uncredited as the Narrator and God)

Premise: While Homer decides to set up his own Internet company, the kids at school go on a field trip with Otto. But the bus crashes into the sea and they are swept away to a desert island where they must fight to stay alive.

Features: Kent Brockman, Chief Wiggum, Mrs Wiggum, Skinner, Otto, Milhouse, Martin, Nelson, Sherri and Terri, Lewis, Wendell, Ralph, Ned Flanders, Android's Dungeon Guy.

Couch: The Simpsons are frogs, with Maggie as a tadpole.

Trivia: Ned and Maude's company is called Flancrest and they sell rugs over the Net. Amongst the names Homer thinks up for his company are CutCo, EdgeCom and InterSlice but at Marge's suggestion he ends up with CompuGlobal-HyperMegaNet. The Android's Dungeon Guy is downloading naked images of Kate Mulgrew from *Star Trek:Voyager* when Homer's advert interrupts him.

Homage: The title comes from *Das Boot* (Wolfgang Peterson, 1981) but, bar the few watery scenes, has little else to do with it. However, the main crux of the adventure on the island is taken from *Lord of the Flies* (Peter Brook, 1963).

Hi, I'm Troy McClure, you may remember me from: such biblical epics as *David versus Super-Goliath* and *Suddenly Last Supper*. He also stars in an untitled version of *Noah's Ark*.

Mmmmm: . . . memo.

Look out for: Homer naming God as his favourite fictional character and a bizarre appearance from Bill Gates of Microsoft fame. The portrayal herein must surely be libellous, or else Bill Gates has a very good, self-deprecating sense of humour!

Notes: A fantastic episode. Ignore the Internet business side, and wallow in the cleverness of the kids trapped on the island. Bart has never been cleverer, Nelson more menacing, and Milhouse more geekish. Great stuff with a delightful ending that is so witty and obvious, that it's annoying you never imagined they'd get away with it.

193
5F10:
'The Last Temptation of Krust'

Written by Donick Carey   **Directed by** Mike B. Anderson
Also starring: Pamela Hayden, Tress MacNeille,
Maggie Roswell
Special guest voices: Marcia Wallace (as Ms Krabappel),
Hank Williams Jnr (as himself), Jay Leno (as himself),
Steven Wright (as himself), Janeane Garofalo (as herself),
Bruce Baum (as himself), Bobcat Goldthwait (as himself)

Premise: Realising that his comedy days may soon be over, Krusty attempts to reinvent himself as an alternative comedian on the club circuit. But just as he triumphs, he faces his greatest temptation: integrity or selling out in exchange for a new car.

Features: Carl, Lenny, Moe, Barney, barflies, Kent Brockman, Chief Wiggum, Agnes Skinner, Skinner, Ms Krabappel, Miss Hoover, Otto, Superintendent Chalmers, Todd, Rod, Mr van Houten, Dr Hibbert, Sylvia, Hans Moleman, Android's Dungeon Guy, Krusty, Sideshow Mel, Apu, Manjula, Gil, Herman.

Couch: The family run in, bums on fire, and douse themselves on the waterlogged couch.

Trivia: The theme for the Canyonero – sung by Hank Williams Jnr – sounds incredibly like that for the sixties TV series *Rawhide*. Krusty is based in Krustylu Studios (a swipe at the Desilu studios set up by Lucille Ball and her husband Desi Arnaz Jnr, where the original *Star Trek* series was filmed). Moe calls his comedy club Brew Ha-Ha, there's a coffee shop called Java the Hut, and a pet shop called All Creatures Great and Cheap. Krusty's drinking binge takes him to The Gutter Room, Blottos, and The Bloated Liver: all this despite Spencer Tracy once dubbing him 'The Most Promising Newcomer of 1959'.

Notes for Brits: They're all comedians, bar Jay Leno, who's a chat show host as well.

Look out for: The headlines on the *Springfield Shopper*: DOG KILLS CAT, SELF. And Krusty with a ponytail and black sweater is soooo cool!

Notes: A good twist on the never-ending Krusty story and, for the most part, you believe he might end up redeemed. Jay Leno turns in a nice cameo but, frankly, the show is stolen by the advert for the Canyonero. Which is, one suspects, rather the point.

194

5F12:

'Dumbbell Indemnity'

Written by Ron Hauge   **Directed by** Dominic Polcino
Also starring: Pamela Hayden, Tress MacNeille
Special guest voices: Marcia Wallace (as Woman in Bar),
Helen Hunt (as Rene)

Premise: Desperate for a life outside his bar, Moe lets Homer take him to a singles' bar where he gets ignored at all turns. But on the way home, they meet Rene, who starts dating Moe. Unfortunately, before long, Moe has maxed out his Players Club credit card and decides to claim the insurance on his car. Trouble is, he relies on Homer to steal and destroy it for him.

Features: Carl, Lenny, Moe, Barney, barflies, Chief Wiggum, Lou, Eddie, Groundskeeper Willie, Otto, Snake, Rainier Wolfcastle, Hans Moleman.

Couch: The Simpsons are caught in a car-crusher.

Trivia: Homer's prison number is 5F124670: note the production number of this episode. Homer watches *Hail to the Chimp* at the drive-in movie. When Moe and Rene date, the soundtrack is 'I'm a Believer', a 1967 hit for The Monkees.

Homage: *Double Indemnity* (Billy Wilder, 1944) is all about an insurance scam, but in that case, it was murder.

Mmmmm: . . . me.

Look out for: The woman who snubs Moe in the bar at the beginning looks curiously like the woman his spin-off double met in 'The Simpson's Spin-Off Showcase' (4F20).

Notes: A case perhaps of life reflecting art as guest star Helen Hunt is now married to Hank Azaria, who is, of course, Moe, which is rather nice as you can't help but feel sad that, by the end of this rather clever and charming episode, Moe has been unlucky in love once more.

195
4F24:
'Lisa, The Simpson'

Written by Ned Goldreyer   **Directed by** Susie Dietter
Also starring: Pamela Hayden, Tress MacNeille,
Maggie Roswell, Russi Taylor
Special guest voice: Phil Hartman (as Troy McClure)

Premise: Lisa has started making mistakes at school and realises, with a little prompting from Grampa, that the Simpsons' gene is kicking in and her brain is going. Before too long she'll be like Homer and Bart. Apu, meanwhile, decides to capitalise on an incident at the Kwik-E-Mart where Jasper tries to place himself into cryogenic suspension.

Features: Carl, Grampa, Jasper, Kent Brockman, Chief Wiggum, Skinner, Ms Krabappel, Miss Hoover, Groundskeeper Willie, Otto, Lunchlady Doris, Milhouse, Martin, Nelson, Jimbo, Dolph, Sherri and Terri, Lewis, Wendell, Ralph, Janey, Helen Lovejoy, Ned Flanders, Todd, Rod, Mr van Houten, Mrs van Houten, Ruth Powers, Dr Hibbert, Apu, Sanjay, Dr Nick Riviera.

Couch: The Simpsons blossom into fruits on a tree.

Trivia: Homer and Bart try to interest Lisa in their current favourite TV show *When Buildings Collapse* (the House of Usher explodes, of course). They also like watching *When Surgery Goes Wrong*. There are a number of Simpson relatives living in the tri-state area. These include Great Uncle Chad (runs an unsuccessful shrimp company); Second Cousin Stanley (shoots birds at airports) and assorted others whose occupations range from getting hit by cars and claiming insurance to impersonating millionaires at parties. On the female side, however, are a surgeon, an architect, and an environmental lawyer.

Hi, I'm Troy McClure, you may remember me from: such medical films as *Alice Doesn't Live Anymore* and *Mommy, What's Wrong with That Man's Face?*

Look out for: The Kwik-E-Mart going through various changes as Frostillicus becomes an attraction. It starts off as the Freak-E-Mart, offering such other delicacies as The Incredible Siamese Hot Dog; The Astonishing Rubber Check from Mysterious Unknown Bank; The Offensive Baseball Cap – Dare You Read It? (for the record it seems to say SHOW ME YOUR TITS). When the freak show is over, Apu and Sanjay open the Nude-E-Mart which does the same – if not better – business. Best bit of the episode is Lisa's dream of becoming an overweight hillbilly with eight kids (one is called Wesley), their father being one Ralph Wiggum. Brrrr.

Notes: A terrific episode, with a good mix of pathos (Lisa's farewell to the Springsonian and her favourite jazz club are inspired) and fun (her Homeresque 'woo-hoo') which comes together to make a refreshing and exciting look at Lisa's life. For us, though, it's the sight of her lying in the hammock with Ralph as her hubby that is the icing on a delightful cake.

196

5F13:

'This Little Wiggy'

Written by Dan Greaney   **Directed by** Neil Affleck
Also starring: Pamela Hayden, Tress MacNeille
Special guest voices: Marcia Wallace (as Ms Krabappel),
Phil Hartman (as Troy McClure)

Premise: Bart becomes friends with Ralph Wiggum, much against his better judgement, until he remembers that Ralph's father not only has files on Homer, but has guns in the house.

Features: Mr Burns, Smithers, Kent Brockman, Chief Wiggum, Skinner, Milhouse, Martin, Nelson, Jimbo, Dolph, Kearney, Sherri and Terri, Lewis, Richard, Wendell, Ralph, the Flanderses, Krusty, Quimby.

Couch: Bart uses a spray can to graffiti the family on to the couch.

Trivia: The boys visit the toy store called J. R. R. Toykin's. The penitentiary looks remarkably like Alcatraz (but then, they probably all do) and the Springfield Knowledgeum is introduced as 'Where science is explained with brightly coloured balls.' Homer watches Ken Wohl playing Inspector Clouseau in *Return of the Pink Panther Returns*. He also records a new answerphone message which is just him humming Van McCoy's 1975 hit 'The Hustle'.

Hi, I'm Troy McClure, you may remember me from: such automated information kiosks as Welcome to Springfield Airport and Where's Nordstrom?

Note for Brits: Nordstrom is a huge chain store of stores; our closest equivalent would be an up-market Marks and Spencer.

Look out for: Ralph explaining that the leprechaun tells him to commit arson. Just when you think he's mad, guess what happens at the end! Outrageously kinky moment of the episode belongs to Waylon Smithers who, after his beloved employer has said 'Smithers! There's a rocket in my pocket!', answers plaintively, 'You're telling me, sir!'

Notes: Marvellous fun as Bart comes to realise there's more to Ralph, or at least his daddy, than he realised. That said, by the time they've seen off Jimbo and the gang at the penitentiary, the two are becoming friends, which is even better. Ralph is, of course, always the star of any episode he's in, this being no exception, his fear of his own night-light being just sublime.

197

3G04:

'Simpson Tide'

Written by Joshua Sternin and Jeffrey Ventimilia
Directed by Milton Grey
Also starring: Pamela Hayden, Michael Carrington
Special guest voices: Bob Denver (as himself), Rod Steiger (as Captain Tennille)

Premise: Homer joins the Navy Reserve and finds himself in charge of a nuclear submarine during a war game. Can he talk his way out of a confrontation with the Russians, the Chinese and some penguins?

Features: Mr Burns, Smithers, Carl, Lenny, Moe, Barney, Grampa, Jasper, Kent Brockman, Skinner, Milhouse, Martin, Nelson, Jimbo, Sherri and Terri, Wendell, Ralph, Janey, Allison, Krusty, Apu.

Couch: The family grow from the ground in a pastiche of the *Rocky and Bullwinkle* title sequence.

Trivia: Amongst the films in Exploitation Cinema are *Blackula* (William Crane, 1972) and its lesser-known cousin *Backenstein*. Lisa reads *Junior Skeptic*, Moe's cat is called Mr Snuggums, and Barney's Mom is also in the Navy Reserve. On board the sub, everyone joins in a chorus of Village People's 1979 hit 'In the Navy' (the group themselves don't seem to survive the sub's dive) and the sub is called the USS *Jebidiah*. The episode plays out with a military band version of the theme.

Homage: The title and the sub come from *Crimson Tide* (Tony Scott, 1995) but not much of the story does. The submarine captain's name is presumably a swipe at the rather unsuccessful American pop duo The Captain and Tennille. The backroom scene at Moe's with Skinner, Krusty and the Asian gangsters is derived from *The Deer Hunter* (Michael Cimino, 1978).

Notes for Brits: *Rocky and Bullwinkle* was an American kids' cartoon series that began in 1959 and was, for its era, quite anarchic; encouraging kids for instance to vandalise the on/off controls on their TVs to ensure they'd still be watching the following week. Ooh, scary stuff!

Mmmmm: . . . donuts.

Look out for: The vast number of Starbucks in Springfield, Homer being unable to pronounce 'nuclear', and the instruction during the war game that they are not allowed to fire upon anyone 'other than Greenpeace'. Very droll.

Notes: A fairly straightforward episode where the biggest laugh comes from Homer being able to talk to penguins and

Bart trying to impress his classmates by doing The Bartman. 'That is so 1991,' comes back Ralph. Indeed.

198

5F14:

'The Trouble With Trillions'

Written by Ian Maxtone-Graham
Directed by Swinton Scott
Also starring: Pamela Hayden, Tress MacNeille, Maggie Roswell
Special guest voices: Marcia Wallace (as Ms Krabappel), Paul Winfield (as Lucius Sweet)

Premise: On New Year's Eve, Ned Flanders is doing his tax returns nice and early. On 15 April, the rest of Springfield is trying to catch the last post. And Homer? He did his last year! When Lisa points out that tax is annual, he tries to get to the Post Office on time, but his parcel comes to the attention of the IRS who pass Homer over to the FBI. They want someone close to Mr Burns to retrieve something he stole from them during the war: the only trillion dollar note in the world.

Features: Mr Burns, Smithers, Carl, Lenny, Moe, Barney, Jasper, Kent Brockman, Chief Wiggum, Skinner, Ms Krabappel, Miss Hoover, Groundskeeper Willie, Otto, Lunchlady Doris, Superintendent Chalmers, Milhouse, Martin, Nelson, Kearney, Snake, Rev. Lovejoy, Helen Lovejoy, the Flanderses, Mr van Houten, Mrs van Houten, Dr Hibbert, Sylvia, Ruth Powers, Quimby, Hans Moleman, Android's Dungeon Guy, Captain McCallister, Krusty, Sideshow Mel, Lionel Hutz, Apu, Manjula, Sanjay, Spotty Boy, Rainier Wolfcastle, Gil, Dr Frink, Dr Nick Riviera.

Couch: The family can't get near the couch because it's now part of an occupied male sauna.

Trivia: The picture over the couch was painted by Marge. In the Cuba portrayed in this episode, not only can you get in if you are there for pleasure, cigar smuggling, or assassinating Castro, but Che Guevara's image is used to promote Duff beer.

Homage: *JFK* (Oliver Stone, 1991) for the scene where the FBI man sidles up to Homer on the park bench.

Notes for Brits: Burns owns a maroon Stutz Bearcat: that's a car.

Look out for: The 'PG' rated FBI film and Ned's proclamation that taxes pay for trees, policemen, sunshine and the people who just don't like working.

Notes: A mediocre episode at best that makes Burns out to be altruistic (which he's not) and very stupid in letting Castro have his money (which he *so* wouldn't). Rather dull and unfunny, although it's nice to see Gil and Lucius Sweet again, albeit both with money troubles.

199

5F15:

'Girly Edition'

Written by Larry Doyle   **Directed by** Mark Kirkland
Also starring: Pamela Hayden, Tress MacNeille, Russi Taylor
Special guest voice: Marcia Wallace (as Ms Krabappel)

Premise: Lisa is made anchor of a new kids' news programme, but it is Bart's charisma that gets noticed and the two start up a battle, both on and off-air, to be the best TV presenter. Homer, meanwhile, decides to adopt a monkey called Mojo, much to Marge's alarm.

Features: Mr Burns, Smithers, Grampa, Jasper, Kent Brockman, Skinner, Groundskeeper Willie, Lunchlady Doris,

Milhouse, Martin, Nelson, Sherri and Terri, Lewis, Richard, Ralph, Janey, Krusty.

Couch: A human hand spins the picture, leaving everything a blur of colour.

Trivia: The place Homer gets Mojo from is called Animal Assistants, and is for disabled people only. A sign on the window reads AS FELT IN BRAILLE WEEKLY. Krusty is also responsible for inflicting upon the world *The Mattel & Mars Bar Quick Energy Chocobot Hour*.

Itchy and Scratchy In: 'The Glass Moan-Agerie' (it's their 5,500th show).

Look out for: The sign on the truck bringing creamed corn to Springfield Elementary that simply says: DANGER CREAMED CORN.

Notes: A great episode, full of more than the normal quota of good jokes, but best of all is Lisa's revenge on Bart, and the mad cat-lady who goes around chucking her cats at people. It's the fact that she keeps cropping up that makes it work so well.

200

5F09:

'Trash of the Titans'

DEDICATED TO THE MEMORY OF
LINDA McCARTNEY

Written by Ian Maxtone-Graham
Directed by Jim Reardon
Also starring: Pamela Hayden, Tress MacNeille,
Russi Taylor, Susie Smith, Paul McGuinness
Special guest voices: Marcia Wallace (as Ms Krabappel),
U2 (as themselves), Steve Martin (as Ray Patterson)

Premise: After insulting the garbage men, Homer finds his rubbish not being collected and sets about challenging the current Sanitation Commissioner to an election. Homer of course wins, and then finds he's blown his annual budget in a month. There's only one thing to do.

Features: Mr Burns, Carl, Lenny, Moe, Barney, Patty, Selma, Jasper, Chief Wiggum, Mrs Wiggum, Agnes Skinner, Miss Hoover, Groundskeeper Willie, Kearney, Ned Flanders, Todd, Rod, Mr van Houten, Ruth Powers, Quimby, Captain McCallister, Sideshow Mel, Apu, Dr Frink, Herman, Cletus.

Couch: The family are in Bart's schoolroom where he has written I WILL NOT MESS WITH THE OPENING TITLES on the blackboard.

Trivia: On Love Day, Marge gives Homer a toy bear, Sir Loves-A-Lot, which is a redress of another Love Day bear, Lord Huggington. U2 sing 'In The Name of Love' at the concert, and Adam Clayton apparently collects spoons. Larry Mullen doesn't actually say anything. Cosingtons the department store have, they proudly proclaim, been over a century without a slogan. Which is their slogan. Oh, and Homer calls Flanders by his first name, which is rather rare. Patty, Selma and Moe are all registered as sex offenders.

Look out for: Loads of good jokes: New York City's garbage is mostly guns and syringes; Bart's clever avoidance of having to empty the garbage and, sickest of all, Mr Bunny's sudden resurrection at his funeral. Brilliant.

Song: Homer sings 'The Garbage Man Can', joined by his fellow garbage men, and Oscar the Grouch from *Sesame Street* joins in.

Notes: Although not a great episode, this one has a series of high points that keep you amused until the end. The song is actually one of the least impressive ones the show has done, simply because it's so like so many others. U2 actually steal the show with their over-the-credits antics on their plane home. Overall, bearing in mind the seriousness of the episode's topic, Linda would probably have approved.

201

5F16:

'King of the Hill'

Written by John Swartzwelder
Directed by Steven Dean Moore
Also starring: Pamela Hayden, Tress MacNeille
Special guest voices: Steven Weber (as Neil),
Brendan Fraser (as Brad)

Premise: As part of an advertising campaign for a new apple-flavoured breakfast bar, PowerSauce, Homer agrees to climb the Murderhorn, Springfield's huge mountain that only Grampa has attempted before.

Features: Mr Burns, Smithers, Moe, Barney, Grampa, Jasper, Chief Wiggum, Lou, Eddie, Miss Hoover, Milhouse, Nelson, Jimbo, Sherri and Terri, Lewis, Ralph, Janey, Rev. Lovejoy, Helen Lovejoy, the Flanderses, Ruth Powers, Rainier Wolfcastle, Dr Hibbert, Don Tony, Android's Dungeon Guy, Apu.

Couch: The couch is inside a snowglobe that then gets shaken.

Trivia: Android's Dungeon Guy is reading *Zebra Girl*, a copy of which he once sold to Bart. Rainier is starring as McBane in another action movie, this one seeing McBane fight off aircraft as he delivers UNICEF parcels to starving children.

Homage: The Murderhorn is clearly inspired by the Matterhorn in the Swiss Alps.

Notes: A quite charming little adventure in which, in an effort to impress Bart, Homer undertakes a dangerous adventure and comes through successfully. It's nice because just for once, to all intents and purposes, Homer actually succeeds in something.

202

5F17:

'Lost Our Lisa'

Written by Brian Scully   **Directed by** Pete Michels
Also starring: Pamela Hayden, Tress MacNeille,
Maggie Roswell
Special guest voice: Marcia Wallace (as Ms Krabappel)

Premise: Lisa wants to visit the last day of an Egyptian exhibition at the Springsonian but her plans are ruined when Bart needs treatment. Lisa opts to get on a bus and go by herself, but ends up on the wrong side of town. Homer tries to rescue her.

Features: Mr Burns, Carl, Lenny, Moe, Barney, Grampa, Jasper, Chief Wiggum, Agnes Skinner, Skinner, Groundskeeper Willie, Superintendent Chalmers, Milhouse, Snake, Dr Hibbert, Android's Dungeon Guy, Cletus.

Couch: As the family sit, Nelson Muntz pulls the couch away from beneath them. Ha-ha!

Trivia: Yukingham Palace is a joke shop where you can get Itching Powder, Heart Attack Powder and Impotence Powder.

Look out for: Homer praying to Superman, the fighting geese, and best of all, Lisa's manipulation of Homer over the phone to ensure she can go on the bus. Her final moments with Homer as they break into the Springsonian are delightful as well.

Notes: A smashing episode, loads of good jokes and clever situations (how come Springfield has a Russian Quarter?) and best of all, Lisa working intelligently. The teaming up of

Father and Daughter has rarely been more enjoyable and lovely. Gives you a warm feeling.

203
5F18
'Natural Born Kissers'

Written by Matt Selman   **Directed by** Klay Hall
Also starring: Pamela Hayden, Tress MacNeille,
Maggie Roswell
Special guest voice: Marcia Wallace (as Ms Krabappel)

Premise: It is Marge and Homer's 11th wedding anniversary but their plans to dine out at the Gilded Truffle are wrecked. Instead, they go away for a weekend and rediscover their primal urges work best under fear of being discovered. They then embark on a series of escapades to almost get caught 'doing it'. Bart and Lisa meanwhile find a new version of the ending of *Casablanca* to show Grampa.

Features: Carl, Lenny, Moe, Grampa, Chief Wiggum, Mrs Wiggum, Agnes Skinner, Skinner, Milhouse, Ralph, Rev. Lovejoy, Helen Lovejoy, the Flanderses, Gil, Sideshow Mel.

Couch: The Simpsons are frogs, with Maggie as a tadpole.

Trivia: The restaurant the Simpsons end up at is Up, Up and Buffet!, a themed restaurant constructed inside an old aircraft. Grampa won the Iron Cross during the war. As well as the version of *Casablanca* (Michael Curtiz, 1942), the old Jewish Guy in the Springfield Retirement Castle – who used to be a film executive – has a rare copy of *It's A Wonderful Life* (Frank Capra, 1946) with a 'killing-spree ending'. And Gil's used car-lot has the slogan OUR PRICES ARE SKY HIGH! The song played over the end credits is 'Rock the Casbah', the 1982 hit by The Clash.

Homage: May not be deliberate, but the sequences where Homer's 'bits' are conveniently covered up seem very similar to those in *Austin Powers: International Man of Mystery* (Jay Roach, 1997).

Look out for: Homer calling his new fridge Cold Faithful, and the dog's reaction to his underwear. We also love Bart's asking whether something is priceless 'like a mother's love or the good kind of priceless?'

Notes: A superb episode which actually makes Marge and Homer's love life seem very real; everyone needs a bit of spice now and again, and they find theirs. The balloon trip is hysterical, and the attempts to explain their behaviour to a very worldly-wise Bart and Lisa are magnificent.

204

5F20:

'Lard of the Dance'

Written by Jane O'Brien   **Directed by** Dominic Polcino
Also starring: Pamela Hayden, Tress MacNeille,
Maggie Roswell, Russi Taylor
Special guest voice: Lisa Kudrow (as Alexis Whitney)

Premise: While Lisa feels put down and shut out by popular new-girl-around-school Alexis, Homer discovers that there's a fortune to be made in lard, without realising that it's already very big business.

Features: Skinner, Miss Hoover, Milhouse, Martin, Nelson, Sherri and Terri, Uter, Lewis, Wendell, Ralph, Janey, Snake, Apu, Spotty Boy.

Couch: As the family sit, Nelson Muntz pulls the couch away from beneath them. Ha-ha!

Trivia: The girls shop at Dingo Junction. Groundskeeper Willie is apparently from Killtown in Scotland and washes with Ajax and Brillo pads. Ouch. Marge sings her own, unique, version of C & C Music Factory's 1990 hit 'Gonna Make You Sweat (Everybody Dance Now)'. Acme Grease later rename themselves Acme Grease and Shovels, just to scupper Homer's plans.

Homage: The title comes from the 'modern' hymn 'Lord of the Dance' (but you knew that). More recently it has become synonymous with Irish dancer Michael Flatley. Alexis, nodding to Lisa Kudrow's more famous role, tells Lisa 'don't be such a Phoebe' (the dippy character Kudrow plays in *Friends*).

Look out for: Visual gems such as Milhouse's lowering of his eyebrows (he's got two lazy eyes, y'know) and Homer's hosepipe wagging like a dog's tail. Also, listen out for Krusty's take on a Speak and Spell machine, and Skinner's bizarre denial that he ever agreed to a school dance.

Notes: The idea of Lisa being unpopular in the light of a new girl in the school hallways is not new (see 'Lisa's Rival') but it is done here with such class. Alexis is very different to Allison, and it is her trendiness that makes her the enemy. Heck, she even has a mobile phone! Again, although Homer looking for new ways to make money from other people's waste isn't new, once more, this is an episode which shows that even he can find interesting ways to do things.

Tenth Season

1998–1999
22 Episodes

205
5F21:
'The Wizard of Evergreen Terrace'

Written by John Swartzwelder
Directed by Mark Kirkland
Also starring: Tress MacNeille, Maggie Roswell
Special guest voice: William Daniels (as Voice of KITT)

Premise: Convinced he is worthless, Homer decides to follow in the footsteps of Thomas Edison and invent something useful. After many attempts, he finally does so – or has someone beaten him to it?

Features: Carl, Lenny, Moe, Barney, Grampa, Kent Brockman, Sherri and Terri, Lewis, Richard, Wendell, Ned Flanders, Dr Frink, Bill and Marty from KBBL.

Couch: The Simpsons find the rest of the cast in their living room watching TV.

Trivia: William Daniels supplied the voice of KITT the talking car on the eighties TV show *Knight Rider*. Bill and Marty use the song 'Oh Yeah', a 1985 single by Swiss popstars Yello, as part of their 'News Flush'. Amongst the T-shirts at the Edison museum is one featuring a lightbulb and the legend 'Screw This'. Just to confuse Simpsons fans who are forever trying to work out where in America Springfield is, the EXIT sign off the freeway directs you to New Jersey, Michigan, Oregon and Texas, none of which are exactly local to each other. Homer invents an electric blanket mobile, Hamburger ear-muffs (Frink has also invented these), and builds an electric hammer, an Everything Is Okay alarm, a double-barrelled make-up gun, and an armchair with flushable commode. Of course, he finally invents the chair with spare legs which is a thoroughly useful invention. There are also flashbacks in this episode to 'Deep Space Homer' (1F13) and 'The Homer They Fall' (4F03) to illustrate Homer's achievements.

Homage: The title is obviously purloined from *The Wizard of Oz* (Victor Fleming, 1939).

Look out for: Homer's dream, where he is being buried as a non-achiever: Lenny is President of the USA, Ned is a vicar, and Homer's mourners include the robot from the sixties TV series *Lost in Space*. Because he feels so wretched after this, Homer eats a bag of flour rather than sugar to punish himself. Homer also reads a pop-up book on Edison's inventions and later runs Edison's ghost down on the freeway.

Notes: A terrific episode, full of wit and sly digs at our expectations of Homer's abilities. The fact that he invents things that other people find useful (and steal the credit for) is both amusing and a little sad. Poor Homer.

206

5F22:

'Bart, The Mother'

Written by David S. Cohen
Directed by Steven Dean Moore
Also starring: Pamela Hayden, Tress MacNeille,
Russi Taylor
Special guest voices: Marcia Wallace (as Ms Krabappel),
Phil Hartman (as Troy McClure)

Premise: When Nelson gets a rifle, Bart thinks it'll be fun to shoot things. Until, that is, he accidentally kills a bird and has to take on the responsibility of rearing its eggs. Of course, nothing is that simple.

Features: Mr Burns, Smithers, Moe, Jasper, Skinner, Milhouse, Nelson, Rev. Lovejoy, Dr Hibbert, Quimby, Apu, Spotty Boy.

Couch: Firemen are using the couch as a net but Homer misses and hits the floor.

Trivia: The Bolivian tree-lizard is responsible for the extinction of the Dodo, the cuckoo, and the ne-ne, and there are fears for the future safety of the titmouse, woodcock and titpecker. Marge was in labour with Bart for 53 hours. Ouch!

Hi, I'm Troy McClure, you may remember me from: such nature films as *Earwigs – Ewwww* and *Man versus Nature – the Road to Victory*.

Mmmmm: . . . loganberry.

Look out for: Gems such as Bart explaining to the eggs about their dad-mother, the repetitive but always funny basement-light joke, and the fact that the Family Fun Center has been featured on *When Disaster Strikes 4*. Oh, and Skinner's various methods of eradicating the lizards: a guillotine, a drill and 'the splatter'.

Notes: Bart's conscience gets the better of him and we see the more sensitive side of his nature (can he be growing up at last? Nah!). We particularly like the moral dilemma at the end, as underlined by Lisa, regarding the eventual culling of the lizards that will need to take place. A good romp, this one, with some nice laughs at Homer's expense.

207
AABF01:
'Treehouse of Horror IX'

Written by Donick Carey and David S. Cohen
Directed by Steven Dean Moore
Also starring: Tress MacNeille
Special guest voices: Ed McMahon (as himself),
Robert Englund (as Freddy Krueger),
Kathie Lee Gifford (as herself), Regis Philbin (as himself),
Jerry Springer (as himself)

Premise: Three stories: 'Hell Toupee', in which Snake's hair attaches itself to Homer to wreak vengeance for his execution; 'The Terror of Tiny Toon', in which Lisa and Bart become embroiled in Itchy and Scratchy's violent world; and 'Starship Poopers', where Lisa's real father returns to Earth after she sprouts tentacles and fangs.

Features: Kang, Kodos, Carl, Lenny, Moe, Barney, Kent Brockman, Chief Wiggum, Lou, Eddie, Miss Hoover, Snake, Mr van Houten, Captain McCallister, Dr Hibbert, Krusty, Apu, Dr Nick Riviera.

Couch: Freddy Krueger and Jason Voorhees wait for the Simpsons – who've died in the garage. 'Hell Toupee' is loosely based on 'The Monkey's Paw', the short story by W. W. Jacobs, as well as *The Hand* (Oliver Stone, 1981). 'Starship Poopers'' title is, obviously, derived from *Starship Troopers* (Paul Verhoeven, 1997).

Trivia: The closing theme bears more than a passing resemblance to shows such as *The Outer Limits* and *The Twilight Zone*. Snake combs Nacho Cheez into his hair. In the Kwik-E-Mart, the NO SMOKING sign is amidst a series of Laramie Cigarette adverts. Homer watches *When Skirts Fall Off*, *Secrets of National Security Revealed* and *The World's Deadliest Executions*, the latter introduced by Ed McMahon.

Nick Riviera is a member of the Back Alley Medical Group. Homer can't spell toolbox (tulebox) and Lisa finds it humiliating to be a character in a cartoon series, particularly one where the police motto is 'Protect and Sever'.

Homage: Freddie Krueger started his slashing spree in *A Nightmare on Elm Street* (Wes Craven, 1984) and starred in all the sequels, of variable quality, and a TV series. Jason Voorhees is from *Friday 13th, Part II* (Steve Miner, 1981) and likewise returned for most of the dodgy sequels and the TV series.

Itchy and Scratchy in: 'Candle in the Wound'.

Look out for: Poochie making a last dramatic bid for fame in Itchy and Scratchy's world and Marge saying she's so f*****g embarrassed when talking to Jerry Springer. Also, we love the idea that the Rigellions consider Earth to be an obscure T-shirt producing planet.

Notes: Another collection of horrors, of varying degrees of wit. The Itchy and Scratchy one is by far the best, and 'Starship Poopers' is only really amusing once the Jerry Springer segment begins.

208
5F19:
'When You Dish Upon a Star'

Written by Richard Appel   **Directed by** Pete Michels
Also starring: Pamela Hayden, Maggie Roswell
Special guest voices: Alec Baldwin (as himself),
Ron Howard (as himself), Kim Basinger (as herself),
Brian Grazer (as himself)

Premise: Homer meets two Hollywood stars on retreat and begins to work for them on the understanding that he keeps their presence in Springfield secret. Of course, he fails.

Features: Smithers, Carl, Lenny, Moe, Barney, Patty, Selma, Chief Wiggum, Skinner, Ms Krabappel, Otto, Milhouse, Wendell, Ralph, Helen Lovejoy, Ned Flanders, Todd, Rod, Mr van Houten, Ruth Powers, Captain McCallister, Android's Dungeon Guy, Krusty, Sideshow Mel, Apu, Cletus, Judge Snyder, Dr Nick Riviera.

Couch: Marge is hanging the family out to dry.

Trivia: Alec Baldwin is allergic to penicillin, and Kim Basinger is obsessed with her Oscar statuettes. Homer dreams of being both Yogi Bear (with Bart as Bobo and Ned as the Ranger) and mentions Magilla Gorilla: both are from series of Hanna-Barbera cartoons. Lake Springfield as formerly Cess Hole 17A. Oh, and in Simpsons-land, the Fox network has been swallowed up by the Disney Corporation!

Homage: *Jurassic Park* (Steven Spielberg, 1993), as the people approach the house and the gin wobbles.

Notes for Brits: The Gersh Agency is a real US actors' agency, with some high-calibre talent on its books.

Look out for: Homer trying to sell *The Terminiser* to Ron Howard, who in turn tries to sell it to Brian Grazer. The boat-hire man telling Homer he can't hire a boat under the influence of alcohol, which Homer takes as a bet. And, best of all, Homer's reason for joining PETA is because he loves animals, to eat.

Notes: Despite three very high-profile guest actors, this episode is really rather dull and uninspired. The only real moment of interest is the car chase at the end, and Kim Basinger's delightfully self-deprecating quips about her constant adoration of her Oscars, Alec Baldwin apparently not having one himself.

209

AABF02:

'D'oh-in' in the Wind'

Written by Donick Carey
Directed by Mark Kirkland and Matthew Nastuk
Also starring: Pamela Hayden, Tress MacNeille,
Maggie Roswell
Special guest voices: George Carlin (as Munchie),
Martin Mull (as Seth)

Premise: Homer meets up with two old friends of his mother, and decides to join them in their hippie lifestyle. They, however, have moved on a bit, and all Homer does is destroy their business and reputation.

Features: Mr Burns, Smithers, Carl, Lenny, Grandma, Grampa, Jasper, Kent Brockman, Chief Wiggum, Lou, Eddie, Skinner, Groundskeeper Willie, Milhouse, Lewis, Ned Flanders, Maude Flanders, Dr Hibbert, Krusty.

Couch: A bar comes down over the couch, locking the family in like a fairground-ride seat.

Trivia: Chief Wiggum's night-sticks have two settings, twirl and whap. There are a number of sixties references in this episode. Musically, there is stuff from the musical *Hair*, 'Incense and Peppermints', a 1967 song by Strawberry Alarm Clock, 'Time of the Season', a 1968 single by the Zombies, and Jefferson Airplane's 1967 tune 'White Rabbit'. At Woodstock, Jimi Hendrix plays his version of 'The Star Spangled Banner', and there is a dog named after Moray Ginsberg. Other guests around include Jill St John, Bob Hope and Phyllis Diller. There is also some imagery borrowed from Pink Floyd's promo video for their 1979 single 'Another Brick in the Wall (Part Two)', as well as items that tend to be dotted around the psychedelic posters of the Grateful Dead. Bringing us up to date, Billy Joel's 1983 hit 'Uptown Girl' gets an airing as well. And we finally find out what the J. in Homer J. Simpson stands for: it's Jay.

Notes for Brits: Dean Rush was the US Secretary for State during the sixties. The famous US brand of ice cream, Ben & Jerry's, was made by a couple of ex-hippies, similar to Munchie and Seth, whose company is called Groovy Groove Juice, the ice cream division being Seth & Munchie's Garden Blast. Mr Burns' film is an Allan Smithee Production: Allan Smithee is a well-used pseudonym in America by writers or directors who want their names taken off a film if they feel the studio has damaged their artistic integrity.

Look out for: The two Homers talking and Yo La Tengo's closing sitar-driven rendition of the theme.

Notes: A dreadful episode that, apart from proving that Grandma Simpson married Abe when she was much younger than him, is notable only for the revelation about Homer's name. Yeah, there are lots of good excuses for sixties psychedelia, and a chance to take pot-shots at the hypocrisy of former hippies being corporate magnates now, but it's all done humourlessly.

210

AABF03:

'Lisa Gets an "A" '

Written by Ian Maxtone-Graham
Directed by Bob Anderson
Also starring: Pamela Hayden, Tress MacNeille, Maggie Roswell, Russi Taylor, Karl Weidergott
Special guest voice: Marcia Wallace (as Ms Krabappel)

Premise: After throwing a few sickies to play Bart's Play-Station, Lisa misses revising for a test on *The Wind in the Willows*. Against her better judgement, she enlists Bart and

Nelson's aid in cheating and wins an A+++, which means the school's success rating is up and it is eligible for a cash reward. But can Lisa stop her conscience forcing her to tell the truth and denying the school its new computers? Homer meanwhile has decided to befriend Mr Pinchy, a lobster.

Features: Carl, Lenny, Moe, Barney, Jasper, Kent Brockman, Chief Wiggum, Mrs Wiggum, Skinner, Miss Hoover, Groundskeeper Willie, Otto, Superintendent Chalmers, Nelson, Ralph, Janey, Allison, Rev. Lovejoy, Helen Lovejoy, Mr van Houten, Mrs van Houten, the Princes, Dr Hibbert, Sylvia, Quimby, Captain McCallister, Gil, Spotty Boy.

Couch: The family have hair transplants: Homer has Maggie's, Marge Bart's, Bart Lisa's, Lisa Homer's and Maggie has Marge's.

Trivia: Luanne van Houten brings Pyro – the Gladiator she's having a relationship with – to the presentation at the end, much to Kirk's annoyance. Lisa plays Dash Dingo on Bart's games console. The vegetarian section of the supermarket has a notice saying SAY IT ISN'T SOY. Amongst the ice cream flavours Lisa tries to avoid freezing to death over (in order to get for Homer) are Milli Vanilli, Cherry Garcia, Desmond Tutti Frutti, Candy Warhol, Xavier Nougat and Sherbert Hoover. Ben and Jerry's, take note.

Homage: Dash Dingo is clearly a substitute for top PlayStation platform game hero Crash Bandicoot.

Look out for: An absolute gem after Timothy Lovejoy's latest boring sermon: leading the dash to escape the church is his wife! Watch out, as well, for Homer's attempts to get the lobster and the fish to live together and, best of all, the different perspectives on Mr Pinchy. Homer sees him all sweet and Disney-esque; Marge sees him as a fierce, ugly, pincer-snapping monster.

Notes: A fabulously defining moment in Lisa's life, showing what happens if you let your guard slip. What makes this work even more is the false ending which shows that everyone in

Springfield is as adept at predicting Lisa's morality as the viewers are. An absolutely inspired piece of comedy.

211

AABF04:

'Homer Simpson in: "Kidney Trouble" '

Written by John Swartzwelder
Directed by Mike B. Anderson
Also starring: Tress MacNeille, Karl Weidergott

Premise: After a visit to a Wild West town, Grampa gets sick and his kidneys explode. The only way to save his life is for Homer, whose fault it is, to donate one of his. Sadly, Homer is not enthralled by the idea and runs away to sea.

Features: Carl, Lenny, Moe, Grampa, Jasper, Rev. Lovejoy, Dr Hibbert, Sylvia, Quimby, Hans Moleman, Captain McCallister, Krusty.

Couch: The Simpsons are frogs, with Maggie as a tadpole.

Trivia: Springfield is two hours' drive from Bloodbath Gulch: 'The Friendliest Town in the Old West'. Between it and Springfield is the world's largest toilet. Larry Hagman of *Dallas* fame reportedly has five kidneys and three hearts, Homer is a big fan of actor F. Murray Abraham, and during the following week, the 20th episode of *Sumo Babies* will be transmitted on TV. Bart rents some of Homer's favourite movies, including *Gorilla Squadron*, *Gorilla Island 6* and *Apes-A-Poppin'*.

Look out for: Grampa getting slapped by a robotic hand, the ship of lost souls and, outside Davey Jones' Locker, a strange boy eating a raw fish who looks like Krusty!

Notes: An odd episode really that goes on a bit too long and could probably have done with an entertaining B story.

Homer's running away is funny the first time, but by the second, it's lost its impact. The biggest joke comes from Grampa's need to go to the lavatory on the way back from the ghost town. Which isn't that funny at all, really.

212

AABF05:

'Mayored to the Mob'

Written by Ron Hauge   **Directed by** Swinton O. Scott III
Also starring: Pamela Hayden, Tress MacNeille,
Maggie Roswell, Russi Taylor, Karl Weidergott
Special guest voices: Marcia Wallace (as Ms Krabappel),
Joe Mantegna (as Don Tony), Dick Tufeld (as Robot),
Mark Hamill (as himself)

Premise: At a science-fiction convention, Homer saves Mark Hamill's life and decides to enrol on a course as a bodyguard. As a result, he starts working for Mayor Quimby and has to save him from Don Tony's attacks.

Features: Mr Burns, Smithers, Carl, Lenny, Moe, Barney, barflies, Chief Wiggum, Lou, Eddie, Skinner, Groundskeeper Willie, Milhouse, Uter, Nelson, Jimbo, Sherri and Terri, Rev. Lovejoy, Helen Lovejoy, the Flanderses, Mr van Houten, Dr Hibbert, Quimby, Dr Frink, Android's Dungeon Guy, Gil, Spotty Boy, Herman, Cletus, Judge Snyder, Bill and Marty from KBBL.

Couch: The Simpsons are caught in a car-crusher.

Trivia: The Bi-Mon-Sci-Fi-Con is a delight for geeks: amongst those there are ALF, Chewbacca from *Star Wars* (George Lucas, 1977), Tom Baker as Doctor Who, Gort from *The Day the Earth Stood Still* (Robert Wise, 1951), *Godzilla* (Ishiro Honda, 1956), Neil Armstrong and Jonathan Harris from the *Lost in Space* TV show, shadowed by the robot.

Skinner has come dressed as Spock, while Edna Krabappel is *Barbarella* (Roger Vadim, 1967). When the 45-year-old virginal Android's Dungeon Guy meets the geeky girl, we hear Alexander Courage's 'Under the Spell' piece of music from the *Star Trek* pilot show, 'The Cage' (and how geeky are we for knowing that!?). Outside the convention is a sign saying SET PHASERS ON FUN and, according to Bill and Marty, one of the weekend's delights is tag team robot wrestling, featuring the Cylons from *Battlestar Galactica* (Richard Colla, 1978) versus the Gay Robots (i.e., C3PO and R2D2) of *Star Wars*. Mark Hamill later stars in a new version of *Guys and Dolls* (Joseph L. Mankiewicz, 1955) where he plays Nathan Detroit, singing 'Luke, Be a Jedi Tonight'. The episode plays out with 'I Will Always Love You', the Dolly Parton song made famous by Whitney Houston.

Homage: Where to begin? Ignoring the science fiction films and series mentioned above, the bodyguard idea is obviously lifted from *The Bodyguard* (Mick Jackson, 1992) and the episode's title comes from *Married to the Mob* (Jonathan Demme, 1988). There are also references to *The Untouchables* (Brian de Palma, 1987), *Weekend at Bernie's* (Ted Kotcheff, 1989), and *The Rock* (Michael Bay, 1996).

Look out for: The fact that Don Tony hangs out at the Legitimate Businessman's Social Club and that at the Bodyguard Academy, Leavelle is shooting the water melons from atop a grassy knoll. Homer, by the way, has to protect Ann Landers, while Kirk van Houten gets to look after Madonna. We also like the idea of a Roger Corman version of *Titanic*. Without a doubt the best moment of the episode – indeed one of the highlights of the entire series – occurs at the convention. In what strikes us as a thoroughly litigious but beautifully observed moment, *Dr Smith* actor Jonathan Harris offers to show Bart something out the back, whereupon in true *Lost in Space* style, the Robot waves his arms about and, in Dick Tufeld's distinctive tones, warbles 'Danger, Bart Simpson, Danger!' Inspired!

Notes: The best bits all involve either the convention or Mark Hamill's repeated attempts to not be mobbed. Sadly, the main thrust of the story – Homer's protection of Quimby from Don Tony – falls a bit flat. Nevertheless, when the jokes run free, they are of exceptionally high quality.

213

AABF06:
'Viva Ned Flanders'

Written by David M. Stern   **Directed by** Neil Affleck
Also starring: Pamela Hayden, Tress MacNeille,
Maggie Roswell, Karl Weidergott
Special guest voices: Marcia Wallace (as Ms Krabappel),
The Moody Blues (as themselves)

Premise: Ned Flanders wants to know how Homer can just enjoy life so much and not have any cares. To show Ned how to have a good time, Homer takes his neighbour away for a weekend of drink, debauchery and gambling in Las Vegas. Oh, and they decide to get married. Again.

Features: Mr Burns, Smithers, Carl, Lenny, Moe, Barney, Grampa, Jasper, Kent Brockman, Chief Wiggum, Agnes Skinner, Skinner, Miss Hoover, Groundskeeper Willie, Otto, Milhouse, Rev. Lovejoy, the Flanderses, Mrs van Houten, Android's Dungeon Guy, Captain McCallister, Sideshow Mel, Apu, Spotty Boy, Gil, Cletus.

Couch: A human hand spins the picture, leaving everything a blur of colour.

Trivia: Homer and Ned drunkenly gain new wives: Homer marries Amber while Ned gets hitched to Ginger. We briefly see the return of Dreaderick Tatum, Ernst and Gunter (this time with trademark white tiger) and Lance Murdock. We hear the Moody Blues perform their 1967 hit 'Nights in

White Satin', and hear Deep Purple's 1972 album track 'Highway Star' as the Springfield duo drive to Las Vegas. Unsurprisingly, we also get a snatch of 'Viva Las Vegas', a hit in 1964 for Elvis. Homer doesn't know Marge's birthday but knows that Barney and Hitler both share 20 April. And the car number plate on the Android's Dungeon Guy's vehicle is NCC1701, the registration number for the *Starship Enterprise* in *Star Trek*.

Homage: When the building explodes at the beginning and everyone runs away, it is reminiscent of both *Dante's Peak* (Roger Donaldson, 1997) and, particularly Homer driving and the flames behind, *Independence Day* (Roland Emmerich, 1996). Outside Rev. Lovejoy's church is the notice that today's sermon will be 'He Knows What You Did Last Summer', clearly inspired by the film *I Know What You Did Last Summer* (Jim Gillespie, 1997), while passing Homer and Ned – but obviously getting away from the big city – are Dr Gonzo and Raoul from *Fear and Loathing in Las Vegas* (Terry Gilliam, 1998). There's also a snatch of the theme from *Mars Attacks* (Tim Burton, 1996) as they dash around escaping the city of lights. And the title comes from the Elvis Presley movie *Viva Las Vegas* (George Sidney, 1964).

Notes for Brits: Don Rickles is a commentator for hockey in America. Joan Rivers and her daughter Melissa are well known these days for doing information commercials more than anything else, usually for fashionable clothes.

Look out for: Jasper and Grampa being carjacked.

Notes: One of the fastest paced episodes ever, this moves at a breathless speed and is enormous fun with more bizarre moments than you can shake a stick at (a hysterical Joan Rivers is our favourite). Excellent stuff!

214
AABF07:
'Wild Barts Can't Be Broken'

Written by Larry Doyle   **Directed by** Mark Ervin
Also starring: Pamela Hayden, Tress MacNeille,
Maggie Roswell, Russi Taylor, Karl Weidergott
Special guest voices: Marcia Wallace (as Ms Krabappel),
Cyndi Lauper (as herself)

Premise: After a night spent celebrating the latest victory by
local baseball team The Isotopes, Homer and his friends trash
the school, but Chief Wiggum blames the kids and brings in a
curfew. Following an abortive attempt to break this, the kids
gang together to make public their parents' darkest secrets.

Features: Mr Burns, Smithers, Carl, Lenny, Moe, Barney,
Patty, Selma, Grampa, Jasper, Kent Brockman, Chief Wig-
gum, Lou, Eddie, Agnes Skinner, Skinner, Miss Hoover,
Groundskeeper Willie, Otto, Superintendent Chalmers, Mil-
house, Martin, Nelson, Jimbo, Dolph, Kearney, Sherri and
Terri, Lewis, Richard, Wendell, Ralph, Janey, Allison, Rev.
Lovejoy, Helen Lovejoy, the Flanderses, Ruth Powers, Mr
van Houten, Mrs van Houten, Dr Hibbert, Quimby, Hans
Moleman, Dr Frink, Krusty, Sideshow Mel, Apu, Spotty Boy.

Couch: The couch drops through the floor, with the cowboy-
hat wearing Simpsons on top, and it drops like a bomb
towards the ground.

Trivia: In the school shower-room, the drunken Homer and
his friends sing Queen's 1977 hit 'We Are The Champions'.
Cyndi Lauper sings 'The Star Spangled Banner' to the tune of
her 1984 hit 'Girls Just Wanna Have Fun'. Luanne van
Houten has begun yet another affair, this time with Pyro's
best friend, Gyro. Agnes Skinner and Superintendent Chalmers appear to be getting romantically involved and Mrs
Prince is a compulsive shoplifter. The sitcom on the TV is

called *Don't Go There* but the kids try and amuse themselves with board games, including Citizenship, Energy Shortage, Lent, and Hippo in the House.

Homage: The couch gag is beautifully lifted from *Dr Strangelove or: How I Learned to Stop Worrying and Love the Bomb* (Stanley Kubrick, 1963). The film the kids sneak out to see, *The Bloodening*, is clearly based on *Village of the Damned* (Wolf Rilla, 1960).

Look out for: Homer's rather deluded memories of the night that led up to his binge and the old man talking all the way through the credits, particularly when he tells the Gracie Films logo to shush herself.

Song: Everyone sings 'Kids', a song inspired by, it sounds like, the musical *Bye Bye Birdie*.

Notes: A curious unmemorable episode with a good chunk in the middle. Neither the opening with The Isotopes nor the finale with the rather dire song help this one at all, and frankly, if it wasn't for the superb parody of *Village of the Damned*, and the kids' revenge by revealing their family's secrets, it'd sink without trace.

215
AABF08:
'Sunday, Cruddy Sunday'

Written by Tom Martin, George Meyer, Brian Scully and Mike Scully
Directed by Steven Dean Moore
Also starring: Pamela Hayden, Tress MacNeille, Karl Weidergott
Special guest voices: Troy Aikman (as himself), Rosey Grier (as himself), Dan Marino (as himself), John Madden (as himself), Pat Summerall (as himself), Dolly Parton (as herself), Rupert Murdoch (as himself), Fred Willard (as Wally Kogen)

Premise: Homer's new friend Wally Kogen can get tickets for the ball game and, with a coachload of their mates, they head off. However, Wally's tickets are fakes and they have to find another way of getting in.

Features: Carl, Lenny, Moe, Barney, barflies, Jasper, Chief Wiggum, Skinner, Milhouse, Martin, Nelson, Sherri and Terri, Lewis, Richard, Wendell, Ralph, Rev. Lovejoy, Ned Flanders, Maude Flanders, Mr van Houten, Dr Hibbert, Bumblebee Man, Android's Dungeon Guy, Captain McCallister, Krusty, Sideshow Mel, Apu, Spotty Boy, Dr Nick Riviera.

Couch: The couch is sunk by an iceberg and only Maggie survives.

Trivia: As the gang race for the stadium, they are accompanied by 'Song 2', a 1997 hit for Blur. Dolly Parton leaves the boys to go and sing a song with actor Rob Lowe and industrial instrumentalists and dancers, Stomp.

Homage: Well, the couch gag owes itself to *Titanic* (James Cameron, 1997). This episode's title is borrowed from *Sunday, Bloody Sunday* (John Schlesinger, 1971) but certainly not the plot.

Notes for Brits: Working on the assumption that neither Ms Parton nor Mr Murdoch need introduction, Aikman, Grier and Marino are sportsmen, and Summerall and Madden are sports commentators.

Look out for: Rupert Murdoch living up to his description as the billionaire tyrant, plus cameos from Vincent Price (no one can quite remember whether he's dead or not) and President Clinton who, in the wake of the Lewinsky affair, is having his curtains measured by Al Gore. Already dated, but nicely observed.

Notes: A thoroughly enjoyable romp through what happens when a bunch of lads go for a Sunday out at the ball game. It's not quite sex, drugs and rock 'n' roll, but both Dolly Parton –

and, bizarrely, Rupert Murdoch – spice things up nicely. By far the most engaging thing is Wally Kogen. A shame he doesn't join our regulars.

216

AABF09:

'Homer to the Max'

Written by John Swartzwelder   **Directed by** Pete Michels
Also starring: Tress MacNeille, Maggie Roswell,
Karl Weidergott
Special guest voice: Ed Begley Jnr (as himself)

Premise: After realising that a TV cop show has a hero named Detective Homer Simpson, Homer is overjoyed. However, reaction to the show is negative and in subsequent episodes the detective is played as a fool. Nevertheless, Homer capitalises on his brief fame, adopts a new name, and becomes part of the Springfield glitterati, even joining in on their ecological protests.

Features: Mr Burns, Carl, Lenny, Moe, Barney, barflies, Grampa, Jasper, Chief Wiggum, Mrs Wiggum, Lou, Eddie, Agnes Skinner, Skinner, Otto, Nelson, Ralph, Janey, Snake, Dr Hibbert, Sylvia, Ruth Powers, Dr Frink, Hans Moleman, Android's Dungeon Guy, Krusty, Apu, Spotty Boy, Herman, Judge Snyder, Dr Nick Riviera.

Couch: Marge is hanging the family out to dry.

Trivia: Krusty has a nephew called Josh (is this who we see in 'Homer Simpson in Kidney Trouble' outside Davey Jones' Locker?). Amongst Homer's other choices for a new name are Hercules Rockefeller, Rembrandt Q. Einstein and Handsome B. Wonderful, before settling on Max Power. Cosingtons the store no longer has a slogan saying it doesn't have a slogan! Other shows in Fox's mid-season line-up include *America's*

Funniest Tornados, Admiral Baby, All in the Family 1999 and *The Laughter Family*.

Homage: *Police Cops* (originally called *Badge Patrol*) is clearly based on the TV show *Miami Vice*.

Notes for Brits: Annie Potts and Jeremy Priven are two US sitcom stars: Potts from *Designing Women*, Priven from *Ellen*.

Look out for: Homer's actual destruction of both the forest and the American eagle. Delightful. And is *The Mule that Saved Spring Bank* a reference to that famous Troy McClure movie *Gladys the Groovy Mule*? We think we should be told! Best in-joke has to be Lisa explaining that in TV pilots, characters that prove unpopular or irrelevant are often dropped, at which point Mr Largo and the Capitol City Goofball from 'Dancin' Homer' (7F05) wander past. There's also a dig at why TV networks like cartoons – so that if an actor leaves, they are easier to replace as no one notices when a voice changes – beautifully underscored by Ned Flanders (voiced by someone who isn't Harry Shearer). This may also have been a bit of a dig at actress Maggie Roswell for whom this was due to be her last series of *The Simpsons*. According to some sources, this was reportedly a result of a salary dispute, meaning all her characters would have to be voiced by a new actress. Keep an eye out at the showbiz party for *Cheers* and *Dumb and Dumber* star Woody Harrelson, President Clinton (who has apparently 'done it' with a pig) and *Saturday Night Live* producer Lorne Michaels.

Song: Homer got the name Max Power from a hairdryer, and the Max Power song is sung to the tune of the Barry/Bricusse/Newley James Bond theme for *Goldfinger* (Guy Hamilton, 1964).

Notes: Funny in all the right places, this is an episode of two distinct stories, neither of which mesh together. The whole Ed Begley Jnr/saving the forest bit seems to have been tacked on, as if the stuff about Homer finding his name being abused (shades of Mr Sparkle again?) ran out of steam. Not a bad show, more a sort of 'So what?' show.

217

AABF11:

'I'm With Cupid'

Written by Dan Greany   **Directed by** Bob Anderson
Also starring: Pamela Hayden, Tress MacNeille,
Maggie Roswell, Karl Weidergott
Special guest voices: Marcia Wallace (as Ms Krabappel),
Jan Hooks (as Manjula), Elton John (as himself)

Premise: Moaned at by their spouses for not being romantic enough, Homer and his friends decide to follow Apu, who is going out of his way to impress Manjula. It's not because they want tips on what he's doing right; it's because they want to stop him, because everything he does makes them look even worse.

Features: Carl, Lenny, Moe, Barney, barflies, Grampa, Jasper, Chief Wiggum, Mrs Wiggum, Lou, Eddie, Skinner, Otto, Milhouse, Martin, Nelson, Jimbo, Sherri and Terri, Ralph, Snake, Rev. Lovejoy, Ned Flanders, Maude Flanders, Dr Hibbert, Sylvia, Captain McCallister, Sideshow Mel, Apu, Sanjay.

Couch: The family have hair transplants: Homer has Maggie's, Marge Bart's, Bart Lisa's, Lisa Homer's and Maggie has Marge's.

Trivia: The chocolate supplier is called Baron von Munchousen. Homer has only once ever placed a small ad; nothing romantic for Marge, but to sell a lawnmower. The parrot in the store sings 'I Love the Nightlife (Disco Round)', a hit for Alicia Bridges in 1978, while Elton John performs a new version of his first ever hit, 'Your Song', from 1971.

Homage: The typing across the screen to identify the location of Homer's car is reminiscent of both *The X Files* and *Millennium*, both Fox shows created by Chris Carter. And Apu going into Tiffany's leads to a direct reference by Chief Wiggum about *Breakfast at Tiffany's* (Blake Edwards, 1961).

Look out for: In a desperate attempt to shut Homer up, Elton John gives him one of his Grammys. It doesn't work.

Notes: Very, very clever and funny, if a little tacky. After all, how nice are these people who want to ruin Apu and Manjula's day just because they're scared of looking bad? Nevertheless, it's executed stylishly and Homer wins in the end; entirely by default of course, but maybe that's his reward for not falling off the skywriting plane until the last minute!

218

AABF10:

'Marge Simpson in: "Screaming Yellow Honkers" '

Written by David M. Stern
Directed by Mark Kirkland
Also starring: Tress MacNeille, Maggie Roswell,
John Kassir, Karl Weidergott
Special guest voices: Marcia Wallace (as Ms Krabappel),
Hank Williams Jnr (as himself)

Premise: When Homer buys a Canyonero 4x4, he finds he can't drive it and so takes Marge's car instead. Left to do the shopping in a strange vehicle, Marge succumbs to road rage and, before long, is caught by Chief Wiggum who sends her on a course to overcome these aggressive urges.

Features: Carl, Lenny, Moe, Barney, Kent Brockman, Chief Wiggum, Mrs Wiggum, Lou, Eddie, Agnes Skinner, Skinner, Ms Hoover, Groundskeeper Willie, Otto, Lunchlady Doris, Superintendent Chalmers, Mr Largo, Nelson, Kearney, Ralph, Snake, Rev. Lovejoy, the Flanderses, Mrs van Houten, the Princes, Hans Moleman, Gil, Krusty, Sideshow Mel, Apu.

Couch: A bar comes down over the couch, locking the family in like a fairground-ride seat.

Trivia: Ms Krabappel does a fan dance, singing 'Fever', a 1964 hit for Helen Shapiro (although the original was by Peggy Lee in 1958). The rest of the teachers pastiche songs from *Fame* (Alan Parker, 1980) in their Edu-Tainment Showcase at the school. There's a sign at the Wild Animal Kingdom that tells us the animals there are BORN FREE – THEN CAGED. Hole singer Courtney Love is advertising Wheaties breakfast cereal. The bear Chief Wiggum uses to demonstrate good driving is called Curtis E. Bear: it's poor Eddie in a suit. Homer buys the Canyonero from Gil at the OK Car-Ral. Except he doesn't. Not quite. Poor Gil!

Homage: The scenes of the animals rampaging through the Wild Animal Kingdom are reminiscent of *Jumanji* (Joe Johnston, 1995), just as Homer says.

Look out for: All the plugs for NBC, a rival TV network, which causes Homer to apologise to Fox over the closing credits. And Hank Williams' Canyonero theme again.

Notes: Very clever, very dry humour and showcasing the last person you might expect to suffer road rage. Some lovely moments (Marge losing patience with Agnes and Kearney is great), especially her drive across the cornfield. Sadly the Canyonero doesn't survive the experience of this episode, which would have been nice, if only to see Marge regularly at the wheel rather than Homer.

219

AABF12:

'Make Room for Lisa'

Written by Brian Scully
Directed by Matthew Nastuk
Also starring: Pamela Hayden, Tress MacNeille,
Maggie Roswell, Karl Weidergott

Premise: After damaging the original handwritten American Constitution in the Springsonian, Homer's fine is paid for by Omnitouch, a mobile communications firm. All he has to do in return is give over part of his house to let them install a new transmitter. Lisa's bedroom is sacrificed and she must move in with Bart, who delights in the torture he can inflict. Seeking peace and quiet, both she and Homer end up in sensory-deprivation tanks, which isn't as relaxing as it sounds, particularly for Homer.

Features: Carl, Lenny, Moe, Chief Wiggum, Mrs Wiggum, Agnes Skinner, Milhouse, Ralph, the Flanderses, Dr Hibbert, Krusty, Don Tony, Bill and Marty from KBBL.

Couch: Firemen are using the couch as a net but Homer misses and hits the floor.

Trivia: Bill and Marty play a 1939 jazz number by Benny Goodman followed by 'The Safety Dance', the 1983 hit for Men Without Hats. The New Age shop is called Karma-Ceuticals, Homer watches *When Animals Attack Magicians*, and we learn that Joan Rivers is only kept alive by foetal-grinding. Omnitouch also tell us that the US government spends its funds on anti-smoking campaigns, pro-smoking campaigns, killing wild doggies. And Israel.

Look out for: Homer's trip in his tank and, indeed, Lisa's dream, both of which are top-notch. We also love Homer's Andy Capp joke and the fact he wins the Sir Drinks-A-

Lot at P. J. O'Harrigans Irish bar. Best bit, though, has to be Marge enjoying listening to everyone else's cellphone conversations.

Notes: Another episode of two distinct halves, although the second far outweighs the first. Homer's adventures in the sensory deprivation tank are inspired in their almost *Keystone Kop* humour as he gets from point A to point B and so on, finally getting back to point A none the wiser. Classic stuff.

220

AABF13:

'Maximum Homerdrive'

Written by John Swartzwelder
Directed by Swinton O. Scott III
Also starring: Pamela Hayden, Tress MacNeille,
Karl Weidergott

Premise: Eating out at The Slaughterhouse steak joint, Homer realises that only two people have ever managed Sir Loin-A-Lot, a full sixteen-pound steak. One is film star Tony Randall, the other 'reliable' Red Barclay, an interstate trucker. Homer challenges Red but loses. Red, however, doesn't celebrate his victory because he dies, and so Homer and Bart set off in Red's truck to honour his memory by delivering his haul. Homer doesn't realise that truckers have their own rules and regulations.

Features: Mr Burns, Smithers, Barney, Milhouse, Nelson, Ned Flanders, Todd, Rod, Dr Hibbert, Sylvia, Bumblebee Man, Gil.

Couch: The family have been reversed so that Bart, Lisa and Maggie are adults with Homer and Marge as kids.

Trivia: The neon sign for The Slaughterhouse shows a cowboy hacking a cow to death with a chainsaw. Dr Hibbert has a 12 per cent share in the restaurant and has installed an automatic Heimlich Manoeuvre machine. Red is placed in a shroud marked I DIED AT THE SLAUGHTERHOUSE. Atlanta, Red's destination, is, apparently, the home of Ted Turner's mood swings. The film Homer and Bart see at the drive-in is *The Monster That Ate Everybody*. In their truck, father and son listen to 'Wannabe', a hit in 1996 for the Spice Girls. Back home, eager to amuse themselves, Marge and Lisa buy a new doorbell that plays Alma Cogan's 1956 hit 'Why Do Fools Fall in Love?'

Homage: *Damien: The Omen II* (Don Taylor, 1978), for the scene where Milhouse is attacked by the birds trying to peck his eyes out. Or maybe it's *The Birds* (Alfred Hitchcock, 1963). Or both. And undoubtedly *Convoy* (Sam Peckinpah, 1978) even down to the fact that none of the truckers gets hurt, even though they should. There is also a good nod to *2001: A Space Odyssey* (Stanley Kubrick, 1969) when the Navitron in Homer's cab apologetically explains, 'I'm afraid I can't let you do that' in the voice of HAL the computer.

Look out for: Homer's diet of peep pills and sleeping pills, a gas station called The Gassy Knoll, and the Jehovah's Witnesses suddenly realising no one likes them, and why. There's also a nice moment when Homer, ill-educated as ever, pronounces touché as 'too-kay'.

Notes: The life of the trucker, as made popular in C. W. McCall's 1976 hit single 'Convoy', is brought to life here in all its glory. For once, Homer is in the right and you cannot help but cheer as the truckers spectacularly fail to stop him getting to Atlanta. A nice, bonding story for Homer and Bart which is diametrically opposed to the one featuring Marge and Lisa.

221

AABF14:

'Simpsons Bible Stories'

Written by Tim Lung, Larry Doyle and Matt Selman
Directed by Nancy Kruse
Also starring: Pamela Hayden, Tress MacNeille,
Russi Taylor, Karl Weidergott
Special guest voice: Marcia Wallace (as Ms Krabappel)

Premise: As the Simpsons fall asleep listening to Rev. Lovejoy's interminable sermons, they each dream a new variation of traditional tales from the Great Book.

Features: Carl, Lenny, Moe, Grampa, Jasper, Chief Wiggum, Lou, Eddie, Agnes Skinner, Skinner, Mr Largo, Groundskeeper Willie, Otto, Milhouse, Martin, Nelson, Sherri and Terri, Lewis, Richard, Wendell, Ralph, Janey, Allison, Snake, Rev. Lovejoy, Helen Lovejoy, the Flanderses, Mr van Houten, Ruth Powers, Dr Hibbert, Dr Frink, Krusty, Dr Nick Riviera.

Couch: The family run in and slip up on banana skins.

Trivia: Marge's dream sees her as Eve, with Homer as Adam, and Ned as God in the Garden of Eden. Unsurprisingly, Snake is the serpent. Homer refers to what happens as Applegate, and God is very upset with them for causing the death of Gary, his unicorn. Homer's dream is a brief one that sees him as King Solomon, with Chief Wiggum as his Chief Guard. Lisa's dream places Milhouse as Moses, Skinner as Pharaoh, Ms Krabappel as Queen Krabapatra, Wiggum again as the Chief Guard and Willie as the slave driver. Lisa and everyone else are Milhouse's fellow slaves driven to fleeing across the Red Sea. In Bart's dream, he is King David to Nelson's Goliath, with Krusty as the jester, Grampa as Methuselah and Ralph as Ralph who likes Bart 'because you kill people'. Nelson then returns to life as a demonised Goliath to the strains of Mussorgsky's 'St John's Night on the

Bare Mountain'. Outside the church, by the way, is the announcement that CHRIST DYED EGGS FOR YOUR SINS. The episode plays out to 'Highway to Hell', a 1979 hit for Australian rockers AC/DC.

Homage: Every biblical epic movie you've ever seen, but particularly *The Ten Commandments* (Cecil B. DeMille, 1956) for the parting of the Red Sea sequence.

Look out for: Too many classic moments, but amongst the best is Homer claiming the burning bush set him up, Wiggum telling Moses and Lisa to give his regards to the British Museum as he seals them inside a tomb, and Marge asking Bart if he's wearing clean underwear as they face the apocalypse. 'Not anymore,' he replies.

Notes: A fantastic twist of the 'Treehouse of Horror' style of storytelling, where each of these is a classic on its own. This is *The Simpsons* at its very best: inventive, irreverent and very, very funny.

222

AABF15:

'Mom and Pop Art'

Written by Al Jean
Directed by Steven Dean Moore
Also starring: Pamela Hayden, Tress MacNeille,
Maggie Roswell, Karl Weidergott
Special guest voices: Marcia Wallace (as Ms Krabappel),
Jasper Jones (as himself),
Isabella Rossellini (as Astrid Weller)

Premise: After a disastrous attempt to build a barbecue, Homer's resultant trash is spotted by an avant-garde art dealer who sees it as true art, an expression of the inner self brought into existence. When it sells for a lot of money at his exhibition, 'Homer's Odyssey', Homer embarks on a creative splurge, but before long he is passé. Until, that is, he finds a new muse.

Features: Mr Burns, Smithers, Carl, Lenny, Moe, Barney, Kent Brockman, Chief Wiggum, Mrs Wiggum, Lou, Eddie, Skinner, Milhouse, Ned Flanders, Maude Flanders, Dr Frink, Don Tony, Spotty Boy, Cletus.

Couch: The couch drops through the floor, with the cowboy-hat wearing Simpsons on top, and it drops like a bomb towards the ground.

Trivia: Homer was voted the 'Most Likely to Be a mental patient or a hillbilly or a chimpanzee', while at school. His car has a bumper sticker declaring him to be SINGLE 'N' SLEAZY and he shaves his shoulders. Homer's anger, which he channels into his art, is inspired by the knowledge that Marge has discovered her engagement ring is candy, Bart has flunked math and is 'a little attracted to Milhouse'. At the Springsonian, Lisa introduces him to the art of Warhol, Dali, Picasso, Turner, Oldenburg, Pollock, and Leonardo da Vinci, amongst others.

Notes for Brits: Jasper Jones is an artist and critic.

Mmmmm: . . . split pea with ham . . . hippo . . .

Look out for: Homer finding an example of Matt Groening at the Springsonian and commenting that he can't draw, whereupon he's attacked by a large eraser! Surreal but all explained wonderfully.

Notes: Well, Marge is justifiably upset when, as an artist herself, it is Homer who is suddenly getting the kudos for producing rubbish. It's a good gag but probably not enough to stretch out for an entire episode. That said, the last few moments are pure joy, and Jasper Jones is a good egg, but it does drag in the middle.

223

AABF16:

'The Old Man and the "C" Student'

Written by Julie Thacker   **Directed by** Mark Kirkland
Also starring: Pamela Hayden, Tress MacNeille, Russi Taylor
Special guest voice: Jack LaLane (as himself)

Premise: It looks as if Springfield will host the Olympic Games, until Bart's jokes anger the selection committee and Springfield is castigated. Angrily, Bart is sent to do his penance by working in the Springfield Retirement Castle. He realises that the old folk need to be entertained and not left to rot, so he and Lisa organise a boat trip.

Features: Mr Burns, Smithers, Carl, Lenny, Moe, Barney, barflies, Patty, Selma, Grampa, Jasper, Kent Brockman, Chief Wiggum, Lou, Eddie, Agnes Skinner, Skinner, Ms Krabappel, Groundskeeper Willie, Otto, Superintendent Chalmers, Milhouse, Martin, Nelson, Sherri and Terri, Lewis, Richard, Wendell, Ralph, Rev. Lovejoy, Ned Flanders, Maude Flanders, Dr Hibbert, Sylvia, Quimby, Hans Moleman, Dr Frink, Apu, Captain McCallister.

Couch: The Simpsons find the rest of the cast in their living room watching TV.

Trivia: Waylon Smithers got thrown out of the navy for drawing naked pictures of his fellow sailors. Jasper has a false leg, and the Springfield Retirement Castle is next door to the Candy & Puppy-Dog Store. The old folk dance around to the Beatles' classic 'Can't Buy Me Love', performed here by NRBQ. The same version plays over the closing credits, which feature a pastiche of the album cover from where it originates, *A Hard Day's Night*, revamped as *A Bart Day's Night*.

Homage: *Gone With the Wind* (Victor Fleming, 1939) is the movie the old folk watch with an alternate ending, and when the boat sinks, there are obvious lifts from *Titanic* (James Cameron, 1997).

Notes for Brits: The vote for 217 campaign was a then-current one to allow Native American Indians to operate casinos in certain states. It was passed.

Look out for: Snowball II's revenge on Homer for encasing him in papier mâché, and Homer's Olympic mascot, Springie of Springfield, winning over Patty and Selma's cigarette man, Ciggie, whom they promptly light up.

Song: 'The Children Are Our Future', choreographed by George Meyer.

Notes: A marvellous feel-good story in which Bart – and eventually Lisa – understand that old folk are not just to be shut away and forgotten about. Very sweet, very endearing, and with the marvellous stereotyped Olympic Committee debate at the start, a terrific episode.

224
AABF17:
'Monty Can't Buy Me'

Written by John Swartzwelder
Directed by Mark Ervin
Also starring: Pamela Hayden, Tress MacNeille,
Maggie Roswell
Special guest voice: Michael McKean (as Jerry Rude)

Premise: When British entrepreneur Arthur Fortune opens yet another megastore in Springfield, everyone adores the ultra-rich businessman, forcing Mr Burns to wonder why no one loves him. After trying to change his public image, he decides to go and capture the Loch Ness Monster to achieve fame and fortune.

Features: Mr Burns, Smithers, Lenny, Moe, Barney, Patty, Selma, Jasper, Kent Brockman, Chief Wiggum, Agnes Skinner, Skinner, Ms Krabappel, Ms Hoover, Groundskeeper Willie, Otto, Nelson, Jimbo, Dolph, Kearney, Ralph, Rev. Lovejoy, Helen Lovejoy, Ned Flanders, Ruth Powers, Mr van Houten, Dr Hibbert, Krusty, Quimby, Android's Dungeon Guy, Dr Frink, Apu, Spotty Boy, Herman.

Couch: The Simpsons rush in to form part of a circus extravaganza.

Trivia: On *Cash in Your Legacy*, Herman has brought a WWI German helmet, Hibbert has a vase, Ms Hoover has books, Android's Dungeon Guy has a polybagged comic called *Sad Sack*, Krusty brings in a candelabra, Apu has a statue of Vishnu, Skinner a blunderbuss, and Moe a rare beertap. Amongst *Jerry Rude and the Bathroom Bunch*'s guests are some lesbian gladiators and Siamese midgets Nick-Nack and Paddiwack. Comedian Adam Sandler is richer than Mr Burns, as the old man discovers upon reading *Billionaire Beat*.

Homage: *The Postman* (Kevin Costner, 1997) is mentioned as something to be avoided.

Notes for Brits: Jerry Rude is clearly based on US shock-jock Howard Stern, while one wonders if Richard Branson was unwilling or unavailable, as Arthur Fortune is him in every way.

Look out for: Mr Burns killing off the crickets, Willie's relatives, the wonderful Nessie monster itself and, best of all, Burns not telling us how he got hold of it!

Notes: Very funny when it's funny, very poor when it isn't, the best part of this episode is the Scottish stuff and the idea that, once again, Burns is actually worried about his public image, as he was in 'The Joy of Sect' (5F23).

225

AABF18:
'They Saved Lisa's Brain'

Written by Matt Selman   **Directed by** Pete Michels
Also starring: Tress MacNeille
Special guest voice: Stephen Hawking (as himself)

Premise: Worried about her intelligence not being recognised or put to good use, Lisa is overjoyed to be welcomed into MENSA. However, when they decide that the best thing they can do is run Springfield themselves, the group fractures and riots ensue.

Features: Mr Burns, Smithers, Carl, Lenny, Moe, Barney, barflies, Patty, Selma, Grampa, Jasper, Kent Brockman, Chief Wiggum, Mrs Wiggum, Lou, Eddie, Skinner, Ms Krabappel, Miss Hoover, Groundskeeper Willie, Otto, Milhouse, Nelson, Jimbo, Kearney, Ralph, Snake, Rev. Lovejoy, Helen Lovejoy, Ned Flanders, Maude Flanders, Mr van Houten, Mrs van Houten, Ruth Powers, Dr Hibbert, Quimby, Hans Moleman, Android's Dungeon Guy, Krusty, Sideshow Mel, Rainier Wolfcastle, Apu, Manjula, Sanjay, Dr Frink, Captain McCallister, Spotty Boy, Herman, Cletus, Bill and Marty from KBBL.

Couch: The couch is sunk by an iceberg and only Maggie survives.

Trivia: DISCRETION GUARANTEED is written in huge letters on the side of the photography van. Dr Hibbert is originally from Alabama, and Springfield is 299th on the list of America's most desirable cities, just below Dawson's Creek. Springfield has eight malls, 32 bars and 13 stores that begin with 'Le Sex'. It has no alternative theatre, no symphonies, and the library's reference department has been replaced by an air hockey table and a make-your-own coffee bar. On TV, Homer watches *Ethnic Mismatch Comedy Series # 644* (which is full of Viagra jokes, much to Marge's amusement), repeats of the Princess of Wales's funeral, and a show called *How Low Will You Go*, sponsored by Grandma Plopwell's Pudding. Homer takes part, obviously. He wears a suit made of popcorn, Bart dresses as Bartman, Barney drinks a six-pack in one go (he actually intended to juggle chickens), and Moe is going to sing like Shirley Temple. Others lined up to do their acts include Mr Burns and Smithers as a pantomime horse, Kirk van Houten as a baby, Apu as a holy cow, and Lenny comes dressed as a urinal! Homer poses in the house to 'I'm Too Sexy', an inexplicable 1991 hit for Right Said Fred.

Notes For Brits: Madeleine Albright, seen here judging the contest, is the current US Secretary of State.

Look out for: Bart riding naked on a wild hog. Later it is riding him!

Notes: It is Stephen Hawking's cameo that saves this retread of 'Lisa the Simpson' from being very boring. Once we're past the *How Low Will You Go* show, the episode takes a nose-dive until the last few minutes. Very, very tedious.

226

AABF20:

'Thirty Minutes Over Tokyo'

Written by Donick Carey and Dan Greaney
Directed by Jim Reardon
Also starring: Tress MacNeille, Maggie Roswell,
Karl Weidergott, Denice Kumagai, Gedde Watanabe,
Keone Young, Karen Maruyama
Special guest voice: George Takai (as Game Show Host)

Premise: In an effort to save money, the family scrimp and save and can eventually afford a last-minute holiday to Tokyo. However, they find the culture there particularly difficult and miss their flight home after Homer insults every-one and everything and loses all their money. Their only chance of escape is to take part in an *Endurance*-like game show and win their freedom.

Features: Mr Burns, Smithers, Carl, Lenny, Moe, Barney, barflies, Patty, Selma, Jasper, Chief Wiggum, Skinner, Miss Hoover, Groundskeeper Willie, Snake, Rev. Lovejoy, Helen Lovejoy, the Flanderses, Mr van Houten, Mrs van Houten, Dr Hibbert, Sylvia, Dr Frink, Android's Dungeon Guy, Apu, Sanjay, Cletus.

Couch: The couch turns into a shredder.

Trivia: At the Mega-Savings Bash (Bring your own chair) is the trademarked character from Monopoly. He leaves on the Monopoly train. Jim Belushi stars in *Kanga Roommate* and is currently filming *Toga 2000*. Homer quotes from 'Pass the Dutchie', a 1982 hit for kiddie group Musical Youth. The Internet café is called The Java Server and bears the legend: wel.com.

Homage: Game shows such as *Endurance* and *Family Fortunes* form the basis of the show the Simpsons must endure to get their tickets home.

Notes for Brits: Godzilla, Gamera, Rodan and Mothra are all famous Japanese movie monsters in gloriously tacky Japanese films from the fifties, sixties and seventies. Hollywood, of course, tried to remake *Godzilla* and failed spectacularly.

Look out for: Black humour at its best is always guaranteed to outrage. The series rarely gets more outrageously tasteless than the Hello Kitty factory.

Notes: A magnificent end to the season, which sees the Simpsons away from familiar turf and having to come together to find a way home. Thoroughly racist – as all overseas Simpsons episodes are – but completely inoffensive because it's simply very funny. And those poor cats.

Futurama

Futurama is a new animated series from the same creative team as *The Simpsons* led by Matt Groening, and employs the same kind of humour: bizarre situations featuring a very distinct but varied set of characters. Each of them is flawed in some way, but strive for greatness, and in everything they encounter, the humour is always topical, cultural and very, very dark. Its main difference to *The Simpsons* is that the characters are coloured naturally rather than Springfield yellow (but they still only have four fingers!).

The first season went out in America to great acclaim, and a second run started in America during September 1999, alongside the eleventh run of *The Simpsons*, one after the other, on Sunday nights.

The characters are:

Fry (Billy West), a pizza-delivery boy from the twentieth century who, just before midnight on 31 December 1999, accidentally got locked in a cryogenic chamber and is awoken on 31 December 2999. By this time (in a sequence lifted superbly from George Pal's 1954 film version of *The Time Machine*), we have seen civilisation rise and fall a few times. By the time Fry awakens, Earth is populated by humans, robots and a few aliens, as well as the Heads: literally the heads of famous people, preserved in jars, imparting their wisdom – or whatever – accumulated over three thousand years.

Fry befriends **Leela** (Katey Sagal), the only one-eyed alien on Earth, whose job is to ensure that Fry remains a delivery boy in this ultra-organised Orwellian society (she is Officer 1-BD-I). He also meets a suicidal, alcoholic robot called **Bender** (John DiMaggio) and moves in with him. Fry's only relative left alive is his great-great-great- (and so forth) grand-nephew, **Professor Farnsworth** (Billy West), who runs a delivery service to other planets and is as mad as trees. Working for the Professor are **Amy**, a co-pilot (Lauren Tom), **Hermes Conrad** (Phil La Marr), his canny financial wizard, and **Dr Zoidberg** (Billy West), whose grasp on human biology leaves a lot to be desired, which is a shame as it's his speciality. On one mission they pick up the cute little alien **Nibbler** (Lauren Tom), who has a voracious appetite and eats anything, although no one seems to twig this fact.

The episodes are:

1ACV01:
'Space Pilot 3000'

Written by David X. Cohen and Matt Groening
Directed by Rich Moore and Gregg Vanzo
Presented in color

Premise: Fry awakens and must avoid Leela's attempts to stamp him with his job ID. While on the run, he befriends Bender and ultimately Leela, after an encounter in the Head Museum. Leela realises her life is no better than Fry's, and the three agree to join up with Professor Farnsworth as a delivery team.

Also starring: Tress MacNeille, Dave Herman, Kath Soucie.

Special guest voices: Leonard Nimoy (as himself as a Head in a jar), Dick Clark (as himself as a Head in a jar).

Introducing: Fry, Leela, Bender, Professor Farnsworth.

Other heads include: Ed Begley Jnr, David Duchovny, Gillian Anderson, Rodney Dangerfield, Elizabeth Taylor, Matt Groening (all bar Groening have been *The Simpsons* guest voices). There are also various US Presidential heads, including Richard Nixon, Gerald Ford, Jimmy Carter, Ronald Reagan, George Bush and Bill Clinton.

1ACV02:
'The Series Has Landed'

Written by Ken Keeler   **Directed by** Peter Avanzio
Presented in Hypno-Vision

Premise: An assignment to the moon excites Fry but bores Leela, until they find themselves stranded on the dark side. Bender meanwhile upsets a local by making it with his robotic daughters!

Also starring: Tress MacNeille, Maurice LaMarche.

And introducing: Amy, Hermes.

1ACV03:
'I, Roommate'

Written by Eric Horsted   **Directed by** Bret Haaland
As seen on TV

Premise: Fry is asked to find alternative accommodation and moves in with Bender, who lives in a broom cupboard. Then they move to a luxurious new apartment, until the money runs out.

Also starring: Tress MacNeille, Maurice LaMarche.

And introducing: *All My Circuits*, the TV soap opera for robots.

1ACV04:
'Love's Labors Lost in Space'

Written by Brian Kelley   **Directed by** Brian Sheesley
Presented in BC [brain control] where available

Premise: While hoping to save endangered species, the crew encounter the vainglorious space captain Zapp Brannigan of the starship *Nimbus*, who sets his sights on Leela.

Guest starring: Maurice LaMarche.

And introducing: Nibbler.

1ACV05:
'Fear of a Bot Planet'

Written by Evan Gore and Heather Lombard
Directed by Peter Avanzio and Carlos Baeze, Ashley Lenz and Chris Suave
Featuring gratuitous alien nudity

Premise: Trapped on a planet of robots who want to destroy all organic life, Fry and Leela go on the run, while Bender wonders if life here ain't so bad.

Also starring: Tress MacNeille, Maurice LaMarche, Dave Herman, Tom Kenny.

1ACV06:
'A Fishful of Dollars'

Written by Patrick M. Verrone
Directed by Ron Hughart and Gregg Vanzo
Loading . . .

Premise: Rich because he has accrued interest over the years, Fry decides to buy a rare tin of anchovies, to taste home. Unfortunately he doesn't realise that crime boss and corporation head Mom will stop at nothing to get the anchovies.

Also starring: Tress MacNeille, Maurice LaMarche, Dave Herman.

Special guest voice: Pamela Anderson (as herself as a Head in a jar).

1ACV07:
'My Three Suns'

Written by J. Stewart Burns
Directed by Jeffrey Lynch and Kevin O'Brien
Presented in double-vision double-vision where drunk

Premise: On a planet occupied by aliens who are liquid, Fry accidentally drinks their Emperor. Now he must become Emperor, which seems fine until he learns what happens to Emperors within the first few days of their reign.

Also starring: Dave Herman, Maurice LaMarche.

1ACV08:
'A Big Piece of Garbage'

Written by Lewis Morton   **Directed by** Susie Dietter
Mr Bender's Wardrobe by Robotany 500

Premise: Professor Farnsworth's new invention, the smello-scope, detects a huge meteor heading towards Earth, constructed entirely of all the waste humanity has been shooting into space for the last three thousand years. Can Fry and Leela deflect its path in time?

Also starring: Tress MacNeille, Dave Herman.

Special guest voice: Ron Popeil (as himself as a Head in a jar).

1ACV09:
'Hell is Other Robots'

Written by Eric Kaplan　　**Directed by** Rich Moore
Condemned by the Space Pope

Premise: Bender finds solace at the Temple of Robotology, but before long, he's back to his old ways. However, this causes him to be consigned to Robot Hell, where he meets the Robot Devil itself.

Also starring: Tress MacNeille.

Special guest voices: The Beastie Boys (as their own Heads in jars), Dan Castellanetta (as Robot Devil).

APPENDIX I

Springfield's Most Wanted

Written by Jack Parmeter   **Directed by** Bill Brown
Cast: John Walsh, Dennis Franz, Andrew Shue,
Courtney Thorne-Smith, Kevin Nealon, Chris Elliott,
Daryl Gates, Jummy Vacarro,
and Elizabeth Hayes (as Dr Lydia Hansen)

Premise: John Walsh and his team on *America's Most Wanted* present a special episode on the crime of the century – the shooting of Mr Burns.

Trivia: The end credits feature some very unusual names (Patty Bourgois, Patty Chayefsky, etc.).

Homage: Er, *America's Most Wanted*, which has been hosted for many years by John Walsh. Pundits include Daryl Gates, former Chief of Police in Los Angeles, Las Vegas bookmaker Jimmy Vacarro, and celebrity psychiatrist Dr Lydia Hansen.

Notes: Certainly the most cleverly conceived of the clip-shows, but rather lost on anybody who hasn't seen *America's Most Wanted* or doesn't know the featured pundits (like us). The use of animation alongside real-life performers is bizarre – but the choice of clips is very good. Cheeky editing includes scenes from the framing sequence of 'Another Simpsons Clip Show'.

APPENDIX II

COMICS

With the implausibility of transferring the success of *The Simpsons* to the prose novel, and with Matt Groening wanting to keep a firm hand on all licensed merchandising, it seemed obvious that setting up his own comic publishing company to produce regular titles would be the answer. But before that was *Simpsons Illustrated*, a quarterly publication put out by Welsh Publishing of New York, an official 'fan' magazine. From that spun out *Simpsons Comics and Stories*, the first issue published in 1993. Rather than produce an Issue #2, Groening took the opportunity to create *Bongo Comics*, part of Bongo Entertainment based in Los Angeles. And from that stable, a veritable glut of official *Simpsons* spin-off comic books has emerged, many of which – in true Bart Simpson style – poke a very large finger at the comics 'establishment' and mercilessly satirise it. And quite right, too.

SIMPSONS COMICS AND STORIES
Issue 1

'Lo, There Shall Come A Bartman'
Story/Art – Steve Vance
Bart ensures that the creator of Radioactive Man receives the proper credit for his work.
(Reprinted in Heroes Illustrated Free Ashcan comic)

'Bring Me the Head of El Barto'
Story/Art – Bill Morrison
Chief Wiggum sets out to find who is spraying graffiti around Springfield.

'Maggie's Excellent Adventure'
Story – Steve Vance and Cindy Vance
Art – Steve Vance and Ray Supreme
Maggie escapes from her room and explores Springfield.

Simpsons Comics published by Bongo Entertainment.

Each issue features a main *Simpsons* story and a backup featuring a 'secondary' character – usually a pastiche of a Marvel/DC Comics hero or the fifties EC horror titles.

Simpsons Comics #1

'The Amazing Colossal Homer'
Story – Steve Vance and Cindy Vance
Art – Steve Vance and Bill Morrison
An experiment by Mr Burns' science team involves Homer becoming an amazing colossal man.

'The Collector'
Story – Steve Vance
Art – Steve Vance and Sondra Roy
Homer becomes trapped in a vault of rare comic books.

Simpsons Comics #2

'Cool Hand Bart'
Story – Steve Vance
Art – Steve Vance and Bill Morrison
Bart and Milhouse go to prison to get a taste of what it's like – only to confront a vengeful Sideshow Bob.

'My Sister, My Homewrecker'
Story – Bill Morrison
Art – Bill Morrison and Tim Bavington
Patty believes that Selma is having an affair with Homer.

Simpsons Comics # 3

'The Springfield Puma'
Story – Steve Vance and Cindy Vance
Art – Steve Vance, Bill Morrison and Tim Bavington
While Principal Skinner is away, someone steals his puma.

'Krusty, Agent of K.L.O.W.N.'
Story – Dan Castellaneta and Steve Vance
Art – Steve Vance, Bill Morrison and Tim Bavington

Simpsons Comics #4

'It's in the Cards'
Story – Steve Vance & Cindy Vance
Art – Steve Vance, Bill Morrison and Tim Bavington
Bart creates an ultra-rare baseball trading card.

'The Gnarly Adventures of Busman'
Story – Steve Vance
Art – Steve Vance, Bill Morrison and Tim Bavington
Otto has to contend with a busload of vampires.

Simpsons Comics #5

'When Bongos Collide Part Two'
Story – Steve Vance
Art – Steve Vance, Bill Morrison and Tim Bavington
Continuing the story from Itchy & Scratchy Comics #3

Simpsons Comics #6

'Be-Bop-A-Lisa'
Story – Bill Morrison
Art – Bill Morrison and Tim Bavington
Otto and Lisa become recording stars.

'The End of El Barto'
Story – Steve Vance

Art – Steve Vance and Tim Bavington
More attempts by Chief Wiggum to bring El Barto to justice.

Simpsons Comics #7

'The Greatest D'oh on Earth'
Story – Andrew Gottlieb
Art – Phil Ortiz and Tim Bavington
To avoid his chores, Bart joins the circus.

'Dead to the Last Drop'
Story – Bill Morrison
Art – Bill Morrison
Aliens try to hijack a charity event and Rainier Wolfcastle must actually become McBain to deal with them.

Simpsons Comics #8

'I Shrink, Therefore I'm Small'
Story – Gary Glasberg with Steve Vance
Art – Luis Escobar and Tim Bavington
Homer, Bart and Milhouse are shrunk to tiny proportions. While Bart and Milhouse explore, Homer is swallowed by Mr Burns.

'Edna, Queen of the Congo'
Story – Bill Morrison
Art – Luis Escobar and Bill Morrison
Bwanna Skinner is saved from the ferocious Congo People by Edna.

Simpsons Comics # 9

'The Purple Prose of Springfield'
Story – Andrew Gottlieb
Art – Luis Escobar and Tim Bavington
Lisa becomes a famous author.

'Asleep at the Well'
Story – Bill Morrison
Art – Stephanie Gladden and Tim Bavington
Barney misses the excitement at Moe's bar and so can't relate stories to the invisible pink rabbit he lives with.

Simpsons Comics #10

'Fan-Tasty Island'
Story – Jeff Rosenthal
Art – Tim Bavington and Luis Escobar with Bill Morrison, Robert Kramer and David Mowry
While on vacation, the Simpsons become involved in a treasure hunt.

'Apu's Incredible 96 Hour Shift'
Story – Bill Morrison
Art – Shaun Cashman
One of Apu's most legendary stories.

Simpson Comics #11

'Fallen Flanders'
Story – Gary Glasberg and Bill Morrison
Art – Stephanie Gladden and Tim Bavington
Sideshow Bob teams up with the aliens and replaces Ned Flanders with an evil twin.

'The Kwik-E and the Dead'
Story – W. E. Holliday
Art – Luis Escobar, Tim Harkins and Tim Bavington
An adventure of the Simpson ancestors in the Old West.

Simpsons Comics #12

'Survival of the Fattest'
Story – Rob Hammersley and Todd J. Greenwald
Art – Eric Moxcey and Tim Bavington

The Simpsons and Flanderses have to co-exist in a biosphere experiment.

'Spare the Rod, Spoil the Grunt'
Story – Scott M. Gimple
Art – Luis Escobar and David Mowry
An adventure of Skinner during his Vietnam tour of duty.

Simpsons Comics #13

'Give Me Merchandising or Give Me Death'
Story – Gary Glasberg
Art – Phil Ortiz and Tim Bavington
Milhouse and Bart create The Oysteriser, a comic character, but it is ripped off by an unscrupulous comic company.

'Rebel Without a Clutch'
Story – Barry Dutter
Art – Shaun Cashman
The adventures of rebellious young Jimbo Jones.

Simpsons Comics #14

'To Heir i$ Homer'
Story – Jon Abel, Glenn Berger and Jeff Rosenthal
Art – Chris Roman and Tim Harkins
Homer takes in a smelly down-and-out. He dies – and only then do the Simpsons discover that he was a billionaire, who leaves the Duff business to Homer.

'Nostalgia Ain't What It Used to Be'
Story – Scott Shaw
Art – Scott Shaw and Tim Bavington
Grampa and Jasper go shopping at a nostalgia mart.

Simpsons Comics #15

'A Trip to Simpsons Mountain'
Story – Mary Trainor and Bill Morrison

Art – Stephanie Gladden and Tim Bavington
Grampa tells a Christmas story that Bart is convinced he's
seen on TV – a few times.

'Kill-Er-Up With Regular'
Story – Bill Morrison
Art – Bill Morrison
A thirties-style Itchy and Scratchy adventure.

Simpsons Comics #16

'Waitress in the Sky'
Story – Lona Williams and Jeff Rosenthal
Art – Phil Ortiz and Tim Harkins
Patty and Selma are sacked from the DMV and become
airline stewardesses.

Simpsons Comics # 17

'What's the Frequency, Simpson?'
Story – Andrew Gottlieb
Art – Phil Ortiz and Tim Bavington
The Simpsons set up their own community television station.

' "Ay, Que Lastima!" '
Story – Scott Shaw
Art – Scott Shaw and Bill Morrison
A day in the life of the Bumblebee Man.

'The Dame and the Clown'
Story – Clay Griffith
Art – Sharon Bridgeman and David Mowry
Moe comes to the aid of a dame in distress.

Simpsons Comics #18

'Get Fatty'
Story – Gary Glasberg

Art – Stephanie Gladden and Tim Bavington
'Diamond' Joe Quimby orders certain Springfield residents to diet – and Rainier Wolfcastle is there to ensure there's no cheating.

'The Quest for Yaz'
Story – Adam Fein
Art – Chris Roman and Tim Bavington
Milhouse uncovers a ring of trading card fraudsters.

Issues 19–22 featured a back-up strip about a new Bongo creation, Roswell, an alien landing on Earth in the fifties. It has no connection with *The Simpsons* TV show. Roswell then ran in his own comic book.

Simpsons Comics #19

'Don't Cry for Me, Jebediah!'
Story – Bill Morrison
Art – Bill Morrison, Luis Escobar, Chris Clements and Steve Steere Jnr
Bart turns Springfield into a tourist attraction by causing the statue of Jebediah Springfield to shed tears.

Simpsons Comics #20

'The Artist Formerly Known as Bart'
Story – Jeff Rosenthal
Art – Phil Ortiz and Tim Bavington
Bart meets a *doppelgänger* who is a superstar and they trade places.

Simpsons Comics # 21

'Stand and Deliverance'
Story – Sib Ventress and Tracy Berna
Art – Phil Ortiz and Tim Bavington

Skinner and Willie take Bart and Martin away for some character building.

Simpsons Comics # 22

'Little Big Mart'
Story – Gary Glasberg
Art – Stephanie Gladden and Tim Harkins
Apu and Mr Burns team up to create a super Kwik-E-Mart.

Simpsons Comics # 23

'Bart De Triomphe'
Story – Jeff Rosenthal
Art – Phil Ortiz and Tim Bavington
Krusty, Milhouse and Bart head for Paris to uncover a criminal ring run by one Sideshow Bob!

'Citizen Shame'
Story – Dan Studney and Jim Lincoln
Art – Bill Morrison and Tim Bavington
Bart sells his soul to the Devil (who makes notes all over the story).

Simpsons Comics # 24

'Send in the Clowns'
Story – Mary Trainor
Art – Stephanie Gladden and Tim Harkins
Political campaign fever hits Springfield and only Lisa sees the opportunity to change the world.

'L'il Homey in Homey Alone'
Story – Chris Simmons
Art – Shaun Cashman and Tim Bavington
A story about young Homer, young Edna and young Grampa.

Simpsons Comics # 25

'Marge Attacks'
Story – Jamie Angell
Art – Phil Ortiz and Tim Bavington
Marge becomes a daytime talk show host.

'Game Called Because of Pain'
Story – Jamie Angell
Art – Phil Ortiz and Tim Bavington
An Itchy and Scratchy tale about baseball.

Simpsons Comics # 26

'Get Off the Bus!'
Story – Rob Hammersley and Todd J. Greenwald
Art – Phil Ortiz and Tim Bavington
Sideshow Bob sabotages the school bus to take revenge on
Bart.

'Diner Violations'
Story – Terry Delegeane
Art – Phil Ortiz and Tim Bavington
Lou and Eddie compare notes on policing in Springfield.

Simpsons Comics # 27

'They Fixed Homer's Brain'
Story – Doug Tuber and Tim Maile
Art – Stephanie Gladden, Tim Harkins and Tim Bavington
Homer is operated on by Frink and his intelligence is magni-
fied. Lisa finally has a father she can relate to.

'Down the Hatches Boys'
Story – Jamie Angell
Art – Phil Ortiz and Tim Bavington
Captain McCallister of the Frying Dutchman tells the Simpsons
how he got his wooden leg.

Simpsons Comics # 28

'I Just Can't Keep It Down'
Story – Scott M. Gimple
Art – Bill Morrison, Chris Clements and Steven Steere Jnr
Krusty decides to set up his own country to avoid paying US taxes and invites people to live there.

'Flanders' Big Score'
Story – Gary Glasberg
Art – Phil Ortiz and Tim Harkins
Ned Flanders sets out to solve the mystery of the empty collection kitty.

Simpsons Comics # 29

'Let's Get Ready to Bumble'
Story – Jeff Rosenthal
Art – Phil Ortiz and Tim Bavington
Homer becomes a WWF wrestler to save Burns.

'Bringing Down Baby'
Story – Bill Morrison
Art – Bill Morrison
Maggie versus Gerald, the one-eyebrowed baby at the annual picnic.

Simpsons Comics # 30

'Smitheres!'
Story – Dan Studney and Jim Lincoln
Art – Stephanie Gladden, Bill Morrison, Tim Bavington and Tim Harkins
To overcome a strike, Mr Burns clones Smithers and creates an army of obedient workers.

'Bore Us The Movie Gruel'
Story – Rob Walton
Art – Phil Ortiz and Tim Bavington

Bart and Milhouse watch Troy McClure in *Gladys the Groovy Mule*.

Simpsons Comics # 31

'Masquerade Ball'
Story – Bill Morrison
Art – Phil Ortiz and Tim Bavington
After a knock on the head, Homer believes he is Radioactive Man.

Simpsons Comics # 32

'Rhymes and Misdemeanours'
Story – Jeff Rosenthal
Art – Tim Bavington, Stephanie Gladden, Phil Ortiz and Bill Morrison
Krusty and Troy McClure open up a celebrity bar and start a talent night.

Simpsons Comics # 33

'Milhouse the Man, Krusty in the Can & the Great Springfield Frink Out'
Story – Scott M. Gimple
Art – Phil Ortiz and Tim Bavington
Frink's monkeys mess about in his lab and, with the aid of a microwave oven, reality is changed and Springfield is populated by alternative versions of its residents.

Simpsons Comics # 34

'Burnsie on Board'
Story – Rob Hammersley
Art – Stephanie Gladden, Erick Tran, Bill Morrison and Tim Harkins
Mr Burns dreams of entering the Winter Olympics, if he can find the right team.

'The Simpsons Supporters Spin Cycle'
Story – Ian Boothby
Art – Phil Ortiz and Tim Bavington
Alternative scripts for the same scene, courtesy of 'readers''
suggestions.

Simpsons Comics # 35

'To Live and Diaper in Springfield'
Story – Billy Rubenstein
Art – Phil Ortiz and Tim Bavington
The horrors of babysitting Springfield's youngest residents.

Simpsons Comics # 36

'The Geek Shall Inherit the Earth'
Story – Ian Boothby
Art – Erick Tran, Julius Preite and Tim Bavington
Homer's nerd friends are found work.

'The Heroic Life and Mortifying Death of Radioactive Man'
Story – Bill and Kayre Morrison
Art – Bill Morrison and Steve Steere Jnr
After Radioactive Man's death, how can Claude Kane still be
alive?

Simpsons Comics # 37

'The Absent-Minded Protester'
Story – Doug Tuber, Tim Maile and Steve Luchsinger
Art – Phil Ortiz and Tim Bavington
To make himself heard, Grampa becomes suburban terrorist
El Grampo.

'The Heroic Life and Mortifying Death of Radioactive Man
(Chapter II)'
Story – Bill and Kayre Morrison
Art – Bill Morrison and Steve Steere Jnr

The Superior Squad set out to contact Radioactive Man's spirit.

Simpsons Comics # 38

'Dullards to Donuts'
Story – Billy Rubenstein
Art – Phil Ortiz and Tim Bavington
In an effort to increase productivity, Mr Burns bans donuts.

'The Heroic Life and Mortifying Death of Radioactive Man (Chapter III)'
Story – Bill and Kayre Morrison
Art – Bill Morrison and Steve Steere Jnr
The forces of Eczema capture the Superior Squad.

Simpsons Comics # 39

'Sense and Censorbility'
Story – Scott M. Gimple
Art – Phil Ortiz and Tim Bavington
After Bart and Homer use comics as research for a school project, the authorities set out to destroy all comic books.

'The Heroic Life and Mortifying Death of Radioactive Man (Chapter IV)'
Story – Bill and Kayre Morrison
Art – Bill Morrison and Steve Steere Jnr
Radioactive Man returns to defeat Eczema, while Plasmo the Mystic pretends to be Claude Kane.

Simpsons Comics # 40

'Sideshow Simpsons'
Story – Bill Morrison
Art – Phil Ortiz and Tim Bavington
After apparently injuring Krusty, the Simpsons must take over his TV show.

'The Incredible Exploits of Lard Lad'
Story – Scott Shaw
Art – Scott Shaw and Tim Bavington
The story behind the donuts.

Simpsons Comics # 41

'Bart Simpson and the Krusty Brand Fun Factory'
Story – Jesse Leon McCann and Robert L. Graff
Art – James Lloyd and Tim Bavington
Bart and Homer join the tour of Krusty's franchise factory.

'The Day the Nagging Stopped'
Story – Ian Boothby
Art – Julius Preite and Tim Harkins
Bart dreams that everyone has become nice to him.

Simpsons Comics # 42

'The Homer Show'
Story – Chuck Dixon
Art – Phil Ortiz and Tim Bavington
Security cameras reveal what a klutz Homer is, and a new TV
star is born.

'Slobberwack'
Story – Jesse Leon McCann
Art – James Lloyd and Tim Bavington
A Simpsons take on the Lewis Carroll poem.

Simpsons Comics # 43

'Journey to the Cellar of the Kwik-E-Mart'
Story – Robert L. Graff and Jesse Leon McCann
Art – Julius Preite, Erick Tran and Tim Bavington
Told via flashbacks, Bart, Lisa and their friends investigate
the legend of Apu's store.

'Poochie!'
Story – Scott Shaw
Art – Scott Shaw and Tim Harkins
New exploits of the cartoon beagle.

Simpsons Comics # 44

'The Prime of Miss Lisa Simpson'
Story – Ian Boothby
Art – James Lloyd and Tim Bavington
When the teachers are deported, Lisa and Martin Prince take over the school.

'Bartman in: "Identity Crisis" '
Story – Terry Delegeane
Art – Phil Ortiz and Tim Bavington
What can Bart do when Marge gives away his Bartman costume?

Simpsons Comics #45

'Hamburger's Little Helper'
Story – Robert L. Graff and Jesse Leon McCann
Art – Phil Ortiz and Tim Bavington
Santa's Little Helper becomes a famous TV star and Bart must go to court when the dog's agent claims the mutt wants to destroy the Simpsons.

'Mr Sparkle in: Destroy All Manga'
Story – Scott Shaw
Art – Scott Shaw and Dan Nakrosis
The corporate image fights the evils of the Manga comic book industry.

Bart Simpson's Treehouse of Horror # 1

'Little Shop of Homers'
Story – Mike Allred

Art – Luis Escobar, Bill Morrison and Mike Allred
Lisa's plant comes to life and threatens Springfield.

'Call Me Homer'
Story – Jeff Smith
Art – Jeff Smith, Stephanie Gladden and Bill Morrison
Homer becomes a sailor searching for a great white whale,
with Mr Burns as Ahab.

'Bart People'
Story – James Robinson
Art – Chris Roman and Bill Morrison
Bart turns into a cat-person late at night and only Lisa can
save him.

Bart Simpson's Treehouse of Horror # 2

'Sideshow Blob'
Story – Paul Dini
Art – Tim Bavington and Bill Morrison
Sideshow Bob is turned into evil goo by Dr Nick Riviera.

'The Exorsister'
Story – Peter Bagge
Art – Stephanie Gladden and Tim Bavington
Lisa is possessed by the spirit of Madonna.

Bart Simpson's Treehouse of Horror # 3

'The Immigration of the Bodysnatchers'
Story – Evan Dorkin
Art – Bill Morrison, Stephanie Gladden, Phil Ortiz and Tim
Bavington
Springfield is taken over by Pod People, and only Homer and
Sideshow Bob are left alive to tell the world.

'Fatal Reception'
Story – Scott Gimple and Bill Morrison

Art – Bill Morrison
Homer steals the kids' Halloween treats, so they seek revenge.

Bart Simpson's Treehouse of Horror # 4

'I Faced Tahn-Enn-Bahm, The Christmas Tree from Another World'
Story – Chuck Dixon
Art – Phil Ortiz and Tim Bavington
Lisa must find a way to prevent Earth being invaded by insidious deciduouses.

'The Illustrative Man'
Story – Batton Lash
Art – Julius Preite and Tim Bavington
Bart and Lisa see stories in a carnival man's tattoos.

Bart Simpson's Treehouse of Horror # 5

'Dark Lisa'
Story – Jill Thompson
Art – Oscar Gonzales Loyo and Steve Steere Jnr
Lisa is given superhuman powers and comes under the tutelage of Mr Burns after she kills everyone at school.

'Xt'tapalatakettle's Day'
Script – Scott Shaw
Story and Art – Sergio Aragones
A Mexican curse and Homer's greed bring Springfield's dead back to life.

'Apu on Rigel 7'
Story and Art – Doug TenNapel
Apu joins forces with Kang in an attempt to overthrow the dictator of Rigel 7, Burnzak.

Lisa Comics # 1

'Lisa's Adventures in Wordland'
Story – Mary Trainor
Art – Mili Smythe, Stephanie Gladden, Bill Morrison and Chris Clements
Lisa finds herself in a curious world of words and pictures.

Radioactive Man was a six-issue mini-series, plus one special, which 'reprinted' classic Radioactive Man adventures from the past. Each one was a clever parody of comics of the time it was 'originally' printed (hence the necessary inclusion of dates and weird numbering system).

Radioactive Man # 1 (November 1952)

'The Origin of Radioactive Man'
Story – Steve Vance and Cindy Vance
Art – Steve Vance and Bill Morrison
The origin of Radioactive Man, plus his first adventure against Dr Crab and his commie comics.

Radioactive Man # 88 (May 1962)

'The Molten Menace of Magmo – The Lava Man'
Story – Steve Vance, Cindy Vance and Bill Morrison
Art – Steve Vance and Bill Morrison
Now a member of the Superior Squad, Radioactive Man fights Magmo, and Fallout Boy recalls his origin.

Radioactive Man # 216 (August 1972)

'See No Evil, Hear No Evil'
Story – Steve Vance, Cindy Vance and Bill Morrison
Art – Steve Vance, Bill Morrison and Shaun Cashman
Radioactive Man and Purple Heart (now called Bleeding Heart) have to rescue Fallout Boy from the clutches of Hypno Head.

Radioactive Man # 412 (October 1980)

'In Ze Clutches of Dr Crab'
Story – Steve Vance
Art – Steve Vance, Bill Morrison and Tim Bavington
With the lightning bolt finally removed from his skull, Radioactive Man becomes a dark and merciless version of his old self.

Radioactive Man # 679 (January 1986)

'Who Washes the Washmen's Infinite Secrets of Legendary Crossover Knight Wars?'
Story – Steve Vance
Art – Steve Vance, Tim Bavington and Bill Morrison
Radioactive Man's alternative selves from the various alternative universes combine – but not all will survive.

Radioactive Man # 1000 (January 1995)

'In His Own Image'
Story – Steve Vance
Art – Steve Vance and Bill Morrison
Radioactive Man is up against lots of his old foes in this milestone spectacular.

Radioactive Man Colossal # 1

'To Betroth a Foe' (originally presented in *Radioactive Man # 72* – January 1961)
Story – Bill Morrison
Art – Chris Roman and Tim Harkins
With guest stars the Superior Squad, can Radioactive Man really be marrying Larva Girl?

Radioactive Man (originally presented in *Radioactive Man* # 84 – January 1962)

'Teen Idol'
Story – Bill Morrison
Art – Stephanie Gladden and John Adam
Larceny Lass is back, but can music stop her?

Radioactive Man (originally presented in *Radioactive Man* # 37 – July 1957)

'The 1,001 Faces of Radioactive Ape'
Story – Scott Shaw
Art – Scott Shaw and Phil Ortiz
A holiday with his old friends in Simian City puts Radioactive Man in danger once more.

Radioactive Man (originally presented in *Radioactive Man's Girlfriend, Gloria Grand* # 10 – August 1959)

'Gloria Grand, Radioactive Girl'
Story – Kayre Morrison
Art – Bill Morrison
For years he has loved her from afar, but does Radioactive Man need a new assistant?

Radioactive Man (originally presented in *Radioactive Man* # 22 – August 1955)

'The Radioactive Man of 1995'
Story – Bill Morrison
Art – Sharon Bridgeman and Abel Laxamana
Gloria Grand takes a trip to the future.

Bartman saw the adventures of Bart Simpson and his alter ego, Bartman.

Bartman # 1

'The Comic Cover Caper'
Story – Steve Vance
Art – Steve Vance, Phil Ortiz, Bill Morrison and Tim Bavington
Bartman foils an attempt by Jimbo's gang to steal comics before they have been given metallic covers, and so create rarities.

Bartman # 2

'Where Stalks the Penalizer'
Story – Jan Strnad
Art – Steve Vance, Bill Morrison, Tim Bavington and Phil Ortiz
Bartman has to stop the Penalizer who is scaring Springfield's young troublemakers half to death.

Bartman # 3

'When Bongos Collide – The Final Collision'
Story – Jan Strnad and Steve Vance
Art – Steve Vance and Bill Morrison
As the fictional and factual worlds come together with Springfield at the epicentre, Bartman teams up with Radioactive Man to stop the aliens' plan.

Bartman # 4

'Bartman'
Story – Gary Glasberg and Bill Morrison
Art – Chris Clements, Luis Escobar and Tim Bavington
Bartman turns his back on his superhero life, but Milhouse is kidnapped.   .

Bartman # 5

Story – Bill Morrison and Gary Glasberg
Art – Luis Escobar, Jim Massara and Tim Bavington

With no Bartman, Milhouse's life is in jeopardy. Maggie and Lisa mount a rescue, but also fall into the clutches of evil. Only one person can rescue them . . .

Bartman # 6

Story – Bill Morrison and Gary Glasberg
Art – Luis Escobar, Tim Bavington and Chris Clements
Joined by Bart Dog the canine crusader, Bartman rescues the others and exposes the real villain of the piece. But who then kidnaps Bart Dog?

Krusty Comics # 1

'The Rise and Fall of Krustyland Part One'
Story – Jamie Angell
Art – Cary Schramm, Mili Smythe, Phil Ortiz and Shaun Cashman
As Krustyland opens to a huge fanfare, Mr Teeny takes the opportunity to bid for his own stardom.

Krusty Comics # 2

'The Rise and Fall of Krustyland Part Two'
Story – Jamie Angell
Art – Cary Schramm
Krustyland ought to be a success, but things are conspiring against Krusty – Tony D'Amico being just one of them.

Krusty Comics # 3

'The Rise and Fall of Krustyland Part Three'
Story – Jamie Angell
Art – Carey Schramm
As Krustyland literally falls apart, will Rabbi Krustofski be there for Herschel?

Itchy & Scratchy Comics # 1

'Around the World in 80 Pieces'
Story – Steve Vance and Cindy Vance
Art – Steve Vance, Mike Milo, Harry McLaughlin and Bill Morrison
A variation on the classic story, with Scratchy winning by a head.

Itchy & Scratchy Comics # 2

'The Itchy & Scratchy Movie II'
Story – Dan Castellaneta and Deb Lacusta
Art – Steve Vance, Bill Morrison, Tim Bavington, Phil Ortiz and Abel Laxamana
The making and première of their new movie.

Itchy & Scratchy Comics # 3

'When Bongos Collide – Labor Pains'
Story – Mike Milo and Steve Vance
Art – Harry McLaughlin, Steve Vance and Bill Morrison
Life carries on as normal for the film makers, until they emerge from the television screen and into Bart and Lisa's living room . . .

Itchy & Scratchy Comics Holiday Hi-Jinx Special # 1

'It's a Wonderful Knife'
Story – Jason Grode
Art – Bill Morrison, Stephanie Gladden and Tim Bavington
It's Christmas and Scratchy just can't seem to make it to a party.

INDEX OF EPISODES